DISABILITY IN THE HEBREW BIBLE

Mental and physical disability, ubiquitous in texts of the Hebrew Bible, receive their first thoroughgoing treatment in this monograph. Saul Olyan seeks to reconstruct the Hebrew Bible's particular ideas of what is disabling and their potential social ramifications. Biblical representations of disability and biblical classification schemas – both explicit and implicit – are compared with those of the Hebrew Bible's larger ancient West Asian cultural context and with those of the later Jewish biblical interpreters who produced the Dead Sea Scrolls. This study helps the reader gain a deeper and more subtle understanding of the ways in which biblical writers construct hierarchically significant difference and privilege certain groups (e.g., persons with "whole bodies") over others (e.g., persons with physical "defects"). It also explores how ancient interpreters of the Hebrew Bible, such as the Qumran sectarians, reconfigure earlier biblical notions and classification models of disability for their own contexts and ends.

Saul M. Olyan is Samuel Ungerleider Jr. Professor of Judaic Studies and Professor of Religious Studies at Brown University. His previous publications include *Biblical Mourning: Ritual and Social Dimensions* (2004), *Rites and Rank: Hierarchy in Biblical Representations of Cult* (2000), *A Thousand Thousands Served Him: Exegesis and the Naming of Angels in Ancient Judaism* (1993), and *Asherah and the Cult of Yahweh in Israel* (1988). He has contributed to, and served as editor of, various publications in the areas of biblical literature and ancient religions.

Disability in the Hebrew Bible

Interpreting Mental and Physical Differences

SAUL M. OLYAN

Brown University

CAMBRIDGE
UNIVERSITY PRESS

CAMBRIDGE UNIVERSITY PRESS
Cambridge, New York, Melbourne, Madrid, Cape Town,
Singapore, São Paulo, Delhi, Mexico City

Cambridge University Press
The Edinburgh Building, Cambridge CB2 8RU, UK

Published in the United States of America by Cambridge University Press, New York

www.cambridge.org
Information on this title: www.cambridge.org/9781107404984

First published 2008
First paperback edition 2011

A catalogue record for this publication is available from the British Library

Library of Congress Cataloguing in Publication Data
Olyan, Saul M.
Disability in the Hebrew Bible : interpreting mental and physical differences / Saul M. Olyan.
p.   cm.
Includes bibliographical references and index.
ISBN 978-0-521-88807-3 (hardback)
1. People with disabilities in the Bible.   2. Bible. O.T. – Criticism, interpretation, etc.
3. People with disabilities in rabbinical literature.   4. Dead Sea scrolls.   I. Title.
BS1199.A25O49   2008
221.8′3624 – dc22   2007035499

ISBN 978-0-521-88807-3 Hardback
ISBN 978-1-107-40498-4 Paperback

Voor Jackie, Mieke en David

Contents

Acknowledgments

It is always a pleasure to recognize the contributions of friends, colleagues, and institutions to the development of a work such as this. Tracy Lemos, David Jacobson, Lynn Davidman, Michael Satlow, Marcy Brink-Danan, Maude Mandel, Michael Gottsegen, Deborah Cohen, Matthew Bagger, Mark Cladis, Stanley Stowers, and Nathaniel Levtow read portions of the manuscript in preliminary form and made helpful suggestions, many of which I have incorporated. Needless to say, any errors of fact or judgment remain my responsibility alone. Frederik Schockaert's advice was crucial at several junctures, as acknowledgments in the notes demonstrate. I would also like to thank the students in my course "Disability in Antiquity" (fall 2004), particularly Debra Scoggins, for their stimulating questions and reactions to my ideas at an early stage in their development. I am indebted to Anke Dorman of the University of Groningen for sending me a bound copy of her dissertation and to Silke Knippschild of the University of Bristol for allowing me to cite an unpublished manuscript. Finally, I am delighted to acknowledge the interest of my editor, Andy Beck, in this project.

A fellowship from the National Endowment for the Humanities and a semester of leave at full pay, plus matching funds, from Brown University made the writing of this book possible. I am grateful to both institutions for this significant support. (Any views, findings, conclusions, or recommendations expressed in this publication do not necessarily reflect those of the National Endowment for the Humanities.) John J. Collins and Steven Weitzman wrote letters supporting my NEH application, and it is a pleasure to thank them once again for their support of my work.

I am grateful to several publishers for allowing me to reproduce materials from earlier publications. Some of the content of my article "'Anyone Blind and Lame Shall Not Enter the House': On the Interpretation of Second Samuel 5:8b," *Catholic Biblical Quarterly* 60 (1998):218–227, appears in chapter 2 in reworked form. I would like to thank the Catholic Biblical Association for permission to reproduce this material. Much of my article "Why an Altar of Unfinished Stones? Some Thoughts on Ex 20,25 and Dtn 27,5–6," *Zeitschrift für die alttestamentliche Wissenschaft* 108 (1996):161–171, appears in revised form in chapter 6. I would like to thank Verlag Walter de Gruyter & Co. for permission to include this material. Some of the content of my article "The Exegetical Dimensions of Restrictions on the Blind and the Lame in Texts from Qumran," *Dead Sea Discoveries* 8 (2001):38–50, appears in chapter 7 in reworked form. I would like to thank Koninklijke Brill NV for permission to include content derived from this article.

Finally, a note on transliteration: I have employed a simplified form of transliteration for Hebrew, Akkadian, and Greek that does not indicate vowel length in many cases.

S.M.O.
Providence, R.I.
June 2007

Abbreviations

The following is a list of abbreviations used throughout the text and notes.

AHw   von Soden, W. *Akkadisches Handwörterbuch.* 3 vols. Wiesbaden, Germany: Harrassowitz, 1965–1981.

BDB   Brown, F., S. Driver, and C. Briggs. *The Brown-Driver-Briggs Hebrew and English Lexicon.* Peabody, MA: Hendrickson, 2000, Reprinted.

CAD   Oppenheim, A. L. et al., eds. *The Assyrian Dictionary of the Oriental Institute of the University of Chicago.* Chicago: Oriental Institute, 1956–2007.

CAT   Dietrich, M., O. Loretz, and J. Sanmartín, eds. *The Cuneiform Alphabetic Texts from Ugarit, Ras ibn Hani and Other Places.* 2nd enlarged ed. Münster, Germany: Ugarit Verlag, 1995.

EM   Cassuto, U. et al., eds. *'enṣiqlopedyah miqra'it.* Jerusalem: Mossad Bialik, 1965–1988.

EncDSS   Schiffman, L. H., and J. C. VanderKam, eds. *Encyclopedia of the Dead Sea Scrolls.* 2 vols. New York: Oxford University Press, 2000.

GKC   Kautzsch, E., and A. E. Cowley. *Gesenius' Hebrew Grammar.* 2nd ed. Oxford, UK: Clarendon Press, 1910.

KAI   Donner, H., and W. Röllig, eds. *Kanaanäische und Aramäische Inschriften.* 4th ed. 3 vols. Wiesbaden, Germany: Harrassowitz, 1979.

LXX   Septuagint

MT   Massoretic Text

NJPS   New Jewish Publication Society Version

NKB   Koehler, L., and W. Baumgartner. *The Hebrew and Aramaic Lexicon of the Old Testament*. Trans. M. E. J. Richardson et al. 5 vols. Leiden, The Netherlands: Brill, 1994.

TDOT   Botterweck, G. J., H. Ringgren et al., eds. *Theological Dictionary of the Old Testament*. Trans. J. T. Willis et al. 14 vols. Grand Rapids, MI: Eerdmans, 1974–2004.

WO   Waltke, B. K., and M. O'Connor. *An Introduction to Biblical Hebrew Syntax*. Winona Lake, IN: Eisenbrauns, 1990.

Introduction

W HETHER IT BE DAVID'S FEIGNED "MADNESS" IN THE PRESENCE of his Philistine overlord, Jacob's limping after wrestling with God, legal restrictions on the ritual participation and leadership of priests and others with physical "defects" (Hebrew *mûmîm*), or the transformation of blind and lame persons into those who can see and walk in prophetic visions of a utopian future, disability is ubiquitous in texts of the Hebrew Bible.[1] Yet, with few exceptions, scholars of the Hebrew Bible have barely acknowledged disability as a subject worthy of serious study.[2] When biblical specialists have discussed disability, it is usually not the focus of investigation, but incidental to the analysis of something else (e.g., priestly or sacrificial law and practice).[3] In contrast, I make the representation of disability itself the focus of my investigation. Acknowledging that disability is our broad (and contested) analytic category – like race, class, sexuality, or gender – but convinced it is a useful analytic focus nonetheless, I seek to reconstruct the Hebrew Bible's particular ideas of what is disabling and the potential social ramifications of those ideas.[4] I consider how biblical ideas of disability relate to notions of disability in the larger ancient West Asian cultural sphere, and also examine some of the ways in which ancient Jewish interpreters of biblical texts perpetuate or reconfigure biblical ideas of disability and biblical models of classification. Although the Hebrew Bible has no term that parallels our term "disability" precisely, it does categorize persons on the basis of physical or mental condition, appearance, alleged vulnerability, and the presence or absence of certain diseases, and such classification may result in the text's demand for the exclusion of affected persons from many aspects of social, economic, and religious life (e.g., participation

1

in sacrificial rites, or living among others in community). Thus, disability as an analytic category has the potential to help us gain a deeper and more subtle understanding of the ways in which the biblical writers construct hierarchically significant difference and privilege certain groups (e.g., those with non-"defective" or "whole" bodies) over others (e.g., those with physical "defects" [*mûmîm*]). Furthermore, disability as an axis of analysis also provides us with insights regarding the ways in which ancient interpreters of the Hebrew Bible preserve or modify earlier biblical notions of disability and patterns of classification for their own particular contexts and their own particular ends.

DEFINING DISABILITY

As a contested category, there is no single agreed-on definition of disability in disability studies, although scholars working in the area have tended recently to opt for broader, more inclusive understandings of what constitutes a disability. This more comprehensive approach to disability is evidently the result of developments within communities of persons with disabilities, and is often justified by the claim that disabled persons share a common stigmatization and marginalization, at least in the contemporary West.[5] There is, however, a virtual consensus among scholars in disability studies that disability, like gender, is a social construction rather than something "natural and timeless," a cultural product that has contributed significantly to the generation and maintenance of inequality in societies.[6] Disability may have some basis in physical or mental difference, but it is the social meaning attributed to such difference that makes it significant.[7] I, too, am inclined to define disability broadly in order to enable me to look at the various categories of persons who are stigmatized and assigned marginal social positions in biblical texts on account of a physical or mental condition or state. Included are persons with physical "defects" (*mûmîm*) such as the blind and the lame, persons who are mentally disabled, persons with diseases cast as polluting (e.g., *ṣaraʿat*, "skin disease"), and the deaf and the mute.[8] These persons are subject to forms of stigmatization and marginalization in biblical texts, analogous in some respects to the common stigmatization and marginalization claimed for contemporary Western persons with disabilities. Furthermore, the biblical text itself will often bring a variety of disabilities into direct association, as in Lev 19:14 (deafness and blindness), Deut 28:28 (mental disability and blindness), and Exod 4:10–11 (impeded speech, muteness, deafness, and blindness), suggesting that they share something in common.[9] Thus, it seems fitting to speak collectively of persons with "defects," with mental disability, with deafness and muteness, with "skin disease" (ṣaraʿat), and with other stigmatized conditions or states, persons whom the text frequently seeks to devalue and marginalize, as the Hebrew Bible's disabled persons. In the setting of this study, therefore, a disability is a physical or mental condition or state impacting negatively on affected categories of persons especially on account of the social meaning and significance attributed to the condition or state in the biblical context. Like other scholars, I understand disability to be preeminently a social production, and therefore, I focus primarily on its social dimensions.[10] In a classic essay, Joan Wallach Scott argued that "gender is a primary way of signifying relationships of power . . .[it] is a primary field within which or by means of which power is articulated."[11] The same, I believe, could be said about disability in the biblical context. Thus, a primary goal of this study is to investigate the social dimensions of disability as it is represented, particularly the ways in which textual castings of disability function to realize and communicate patterns of social inequality.

TEXTUAL REPRESENTATIONS

It is worth emphasizing that the focus of this project is the textual representation of disability in several ancient corpora rather than the study of disabled individuals or groups from Israelite and Jewish antiquity. Because we know little or nothing about the lives of ancient persons with disabilities, textual representations of disability are virtually all that we have to work with.[12] Of these, many, if not most, focus on categories of disabled persons (e.g., "the blind," "the lame") rather than particular, historically situated individuals or groups. Biblical representations of disability come from different time periods and geographic/social locations, and are found in a variety of literary contexts, including prescriptive legal discourse, ancestral lore, historical narrative, prophetic oracles, and nonprophetic poetic compositions. In many cases, it is difficult if not impossible to date our texts, and questions of provenance must often remain unanswered. In short, our data are exceedingly limited, and in the main, not conducive to reconstructing individual lives, regional or local ideological differences, or historical change over time.[13] However, representations are central to our enterprise nonetheless because they are ideologically charged and function themselves to mold patterns of thought among those for whom they are intended. From them, we can learn something about how disabilities were constructed by the elusive writers of our texts, and how our writers' textual productions might have resonated with and shaped the thinking of their audiences. The study of the textual representation of topics such as the past, ritual, and gender in biblical and cognate materials has become increasingly attractive to biblical scholars in recent years, as the impact of the cultural turn in the humanities has spread in the international academy over the past several decades.[14] Given that representations of disability must have played a part in the creation and shaping of social categories and therefore, social differentiation in ancient Israel, the study of such representations is an urgent desideratum if we hope to develop a more nuanced understanding both of disability and inequality in the literary works under considera-tion and in the ancient contexts that produced them. Hayden White's observation is in the main true for an investigation such as this: "The historically real, the past real, is that to which I can be referred only by way of an artifact that is textual in nature."[15] Thus, I focus on *representa-tions* of disability in the biblical text. Although these representations are anything but an unproblematic window providing direct access into the day-to-day lives of ancient persons, they do teach us something about the ways in which disability was constructed and infused with meaning in biblical and related contexts, and therefore, some of the ways in which ancient writers thought about disability and sought to shape the thinking of others.

CLASSIFICATION AND STIGMATIZATION

Classification has been much discussed over the past several decades in scholarship in the humanities. To classify or differentiate has been called "a process of making meaning" (J. W. Scott), classification has been described as "a necessary prerequisite" to explanation (J. Z. Smith), and taxonomies themselves have been characterized as both "epistemological instruments" and "instruments for the organization of society" (B. Lincoln).[16] Religions, in particular, have been described as "powerful engines for the production and maintenance of classificatory systems" (J. Z. Smith).[17] As more than a few scholars have noted, binary oppositions such as clean/unclean or holy/common are central to many classificatory systems, and those evidenced in the Hebrew Bible are no exception to this pattern. I have argued elsewhere, in fact, that such dyads are frequently productive of hierarchy in biblical representations of cult.[18] The representation of disability in the Hebrew Bible is in part the product of the operations of a number of native dual oppositions. These include non-"defective" or "whole"/"defective," clean/unclean, holy/common, honored/shamed, blessed/cursed, beautiful/ugly, and loved/hated. The discourses that deploy these oppositions, discourses of valorization and stigmatization, are at times overlapping. Blindness, a "defect," may also be cast as a curse, as it is in Deut 28:28. In the same way, the person classified as "without defect" might also be categorized as "beautiful," as in Dan 1:4 and Song of Songs 4:7 ("You are entirely beautiful, my companion," // "there is no 'defect' in you").[19] When deployed by the writers of our texts, these oppositional discourses function to create unequal categories of persons. For example, those whose bodies are understood by the text as lacking "defects" (mûmîm) are privileged in any number of ways over those whose bodies are cast as "defective." According to Lev 21:17–23, priests with physical "defects" such as blindness, lameness, damaged genitals, or broken limbs may not offer sacrifices to Yhwh as other priests do; they constitute a distinct, secondary, stigmatized, and, in part, marginalized category of priests who are not allowed to perform the central, most highly esteemed priestly function according to this source: offering the deity sacrifices.[20] This privilege belongs exclusively to priests whose bodies lack "defects." Similarly, serious polluters are stripped of opportunities for cultic activity and social intercourse that would be readily available to those cast as clean. For example, persons with "skin disease" (ṣāraʿat) are constructed as highly polluting, and are therefore portrayed as physically and socially separated from the community, living on their own or with others similarly afflicted, and unable to participate in communal life (Lev 13:45–46; Num 5:1–4). Thus, through the deployment of disabling and enabling binary discourses alone or in combination, texts create categories of stigmatized persons whom they seek to marginalize, as well as their antitype: categories of privileged persons who lack negatively constructed, stigmatized characteristics and possess valued traits (e.g., those with non-"defective" or "whole" bodies, those who are blessed or honored, those who are clean and fit to participate in communal or familial cultic rites).

Biblical authors also seek to classify, stigmatize, and marginalize through several other moves. They deploy denigrating comparisons to devalue disabled persons (e.g., likening them implicitly to a parched desert) and speak of an ideal future in which Yhwh acts to eliminate disability entirely (Isa 35:4–10). Perhaps the most common way in which authors seek to categorize, devalue, and marginalize persons with disabilities is through association. Disabled categories of persons are brought into association with other stigmatized and socially marginal types, such as the poor, the widow, the fatherless, the alien, and, in the case of persons with non-"defective" disabilities, those cast as having "defects" (*mûmîm*); with devalued personal characteristics such as weakness, vulnerability, dependence, ineffectuality, ignorance, and bad judgment; with ideas such as divine rejection and contempt; and, in the case of males, with categories of women, suggesting their feminization. Job 29:12–16 illustrates some of these associations at work. In this text, the blind and lame are listed with the poor; the afflicted; the widow; and other categories of persons cast as weak, vulnerable, and dependent, who are helped by a vigorous, autonomous Job before his own calamities incapacitate him:

> I was eyes for the blind,
> feet for the lame was I.
> I was a father for the poor,
> and the lawsuit of the stranger I researched.[21]
>
> (vv. 15–16)

By mentioning the blind and the lame with the poor, the widow, the stranger, and other dependent sufferers, Job 29:12–16 implicitly classifies blind and lame persons with these marginal groups, suggesting that they share the same devalued characteristics (e.g., weakness, dependency). These persons serve as a foil for Job, the ideal man, the paradigm of agency, strength, and autonomy.[22] Ps 146:5–9 is similar. Here, the blind and other vulnerable categories of persons are said to be helped directly by Yhwh:

> He executes justice for the oppressed,
> provides food for the hungry.
> Yhwh frees prisoners,
> Yhwh gives sight to the blind,
> Yhwh raises up the prostrate,
> Yhwh loves the innocent,
> Yhwh watches over the resident aliens,
> The fatherless and widow he helps.
> But the way of the wicked he subverts.
>
> (vv. 7–9)

Although texts such as these may have been intended to challenge negative representations of the blind and other dependent sufferers by suggesting that such persons are of special interest to the powerful, including the deity, they nonetheless affirm their weakness, vulnerability, dependence, and lack of agency, thereby stigmatizing them.[23] Other biblical texts associate disabilities such as blindness and deafness with ignorance, and muteness with ineffectuality. An example is Isa 56:10, in which dysfunctional Judean "watchmen" (presumably, Judah's prophets) are described: "His watchmen are blind, all of them, knowing nothing," // "All of them are mute dogs, unable to bark."[24] In this passage, blindness signals ignorance, and muteness a dysfunction in communication. Two related legal formulations associate blindness with bad judgment and corruption: "A bribe you shall not take, for the bribe blinds (ye'awwer) the sighted, and twists (yesallep) the cause of the innocent" (Exod 23:8; cf. Deut 16:19). Many of these associations are also present in non-Israelite West Asian texts. For example, Babylonian *kudurru* (boundary) inscriptions often contain a formula suggesting that groups such as the deaf, the blind, and the mentally disabled can be manipulated into offenses on account of their ignorance and lack of judgment.[25] Furthermore, words for physical disabilities such as *akû* and mental disabilities such as *lillu* can be used in cuneiform texts as synonyms for "poor," suggesting a close association between disability and impoverishment.[26]

The stigmatizing association of disability with weakness, vulnerability, dependence, and ineffectuality constitutes an exceedingly widespread literary topos in biblical texts. It is present even in materials that do not deal directly with disabled persons, such as the so-called idol polemics found in prophetic texts and the Psalms, in which divine images opposed by the writers are denigrated through the listing of their various physical disabilities and through emphasis on their dependence and inability to act.[27] Although texts such as these do not speak directly of disabled persons, their stigmatization of a variety of physical disabilities and of weakness and dependency is well worth our careful attention because it tells us something of the authors' thinking about these issues. Jer 10:5 is a primary example of the polemical denigration of "idols" by bringing their disabilities and lack of agency into relief: "Like a scarecrow in a cucumber patch are they. They cannot speak; they must be carried for they cannot walk. Do not fear them, for they can do no harm. Nor is it in their power to do good." The following verses, in contrast, speak of Yhwh's greatness, might, and incomparability (vv. 6–7). The "idols" under attack in Jer 10:5 are false gods according to the writer, lacking essential qualities of a real, living god; likewise, the scarecrow to which they are compared is an artificial substitute for a human being, lacking fundamental human characteristics. The quintessential qualities of the living – whether deity or human – privileged by this text are the capacity to speak; the capacity to walk; the capacity, in short, to function as an independent agent. The implication of the text is that those who lack these abilities, like the "idol" and the scarecrow, lack fundamental divine and human characteristics. The polemic of Psalm 115 is similar, contrasting the agency of Yhwh (v. 3, "all that he desires he does") with the disabilities of the "idols" of the nations (vv. 5–8):

> They have mouths but cannot speak,
> they have eyes but cannot see,
> they have ears, but cannot hear,
> they have a nose but cannot smell,
> their hands cannot feel,
> their feet cannot walk,
> they utter no sound in their throat.
> Like them are those who made them,
> all who trust in them.

In marked contrast to Yhwh, who can do anything he wants to do (v. 3), the "idols" can do nothing at all. Any voluntary association with such ineffectual, false gods reduces the votary's own status. He also becomes a target of derision, said to share the ineffectuality of the "idols" themselves.

The evident resonance of what I call the weakness and ineffectuality topos with ancient audiences affords biblical authors the opportunity to use disabled characters to develop and complicate a plot, often in order to bring into relief a favorite theme: the magnificent power and agency of Israel's god Yhwh.[28] Because of Samson's blinding and fettering after his capture and his evident loss of superhuman strength, the Philistines believe that he is no longer a threat to them.[29] In fact, the narrative comes to focus on Samson's blindness as emblematic of his weakness and ineffectuality.[30] Philistine assumptions about Samson's disability allow them to forget his previous god-given physical strength connected to the growth of his hair, and they perish as a result when Samson is given an opportunity to grasp the pillars supporting the temple of Dagon and pull it down on them and on himself (Judg 16:25–30). The fact that Samson is able to wreak havoc among the Philistines and kill even more of them at his death than he killed previously – to paraphrase Judg 16:30 – does not suggest anything positive about his blindness; it only serves to underscore the deity's might, his receptivity to Samson's petition for revenge, and the foolish overconfidence of the Philistines. Even though he was blind and would have been ineffectual as an adversary under normal circumstances, Samson was nonetheless able to accomplish one last mighty feat against the Philistines as a result of Yhwh's willingness to intervene on his behalf.

A second example of blindness functioning in a narrative to bring into relief Yhwh's exceptional ability and agency is the story of the visit of King Jeroboam's wife to the prophet Ahijah of Shiloh in 1 Kgs 14:1–18. After Jeroboam's son Abijah becomes ill, Jeroboam sends his wife – who is never named – in disguise to consult the prophet Ahijah regarding the boy's future. Ahijah the prophet, we are told, is blind on account of old age. Before Jeroboam's wife arrives at Ahijah's house, Yhwh tells him that she is coming in disguise to seek information about her sick son's fate (v. 5). As Jeroboam's wife enters Ahijah's house, Ahijah says "come in wife of Jeroboam. Why do you pretend to be someone else? As for me, I am sent with hard (news) for you" (v. 6). Ahijah's blindness would, under normal circumstances, make him ignorant of the identity of his visitor who had not as yet uttered a word to him, even if she were not disguised. The fact that she is disguised and that he is able nonetheless not only to recognize her, but also to identify her mission (v. 5), underscores Yhwh's outstanding capacity to know all, and to communicate this privileged knowledge to his blind mouthpiece, the prophet.[31] Ahijah's inability to see, which would have placed him at a disadvantage vis-à-vis Jeroboam's wife were he not a prophet of Yhwh, is rendered irrelevant in light of Yhwh's supreme knowledge and his choice to communicate it to his representative.

Several other biblical texts in which the central character has a disability of some kind function similarly to the Samson and Ahijah narratives. As in Judges 16 and 1 Kings 14, where Samson's and Ahijah's blindness provide an opportunity to bring Yhwh's own outstanding agency, knowledge, and power into relief, Moses' protest in Exod 4:10 that he is "heavy of mouth and heavy of tongue," and so inadequate to the task of leading the people out of Egypt, provides the writer with an opportunity to emphasize the deity's contrasting ability and Moses' complete dependence on it: "Who gives a human a mouth, or who makes (someone) mute, deaf, sentient, or blind? Is it not I, Yhwh? Now then, go, and I myself shall be with your mouth, and shall teach you what you will say" (Exod 4:11–12).[32] The fact that disability is characteristic of Moses in this text, as it is of Samson in Judges 16 and Ahijah in 1 Kings 14, does not pose a challenge to disability's stigmatization in the larger biblical narrative; if anything, it reinforces it. Disability in these texts remains associated with inadequacy, insufficiency, and dependence, and functions to provide the texts' writers with opportunities to emphasize Yhwh's contrasting ability, knowledge, and agency. Even Jacob's limping as a result of his wrestling with Yhwh in Genesis 32:25–33 (Eng. 24–32) signals the deity's unequaled strength and ability rather than something positive about Jacob: Jacob is disabled by Yhwh in order to allow the deity to prevail in his wrestling match with him and escape before the sun's rise. Jacob's lameness therefore demonstrates Yhwh's power over even the most capable of human adversaries, and is emblematic of his ultimate weakness vis-à-vis the deity.

CONTESTING DISABILITY'S STIGMATIZATION

Few alternative voices survive that contest the stigmatization of disability evidenced so broadly in extant biblical texts, in contrast to the wealth of material that challenges negative representations of the poor, the widow, the fatherless, and the resident alien. Although the poor are not infrequently cast as weak, victimized, marginal, dishonored, and worthy of pity (e.g., 1 Sam 18:23; 2 Sam 12:6; Amos 2:6–7; Ps 113:7; Prov 13:18; 22:7), narratives such as those that insist that Yhwh affords them special protection or takes a special interest in them (e.g., 1 Sam 2:8; Ps 72:4, 12–14), or texts that suggest that the poor might possess honor not based on wealth (e.g., Sir 10:30), challenge this characterization, although not always effectively, as I have pointed out.[33] The same is true of the many biblical texts that insist that Yhwh has a special interest in helping the widow, the fatherless, and the resident alien, and that demand that these persons be protected from oppressors and be provided for by those with means.[34] Yet, similar materials contesting the stigmatization of disabled persons are much rarer, although they do exist (e.g., laws protecting persons with disabilities in Lev 19:14 and Deut 27:18, or Ps 146:8 on Yhwh's special concern for the blind as well as other dependent sufferers).[35] One text, however, stands out in this regard: Isa 56:3–7. This pericope, likely a product of the late sixth or fifth centuries BCE, is clearly a direct challenge to Deut 23:2–9 (Eng.1–8), which excludes males with damaged genitals and certain male aliens from entry into the "assembly," an idiom probably to be understood as entry into the sanctuary sphere for worship.[36] In response, Isa 56:3–7 states that both the pious alien and the devout eunuch have a central place in Yhwh's temple and community.[37] The eunuch's inability to produce offspring ("I am a dried up tree") does not prevent Yhwh from giving him a memorial monument in the temple and an everlasting name (vv. 4–5):

> For thus says Yhwh,
> to the eunuchs who observe my Sabbaths,
> and choose that which I delight in,
> and grasp onto my covenant.
> I shall give to them in my house and within my walls
> a memorial monument
> better than sons and daughters.
> An everlasting name I shall give to them,
> which shall not be cut off.

Marginalization and stigmatization of the eunuch are challenged here through the strategic use of Yhwh's authoritative voice made manifest through a prophetic oracle. The effect is to present a counternarrative of the eunuch's inclusion and even privilege.[38] Far from being cut off from the temple and the community of worshipers on account of his "defect," the pious eunuch will be fully included in the cultic community, and his inclusion will be marked by a memorial monument in the deity's house and by an everlasting name.[39] The fact that the memorial monument is said to be "better than sons and daughters," and that the eunuch's name shall last forever, suggest the eunuch's position of privilege vis-à-vis others who do not have "defects" (mûmîm). The eunuch is not their equal, asserts the text; rather, he is treated with greater favor than they are. Unhappily, truly countervailing texts such as Isa 56:3–7, texts that vigorously contest disability's stigmatization in the dominant biblical narrative without reinforcing it indirectly at the same time, are all too rare. Nonetheless, they do provide us with a glimpse of some of the ways in which the hegemonic shaping of disability might have been challenged through the production of alternative, validating representations.

NATIVE AND NONNATIVE MODES OF CLASSIFICATION

It will be evident to any reader that I intend to engage both native and nonnative modes of classification in this study. Native modes of classification such as the contrast non-"defective" or "whole"/"defective" or clean/unclean allow us to learn something about the ways in which the ancients represented themselves and others, and thought about the organization of their society. Nonnative modes of classification such as disabled/able bodied help contemporary scholars gain greater insight into the ancient society we seek to understand from its literary and nonliterary remains, and allow us to contextualize more effectively its particular social and cultural configurations. Both native and nonnative taxonomic categories are socially constructed, the native – in the case of this study – in an ancient West Asian setting, the nonnative in our contemporary Western academic context. A primary goal of this investigation is to determine the extent to which the native and nonnative taxonomic systems in question overlap, and the degree to which they differ. Although disability, like race, class, gender, and sexuality, is a contemporary category of analysis, and although no equivalent or even roughly parallel term survives in extant ancient texts, I seek nonetheless to determine whether the texts of interest to us suggest the possibility of an implicit, larger native classification that brings together various types of persons we might refer to as disabled. As mentioned previously in this introduction, the biblical text does indeed bring into direct association a variety of disabilities – both "defects" (*mûmîm*) and non-"defects" – suggesting that they share something in common from the perspective of native taxonomy.

CHAPTER OUTLINE

This study is divided into seven chapters, excluding this introduction and the conclusion. In chapter 1, I reconstruct ideas of beauty and ugliness as they are represented in biblical texts, and seek to identify which somatic and nonsomatic qualities and characteristics were valued by the writers of biblical texts, which were understood to be somehow wanting, and which provoked little or no strong response. I also explore the biblical deployment of the Hebrew vocabulary of beauty and ugliness, perfection and "defect," and consider evidence for dissenting views on beauty and its importance. My examination of biblical ideas of beauty and ugliness underscores their culture-specific nature. Because notions of beauty and ugliness often contribute to the shaping of biblical discourse on "defects" (*mûmîm*) and other disabilities, this chapter serves as a preamble to further investigation in this work. Chapter 2 consists of a systematic inquiry into biblical treatments of congenital or acquired alterations to the body that are classified as "defects" (*mûmîm*). To these I compare circumcision, a physical alteration cast as enabling, as well as other physical disabilities not classed as "defects" (e.g., deafness, muteness, several diseases) in an attempt to explain what makes a "defect" a "defect." The potential social ramifications of "defects" are also a central concern. Finally, this chapter considers "defects" and other "mutilations," both permanent and temporary, imposed as a form of punishment on living persons, corpses, and even the iconic representations of an enemy's gods and rulers (e.g., cutting off limbs), and their relationship to congenital and acquired "defects." Chapter 3 is a study of disabling diseases and physical conditions ("skin disease" [*ṣaraʿat*], genital "flows," deafness, muteness, menstruation, parturition) not categorized as "defects" (*mûmîm*) in the biblical text, their relationship to "defects," and the potential social ramifications of their representation. Of particular interest is comparison of the stigmatizing and marginalizing strategies deployed by biblical authors in their representations of non-"defective" physical disabilities on the one hand, and "defects" on the other. Chapter 4's focus is an analysis of the ways in which mental disability is represented and classified, and how this both differs from and shares characteristics in common with the representation and classification of physical disabilities. Chapter 5 seeks to understand the role disability plays in prophetic utopian visions such as Isa 35:4–10. In some of these texts, the circumstances of disabled persons are changed in the ideal future; in others, disability itself is eliminated; in still others, there are no disabled persons, but disability has a central, metaphorical function. Chapter 6 is an investigation of nonsomatic analogues to bodily wholeness and "defect" (e.g., "whole" altar stones). Here, I trace the larger cultural resonance of the "whole"/"defective" contrast. Finally, chapter 7 considers the ways in which ancient Jewish interpretive texts from the period before the destruction of the Second Temple in 70 CE (specifically, the Dead Sea Scrolls) perpetuate, elaborate on, or transform biblical notions of disability and biblical models of classification, and the ramifications of such elaboration or modification with respect to stigmatization and marginalization.

In addition to contributing to the mainstreaming of disability as a significant area of biblical study, it is my hope that this book contributes to disability history more broadly. Given that most historians working on disability have focused on Euro-America after 1789, this investigation should provide some potentially useful comparative perspectives to those working in other areas of disability history, and complement recent work in related fields such as Classics and Rabbinic literature.[40]

1

ॐ

Constructions of Beauty and Ugliness

*M*Y GOAL IN THIS CHAPTER IS TO RECONSTRUCT BIBLICAL notions of beauty and ugliness from their representations in various biblical texts. This investigation of biblical ideas about beauty and its antitype serves several purposes. It allows us to get a sense of which particular physical and nonphysical qualities and characteristics were esteemed by the writers of our texts, which were deemed deficient in some way, and which elicited little or no strong reaction. It also permits us to identify the particular vocabulary of beauty and ugliness native to the biblical text and to examine carefully its deployment by biblical authors, and it allows us to consider dissenting perspectives on beauty and its importance. Finally, a consideration of biblical representations of somatic and nonsomatic ideals and their opposites brings into relief the degree to which all notions of beauty and ugliness are culture specific. Although certain characteristics of biblical constructions of male and female beauty are not unlike some of those familiar in some contemporary Western contexts, others will likely strike readers as alien to their own understandings of beauty. This chapter serves as a preamble to my investigation of biblical constructions of disability, particularly physical disability, for ideas of beauty and ugliness are not infrequently related to "defects" (*mûmîm*) and other biblical disabilities.[1]

MALE AND FEMALE BEAUTY

I begin with qualities of the beautiful male mentioned in texts that describe the physical appearance and behavior of heroic leaders such as Saul and David, of the ideal male lover of the Song of Songs, and of

David's rebellious son Absalom. Although these descriptions privilege one or another physical or nonphysical trait (e.g., exceptional height, ruddy skin, agility of movement), they tend to use the same technical vocabulary to communicate their notions of beauty and ugliness. Saul is introduced in 1 Sam 9:2, the beginning of the second of two narratives that focus on how he came to be Israel's first king.[2] He is described as "a handsome young man" (*baḥûr waṭôb*), an expression drawing together the notions of youth and physical attractiveness.[3] In fact, the text goes on to state that "there was no man of the children of Israel more handsome (*ṭôb*) than he; from his shoulder upward he was taller than all the people." The characteristic of significant height, cast as exemplary of Saul's attractiveness in this passage, is also a singular and attractive attribute of Saul emphasized in the other literary version of his rise to kingship: "When he stationed himself in the midst of all the people he was taller than all the people from his shoulder upward. And Samuel said to all the people: 'See the one whom Yhwh has chosen, for there is none like him among all the people'" (1 Sam 10:23–24). Other texts suggest qualities associated with the beautiful male in addition to noteworthy height and youth. In 1 Sam 16:12, the young David is introduced for the first time in the narrative. He is described as "ruddy, with beautiful eyes, and handsome with respect to appearance" (*'admônî 'im yepeh 'ênayim weṭôb ro'î*). Later, we are told that Goliath despised David because "he was a youth, and ruddy, with a handsome appearance" (1 Sam 17:42).[4] Ruddiness is also a quality of the male lover praised in Song of Songs 5:10: "My beloved is gleaming and ruddy, outstanding among ten thousand." A male youth's clear skin is contrasted favorably with the diseased skin of the Syrian general Naaman in 2 Kgs 5:14; it is the ideal into which Naaman's skin is transformed by Yhwh's miraculous intervention. Thus, it seems likely that handsome, ruddy youths also have clear, blemishless skin. In addition to a reddish, clear complexion, plumpness is mentioned as an attractive somatic characteristic of males in Dan 1:15, the expected result of a rich diet; the same idiom used of attractive, well-fed animals elsewhere (e.g., Gen 41:2) is used of the youths in question (*berî'ê baśar*, "fat with respect to flesh").[5] Certain qualities of a man's hair and beard are praised in several texts. 2 Sam 14:26, describing Absalom's habit of cutting his hair at regular intervals, suggests implicitly that thick, heavy hair on the head is emblematic of male beauty.[6] Song of Songs 5:11 suggests that raven black is an ideal hair color. The wearing of a full beard by mature men is assumed (e.g., Ps 133:2), and its manipulation through depilation or shaving is associated with forms of debasement, including mourning rites. The same is true of shaving or depilation of the hair on the head.[7] Qualities other than those related to physical appearance are also associated with male attractiveness. In Song of Songs 2:8–9, the male lover is compared to a gazelle or hart leaping in the mountains and bounding in the hills (cf. 2:17; 8:14). Thus, the text associates ease of ambulation, agility, and speed in movement, qualities of the gazelle or hart, with male attractiveness; it implies that a lack of such qualities is indicative of, at minimum, a deficit with respect to beauty. The speed and physical strength of the ideal male warrior is extolled in 2 Sam 1:23. In that verse of David's Lament, Saul and Jonathan, the dead warriors in question, are said to have been "swifter than eagles, [and] mightier than lions."[8] Some texts mention other desirable qualities, such as musical and vocal ability, and adroitness in speech (1 Sam 16:18; Ezek 33:32).[9] Characteristics such as exceptional height; youth; ruddy, clear skin; beautiful eyes; plumpness; thick hair on the head; a beard in the case of a mature man; rapid, agile movement; and physical strength are constructed as emblematic of male beauty in biblical texts. These are the qualities that define technical expressions such as "handsome" (*ṭôb*) and "beautiful" (*yapeh*).

Female beauty is frequently described using idioms similar to those used of males who are categorized as beautiful, and the attractive qualities of women are frequently not unlike those of men. Abigail, the wife of a foolish clan chieftain of Caleb, is characterized as "beautiful with respect to appearance" (*yepat to'ar*) in 1 Sam 25:3, as is Rachel in Gen 29:17. Joseph is described using the same expression in Gen 39:6, and a similar idiom is used of David in 1 Sam 16:12 (*ṭôb ro'î*). Just as David's eyes were mentioned as emblematic of his attractiveness, so too are those of Rachel (by implication), in contrast to those of her unattractive sister Leah, whose eyes are described as "weak" (*rakkôt*) (Gen 29:17). The eyes of the female lover in Song of Songs 4:1 are also mentioned as evidence of her beauty: "Behold, you are beautiful, your eyes are doves behind your veil." Thick hair and smooth skin are most likely the meaning of expressions such as "your hair is like a flock of goats" and "your temples are like slices of pomegranate," mentioned in Song of Songs 4:1, 3 as beautiful qualities of the female lover; such attractive traits are also shared by men, as we have seen. A good-looking woman's eyelashes can be illustrative of her beauty, as Prov 6:25 suggests. Symmetrical teeth are mentioned as emblematic of female beauty in Song of Songs 4:2 and 6:6, as is a concave navel (7:3 [Eng. 2]) and a pleasant voice (2:14).[10] Qualities of beauty distinct to women share the theme of symmetry: "Your two breasts are like two fawns, twins of a gazelle . . ." (4:5; 7:4 [Eng. 3]). It seems likely that symmetrical paired body parts were equally associated with male beauty, although extant texts are less vocal in that regard. Finally, a woman may beautify herself by applying makeup, manipulating her hair in some way, and wearing fine, ornamented clothing (2 Kgs 9:30; Jer 4:30; cf. 2 Sam 1:24).

In addition to such positively constructed characteristics as plumpness; thick hair on the head; ruddy, clear skin; beautiful eyes; symmetrical teeth and breasts; significant height; quickness and agility of movement; and physical strength, male and female beauty are not infrequently associated with a lack of "defects" (*mûmîm*). Absalom, according to 2 Sam 14:25–27, was the most handsome man in Israel: "There was no attractive man (*'îš yapeh*) in all Israel as worthy of praise as Absalom. From the bottom of his foot to the top of his head, there was no 'defect' (*mûm*) in him." A lack of "defects" and physical beauty are also associated directly in Dan 1:4, which describes the characteristics of the Judean youths, including Daniel and his compatriots, who are brought to the royal palace to serve the king of Babylon: They are "boys who have in them no 'defect,' and are beautiful with respect to appearance." In Song of Songs 4:7, the female lover is said to be beautiful, and lacking in "defects"; in 6:9, she is described as "my perfect one" (*tammatî*), a derivative of the root "to be whole," or "perfect" (*tmm*), the antonym of idioms of "defect" (*mûm*).[11] What constitutes a "defect" in the biblical context? Although specific "defects" are not mentioned in these descriptions of beauty, we learn from texts such as Lev 21:18–20 that they include blindness, lameness, genital damage, broken or crushed limbs, limbs of uneven length, a blurred iris, two nonpolluting skin conditions, a hunch in the back, and several other conditions, some of which are difficult or impossible to identify with any confidence.[12] Lack of symmetry and blurring of physical boundaries are features of "defects" such as crushed or broken limbs or an indistinct iris; physical dysfunction distinguishes others such as some forms of blindness, lameness, and types of genital damage; others still are characterized by both dysfunction and asymmetry (e.g, a crushed arm or foot). Not all physical conditions that contemporary Westerners associate with disability are constructed as "defects" (*mûmîm*) in the biblical context. Deafness and muteness are never classified as "defects" in any biblical text, nor is mental disability cast as a "defect." In short, biblical "defects" overlap with certain conditions we characterize as disabilities, but not with others. Thus, "defect" is a technical term in biblical usage, referring to a specific set of negatively constructed physical characteristics inconsistent with biblical notions of beauty.[13]

UGLINESS

Just as it is possible to reconstruct biblical ideas of the beautiful, we can turn now to descriptions of the unattractive to get a sense of what constituted ugliness in the biblical context. Depictions of ugliness are much less common in biblical texts than are those of beauty, and most focus on animals rather than humans. However, because the idioms for animal attractiveness are much like those for human beauty, we can assume with some confidence that surviving descriptions of animal ugliness would have had some similarities to the descriptions of human unattractiveness that we now lack. Gen 41:2 speaks of Joseph's dream of seven beautiful, fat cows (*yepôt mar'eh ûberî'ot baśar*) rising up from the Nile followed by seven ugly, thin cows (*ra'ôt mar'eh wedaqqôt baśar*). In this description of Joseph's symbolic dream of 7 prosperous years followed by 7 lean years, a common adjective for "beautiful" (*yapah*) is contrasted with an adjective best translated "ugly" in this and related contexts (*ra'*). Gen 41:19 builds on the initial contrast drawn in 41:2, further describing the unattractive cows as "poor" or "weak" (*dal*) in addition to "thin" (*daq*; probably, "emaciated") and "ugly" (*ra'*). Their unattractiveness is emphasized in Joseph's summary statement about them: "I had not seen the like of them for ugliness in all the land of Egypt." In these passages, ugliness is characterized by thinness (probably, emaciation) and, perhaps, weakness[14]; these stand in opposition to plumpness, an attractive human characteristic according to Dan 1:15. Several texts concerned with the quality of animal sacrifices associate "defects" (*mûmîm*) with ugliness. A gloss on Deut 15:21 speaks of "defects" in a sacrificial animal (specifically, a firstling) as "ugly" or "disfiguring" (*ra'*): "If there is a 'defect' in it – lame or blind, any ugly 'defect' (*kol mûm ra'*) – you shall not sacrifice it to

Yhwh your god." A gloss on Deut 17:1 is similar: "You shall not sacrifice to Yhwh your god ox or sheep which has in it a 'defect' – any ugly thing (*kol dabar ra'*) – for it is an abomination of Yhwh your god."

Qualities constituting human ugliness are suggested by a number of texts. In Gen 29:17, Leah's "weak eyes" are emblematic of her lack of beauty. The presence of a foreskin is associated with disgrace (*ḥerpah*) in two passages (Gen 34:14; Jos 5:9); although no idiom of ugliness per se is used in these texts, it seems nonetheless evident that a lack of circumcision is constructed as an unattractive, even repellent quality in a male.[15] The same association of "defects" with ugliness was very likely the case for humans as it was for animals, although no text is explicit about this. Baldness may well have been characterized as unattractive, given the story of the youths who mocked the prophet Elisha on account of his bald head and Elisha's intemperate reaction to them: "When he turned around and saw them, he cursed them in the name of Yhwh. Then two bears emerged from the forest and mauled forty two of the children" (2 Kgs 2:23–24).[16] Shaving the head or part of the head as a form of self-debasement in mourning rites also suggests that baldness may have been considered an ugly trait (e.g., Jer 16:6; Mic 1:16). The fact that thick, luxuriant hair is a source of praise in several passages may indicate this as well. Thus, physical qualities such as weak eyes, thinness (probably, emaciation), the presence of a foreskin or a "defect," and possibly baldness, very likely constitute human ugliness in the biblical context.

PHYSICAL CHARACTERISTICS THAT ARE NEITHER BEAUTIFUL NOR UGLY

Several physical qualities that might potentially be categorized negatively or positively elicit little or no strong reaction in our texts. A short or average stature is one example. Although David is praised for his appearance in several passages, tallness, an esteemed quality of Saul in the narratives of 1 Samuel, is never an attribute mentioned among David's various attractive qualities. Yhwh's admonition to Samuel to look beyond attractive characteristics such as significant height in 1 Sam 16:7, a narrative of Yhwh's choice of David, can be taken as an indirect comment on David's stature.[17] Several texts state that David was a handsome man, even though significant height was not among his attractive attributes. His short or average stature is apparently viewed as neither an attractive nor an unattractive characteristic. Left-handedness is another example of a trait that is typically constructed neither positively nor negatively in biblical materials. Although the right hand, and a preference for it, is sometimes privileged in biblical discourse (e.g., Gen 48:13–14; Exod 15:6), partiality for the left hand is generally not denigrated; occasionally, it is even presented as an asset. One example of a left-handed hero is the crafty Ehud, who uses his left-handedness to advantage in Judg 3:15–30; other notable warriors include the highly skilled, left-handed Benjaminites mentioned in Judg 20:16. With respect to behavior, the straight path is typically praised, with deviation to the right or left denigrated: "Do not incline to the right or the left," // "Remove your foot from evil" (Prov 4:27; cf. Deut 2:27; 5:32). Eccl 10:2 disparages the left hand, associating it with the fool, but this is unique in the Hebrew Bible, and likely reflects Hellenistic influence.[18] An addition to the Septuagint of Prov 4:27, associating the left with perversity and ungodliness, and the right with the deity, may be viewed similarly.[19]

BEAUTY AND PERFECTION: THEIR RELATIONSHIP

Although somatic beauty and physical perfection (= a lack of "defects" [*mûmîm*]) are not infrequently brought into association in biblical texts, they are not equivalent ideas. A person might be sighted (= lacking blindness, a "defect") without having beautiful eyes (e.g., Leah in Gen 29:17); another who walks without a limp might not necessarily be swift and agile; one's legs might be fully functional, but nonetheless not be understood to be attractive (cf. Song of Songs 7:2 [Eng. 1]). It is therefore possible to lack "defects" and still be deficient with respect to beauty, but those who are described as beautiful must be without "defects," as texts such as 2 Sam 14:25, Song of Songs 4:7, and Dan 1:4 insist. Similarly, it appears that it is possible to be ugly without having "defects," although the presence of "defects" probably means that one is understood to be ugly. The ugly cows of Gen 41:2, 19 are not characterized as having "defects," but the "defects" of sacrificial animals mentioned in Deut 15:21 and 17:1 are described as ugly. Thus, beauty and perfection, although frequently associated in biblical descriptions of the physical, are not equivalent notions, and the same is true of ugliness and "defect." Perfection is required in order to be beautiful, although not all who are perfect possess the attributes of attractiveness. "Defects" are constructed as ugly, although not all who are ugly possess "defects." The overlap between beauty and perfection, ugliness and "defect," is therefore only partial, with perfection and ugliness as the larger fields. The difference between the two pairings is that all persons who are "defective" are likely ugly, whereas not all persons who are perfect are beautiful.

TECHNICAL VOCABULARY OF BEAUTY AND UGLINESS

The technical vocabulary of beauty and ugliness in the Hebrew Bible is not especially rich or complex, and tends to be organized around dyadic pairs such as "beautiful" or "handsome" (*na'im, yapeh, tôb*) on the one hand, and "ugly" (*ra'*) on the other. What is particularly interesting about this vocabulary, however, is the semantic range of the pair that I have translated "handsome" and "ugly" (*tôb* and *ra'*).[20] As C. Dohmen stated, "the semantic spectrum of these polar terms is very broad, as is the range of their syntactic variation. The meaning of the contrast extends from a general 'positive – negative' response of emotions, feelings, and sense perceptions ... to describing ethical knowledge in its totality and the ability to decide between right and wrong. ..."[21] The first member of the pair has a generally positive thrust and is frequently to be translated as "good," sometimes in a moral sense (e.g., Mic 6:8); the second member of the dyad has a generally negative thrust and is often appropriately rendered "bad" or "evil." The two components of the opposition are brought together in the expression "to spurn the evil and choose the good" (Isa 7:16), an idiom that refers to discernment of right from wrong, appropriate from inappropriate; they are also famously paired in Gen 2:17; 3:5, 22. For the purposes of this investigation, it is not insignificant that the same word used for "good," "appropriate," "right," and even "happy" (e.g., Eccl 7:14) can also mean "handsome" or "beautiful," and the same word used for "bad," "inappropriate," "wrong," "evil," and "sad," (e.g., Neh 2:1–2) is also used to mean "ugly." The semantic range of these technical terms serves to underscore the positive casting of beauty in the biblical context, and the negative casting of ugliness. Beauty, like all things "good," is desirable and to be welcomed; ugliness, like all things "bad," is undesirable and not to be sought after.

ASSESSMENTS OF BEAUTY

In more than a few of the texts under consideration, Yhwh's choice of handsome young men such as Saul and David to lead Israel lends to the text's notions of beauty an additional dimension of divine approbation and even favor.[22] Ps 45:3 (Eng. 2) even goes so far as to state that the king is the most beautiful of humans, and articulate; as a result, he is blessed by God forever.[23] Thus, when Yhwh makes choices among humans, texts such as these suggest that he has a preference for the beautiful.[24] Humans, too, prefer the beautiful according to some biblical texts. Kings choose attractive men to serve at court (Dan 1:3–4), and beautiful women as wives and attendants (Esther 2:2–4; Ps 45:11–12 [Eng. 10–11]). Common people also favor that which is beautiful. Isa 53:2 characterizes the servant as one lacking an attractive appearance from the beginning, and so lacking attention and interest from members of his community: "He had no form (*to'ar*) or honor, that we might look at him" // "Nor appearance (*mar'eh*), that we might take pleasure in him." The words for "form" and "appearance" in this passage are used commonly in descriptions of beauty (e.g., Gen 39:6), so it is clear that the text is speaking of someone who lacks physical attractiveness, and therefore, notice in the community.[25] Needless to say, beauty is directly associated with sexual desire in more than a few passages (e.g., Gen 6:2; Deut 21:11; 2 Sam 11:2–4; 13:1–2, 15).

Yet, majority voices in the biblical anthology that privilege beauty and denigrate or ignore ugliness are not representative of the collection as a whole. A case in point is the so-called servant song of Isa 52:13–53:12, discussed in the previous paragraph. In that text, the servant, whose physical appearance was initially not deemed worthy of notice by his community, was nonetheless chosen by Yhwh, who refers to him as "my servant," and promises that he shall prosper and be exalted exceedingly (Isa 52:13), winning a portion with the great (53:12). The Yhwh of this text chooses an unattractive person as his servant and favors him with esteem, much in contrast to the Yhwh who prefers the beautiful in texts, such as 1 Sam 9:2. Other passages also depart from the typical view either by insisting that beauty be coupled with wisdom or piety in order to be of worth, or by taking a generally skeptical or even negative position on beauty. Some texts praise a combination of physical beauty and wisdom, knowledge or piety in the same individual, instead of focusing exclusively on physical attractiveness. In 1 Sam 25:3, Abigail is described as both a woman of good sense (*ṭôbat śekel*) and beautiful with respect to appearance. Likewise, the Judean youths selected for the Babylonian court in Dan 1:4 are described as without "defect," attractive in appearance, proficient in every type of wisdom, and knowledgeable. A lack of wisdom or piety renders beauty worthless according to Prov 11:22: "Like a ring of gold in the nose of a pig is a beautiful woman without sense." Other voices in the wisdom tradition express more skepticism about beauty.[26] In speaking of the capable wife, Prov 31:30 states that "Grace is false and beauty is empty," // "But a woman who fears Yhwh is to be praised." Sir 9:8–9 (G, 8) casts female beauty as the potential cause of male ruin, as does Prov 6:25.[27] These passages not only privilege wisdom and piety over physical attractiveness; they have little good to say about beauty. Some texts even go so far as to blame beauty for the corruption of wisdom. In Ezek 28:12, the king of Tyre is said to be both full of wisdom, and perfect in beauty. Yet, it is precisely his beauty that corrupted his wisdom according to 28:17: "Your heart was haughty because of your beauty" // "You perverted your wisdom on account of your splendor." Thus, although many biblical texts esteem beauty most highly, and even portray a deity who does the same, other texts, particularly those with a wisdom background, present strikingly different views of beauty, its value, and Yhwh's attitude toward it. These alternative voices remind us that the Hebrew Bible is an anthology of literature spanning a millennium, and that even if it is difficult or impossible to date or contextualize particular texts, at minimum a range of voices on issues of interest to this study (e.g., the beautiful) can sometimes be identified and compared.

CONCLUSION

In this chapter, I sought to identify both qualities related to human physical appearance and other human qualities (e.g., agility in movement) most highly esteemed by the writers of biblical texts. I also discussed denigrated characteristics and those generally eliciting little reaction (e.g., left-handedness, short or average stature). The list of privileged qualities that constitute beauty in the biblical context includes characteristics that will likely resonate with many members of contemporary Western societies (e.g., symmetry of female breasts and teeth, attractiveness of female eyelashes, male youth and vigor). It will also include those that will appear alien to some (e.g., extreme height among male leaders, male plumpness).[28] Some qualities often associated with female or male beauty in many contemporary Western contexts (e.g., substantial female breast size) appear to elicit no evident response in biblical descriptions of the attractive, and other characteristics emphasized in biblical texts (e.g., striking eyes in men and women) do not necessarily play an equivalent role in contemporary Western discourses on beauty. Thus, beauty is a construction specific to particular contexts, as is ugliness. In addition to examining privileged and nonprivileged human characteristics and their cultural resonances, I also investigated the technical vocabulary of beauty and ugliness in order to develop a more nuanced understanding of biblical discourses of attractiveness and unattractiveness. The most striking aspect of the biblical vocabulary of beauty and ugliness is the use of common terms for good and bad, with a specialized meaning of beautiful and ugly. Thus, the beautiful is indirectly associated with what is good, happy, right, appropriate, and desirable, and the ugly is indirectly associated with what is bad, unhappy, wrong, inappropriate, evil, and undesirable, thereby underscoring the positive casting of beauty and the negative casting of ugliness. Yhwh's favoring of the beautiful in the dominant stream of the biblical tradition also serves to bring into relief beauty's privileging, although dissenting voices, many from the wisdom tradition, demonstrate clearly that this construction of the importance of beauty was not universally embraced.

༅

2

Physical Disabilities Classified as "Defects"

I N THIS CHAPTER I UNDERTAKE A SYSTEMATIC INVESTIGATION OF congenital or acquired alterations to the body that are classified by biblical texts as "defects" (*mûmîm*).[1] "Defects" constitute a significant, although by no means comprehensive, category of disability in the biblical anthology. Even though blindness, lameness, and several other physical conditions are included among biblical "defects," deafness, muteness, and various diseases, as well as mental disability, are not categorized as such, and this chapter attempts to identify the rationale behind what constitutes a "defect." Biblical "defects" tend to have negative social ramifications for those who possess them, and therefore, the social dynamics of "defects" are explored in some depth. Persons with "defects" are frequently stigmatized by biblical authors, who also assign them marginal social positions. This is accomplished through the deployment of discourses of profanation, curse, and hatred, among others, as well as through association with devalued characteristics (e.g., weakness, vulnerability, ignorance) and other marginal categories of persons (e.g., the poor, the alien). The degree to which the stigmatizing and marginalizing "defect" is a particular social construction native to a specific cultural context is brought into relief by the exceptional case of male circumcision. Constructed by biblical texts as normative, although it is an imposed alteration to the body not unlike other imposed alterations cast as "defects" (e.g., the cutting off of a lip or an eyelid), circumcision is socially and ritually enabling rather than disabling. Finally, this chapter examines the evidence for "defects" and other mutilations imposed as a form of punishment on living persons, corpses, and even on iconic representations of an enemy's gods and rulers (e.g., cutting off limbs), and considers what such mutilations are intended to accomplish.

A NATIVE CATEGORY

The "defect" (*mûm*) is a native category of classification found primarily, although not exclusively, in legal materials that focus on the cult and its requirements. The primary texts dealing with "defects" in persons are Lev 21:17–23; 24:19–20; and Deut 23:2 (Eng. 1); these are supplemented by texts such as Isa 56:1–8 and the saying in 2 Sam 5:8b, and by a variety of texts that concern "defects" in sacrificial animals (e.g., Lev 22:18–25; Deut 15:21–23; 17:1; Mal 1:6–14). Lev 21:17–23 is the most extensive treatment of human "defects" preserved in the biblical anthology. A part of the so-called Holiness Code, it concerns priests with "defects" whose ritual activities are restricted in two ways on account of their condition: They are forbidden to offer sacrifices to Yhwh, and those priests in the high priestly line are excluded from service as high priest.[2] Verse 17 introduces the issue of altar service, a most highly esteemed priestly activity according to cultic texts: "Speak to Aaron as follows: 'Any man of your descendants for their generations who has in him a 'defect' (*mûm*) shall not approach to bring near the food of his god.'"[3] The "defects" that exclude "defective" priests from offering sacrifice are then listed, and include blindness, lameness, an improperly healed broken leg or arm, limbs of uneven length, a hunch in the back, a loss of distinction between the iris and the white of the eye, two nonpolluting skin conditions, and genital damage of some kind (probably a crushed testicle), as well as several conditions impossible to identify.[4] Lev 24:19–20, part of the same Holiness legal collection as Lev 21:17–23, adds the loss of an eye and the loss of a tooth as "defects," citing the talion formulation in a way as to suggest that these are to be understood as such: "As for the man who imposes a 'defect' on his fellow, as he has done, so shall it be done to him: break for break, an eye for an eye, a tooth for a tooth. Because he imposed a 'defect' on a person, so it shall be imposed on him." Deut 23:2 (Eng. 1), a text unrelated to Lev 21:17–23 and 24:19–20, does not use the rhetoric of "defect" as these texts do, but nonetheless excludes men with two kinds of genital damage – a type of "defect" – from entry into "the assembly of Yhwh," likely a reference to cultic participation, as suggested by the earliest interpretations of and responses to the restriction itself and the larger pericope in which it is embedded (Deut 23:2–9 [Eng. 1–8]): "A man with crushed testicles or a cut off penis shall not enter the assembly of Yhwh."[5] In a later time, Isa 56:3–5 responds critically to the proscription of men with genital damage from entering the sanctuary found in Deut 23:2 (Eng. 1). It assumes the prohibition's broadening to include the eunuch and asserts that the eunuch does indeed have a place in Yhwh's cultic community.[6] Finally, 2 Sam 5:8b, presented as a popular adage, appears to bear witness to an interdiction on entry of blind and lame Israelites into a sanctuary – likely the Jerusalem temple – for the purposes of worship: "Anyone blind or lame shall not enter the house."[7]

The biblical texts of varying provenance and date that I have introduced provide some insight into the range of physical conditions constructed as "defects" (*mûmîm*) by biblical authors. They also treat "defects" in persons in a variety of ways. The "defects" mentioned in these texts include both those visible to the eye and those not normally seen (e.g., genital damage).[8] Some "defects" are presumably congenital, whereas others are clearly acquired in one way or another (e.g., Lev 24:19–20).[9] No distinction is made in extant biblical texts between temporary "defects" and those that are permanent or long lasting, although most, if not all, "defects" were probably thought to be long lasting or permanent.[10] A lack of symmetry or the blurring of physical boundaries are characteristic of some "defects" (e.g., limbs of uneven length, a missing eye or tooth, an indistinct iris); physical dysfunction is characteristic of others (e.g., some forms of genital damage or blindness); still others feature both somatic dysfunction and asymmetry/blurring of physical boundaries (e.g., a crushed arm or foot, a blind eye with an indistinct iris). Although several texts concern the "defects" of common Israelites (Lev 24:19–20; Deut 23:2 [Eng. 1]; 2 Sam 5:8b; Isa 56:3–5), one focuses on those of priests (Lev 21:17–23). And even though a number of the texts concern males exclusively (Lev 21:17–23; 24:19–20; Deut 23:2 [Eng. 1]; Isa 56:3–5), one is apparently broader in its interests (2 Sam 5:8b). All but one of these texts concern cultic matters. Several proscribe entry into the sanctuary and participation in cultic rites such as sacrifice for persons with particular "defects" (Deut 23:2 [Eng. 1]; 2 Sam 5:8b), and one challenges such a prohibition in the case of the eunuch (Isa 56:3–5). Lev 21:17–23 limits the cultic activity of priests with "defects" without excluding them from the temple sphere per se, much in contrast to exclusionary texts such as Deut 23:2 (Eng. 1) and 2 Sam 5:8b, which prohibit entry into the sanctuary sphere to persons with particular "defects." (It is possible that 2 Sam 5:8b uses "blind and lame" as a synecdoche or an idiom of inclusion, and therefore refers to all persons with "defects."[11]) Thus, these texts bear witness to a variety of approaches to persons with "defects" and even to debate over their inclusion or exclusion from the cult and its familial and communal dimensions. All but one text construct the "defects" in question negatively and impose restrictions on "defective" persons, but the nature of the restrictions differ from text to text, as do their social ramifications.

The criteria that determine whether biblical sources classify physical conditions or qualities as "defects" (*mûmîm*) remain obscure. Some have argued that all "defects" are visible to the eye; thus, deafness, muteness, and mental disability are not constructed as "defects." Although this explanation works well for the "defects" of animals, among humans it fails because genital damage of whatever sort will normally be covered by clothing and, therefore, will not be visible to the onlooker.[12] Also, a condition such as "skin disease" (*sara'at*) would often be visible, yet it is never classified as a "defect" in any biblical text.[13] The same appears to be the case with respect to tattoos and related phenomena.[14] Although asymmetry is characteristic of some "defects" (e.g., a limp, an improperly set broken leg, the loss of an eye or a tooth), it is not characteristic of all (e.g., forms of complete blindness that do not affect the appearance of either eye, the loss of a penis or a nose). Furthermore, asymmetry is apparently characteristic of "skin disease" (*sara'at*) as it is described in Lev 13:12–17 and Num 12:12, yet "skin disease," as mentioned, is never classified as a "defect." The blurring of physical boundaries is a feature of "defects" such as blindness accompanied by an indistinct iris, although certainly not of all "defects." Somatic dysfunction is a quality shared by many if not most "defects," but a number of non-"defective" disabilities (e.g., deafness, muteness) also share this characteristic. The permanence or long-lasting nature of most, if not all, "defects" can also be shared by conditions that are not classified as "defects" (e.g., mental disability, "skin disease"). This leaves us with no evident rationale that can explain what every "defect" shares in common, and why conditions such as deafness, muteness, mental disability, and "skin disease" are not constructed as "defects" in any biblical text. Most "defects" are, however, visible to the eye, long lasting or permanent in nature, and characterized by physical dysfunction, and more than a few share asymmetry as a quality.

Texts that focus on "defects" among sacrificial animals add some important information about the way "defects" are constructed that likely applies equally to human beings with "defects." Lev 22:18–25, like a number of passages that deal with animal "defects," refers to sacrificial animals that lack "defects" as "whole" or "perfect" (*tamîm*), an adjective from the same root (*tmm*) as the expression "my perfect one" (*tammatî*), which is used to describe the female lover in Song of Songs 6:9, who is said elsewhere (4:7) to be lacking in "defects."[15] Thus, it seems evident that persons lacking "defects" are understood to be "perfect," not unlike animals without "defects." Lev 22:25 casts "defects" as a source of "ruin" or "destruction" in sacrificial animals (*mošḥat*), and other verses of Lev 22:18–25 make clear that almost all animals with "defects" are unacceptable to Yhwh as a sacrifice (vv. 20, 21, 22, 23, 24, 25).[16] Glosses on Deut 15:21 and 17:1 establish an explicit association between the presence of a "defect" and ugliness: "If there is a 'defect' in it – lame or blind, any ugly 'defect' – you shall not sacrifice it to Yhwh your god" (Deut 15:21). A gloss on Deut 17:1 defines the "defect" as "any ugly thing," and the verse itself refers to a sacrificial animal with a "defect" as an abomination of Yhwh.[17] Mal 1:6–14, a text of the fifth century, speaks of sacrificial animals with "defects" as "ruined things," not unlike Lev 22:25, and adds a new dimension to the rhetoric of rejection applied to such animals: they are "polluted food" (*leḥem mego'al*), impure and like all impure things or persons, utterly unacceptable in a sanctuary setting. This association of impurity and "defect" will eventually be applied explicitly to the human "defect" of blindness in the Temple Scroll from Qumran; it is possible that such an association is also evidenced in 2 Sam 5:8b, although this must remain uncertain. The devaluing of sacrificial animals with "defects," and their stigmatization as unacceptable, ruined, ugly, abominable, and even unclean in the case of Mal 1:6–14, likely had at least some parallels in the treatment of humans with "defects," although texts are rarely as direct in this regard. Nonetheless, devaluing discourses of curse, dishonor, and profanation, among others, are brought to bear on biblical persons with "defects," as they are on others with disabilities, as we shall see. These discourses have the effect of stigmatizing persons with "defects" in a variety of ways, and seek to marginalize them.

STIGMATIZATION AND MARGINALIZATION

The stigmatizing and marginalizing of priests with "defects" is only partial according to Lev 21:17–23. As v. 22 makes clear, the afflicted priest may remain in the sanctuary sphere, and may continue to eat from his allowance of most holy and holy foods. He is neither expelled from the sanctuary and priestly service, nor must he give up his normal sources of food, even the exclusive most holy offerings.[18] However, as v. 23 states, "defects" disqualify a priest from altar service and a potential high priest from serving as high priest for fear that such persons might profane (ḥll) Yhwh's sanctuaries, which he sanctifies (qdš). It would appear that this potential, undesirable profanation is action or situation specific in this particular text. As long as the afflicted priest refrains from two specific ritual actions – offering sacrifice as priests normally do and approaching the tabernacle curtain, the responsibility of the high priest – his condition does not threaten the holiness of the sanctuary and its offerings. However, should he flout the restrictions imposed on his service, his actions would result in profanation of the sanctuary, meaning the loss of its holiness, the divine quality par excellence and essential to the sanctuary's continued operation. Thus, the priest or potential high priest of Leviticus 21 who has a "defect" is stigmatized in the sense that his potential to profane the sanctuary's holiness is greater than that of his fellows who lack "defects," and an ever-present threat; he is both stigmatized and marginalized in that he is cut off from the most highly esteemed ritual activity normally open to him, although presumably he may participate in other priestly activities. He retains some priestly prerogatives (e.g., access to the most holy foods), but loses several of the central, most honorable privileges. Socially, the priest with a "defect" in Leviticus 21 continues to enjoy perquisites and honor unavailable to the nonpriestly Israelite male, such as access to holy and most holy foods, which are generally off limits to nonpriests, but he is no longer the equal of his non-"defective" peers.[19]

The social marginalization and stigmatization experienced by blind and lame persons who are excluded entirely from the sanctuary, according to the saying preserved in 2 Sam 5:8b, is far more severe than that of the priest with a "defect" in Lev 21:17–23 because the blind and the lame of 2 Sam 5:8b are not able to gain admittance to the temple at all, in contrast to the priest, who remains in the sanctuary sphere, albeit with a limited range of ritual action open to him. This means that the blind and the lame of 2 Sam 5:8b are effectively cut off from temple-based rites of atonement, petition, thanksgiving, and purification, and excluded from the social dimensions of cult as well (e.g., sanctuary-based family dynamics) in a way that the priest of Leviticus 21 is not. Exclusion from the sanctuary represents a very serious social and religious disadvantage in the Hebrew Bible's cultural context that should not be underestimated for the sanctuary is the locus par excellence for encounters with deity.[20] The reason for the total exclusion of the blind and the lame of 2 Sam 5:8b is unclear, although the text, through its proscription, may be suggesting that the affected individuals are understood to be polluters, not unlike the "defective" sacrificial animals of Mal 1:6–14. This, however, is uncertain, given that no rhetoric of impurity is used in the text. It is also possible that the blind and the lame are understood to profane the holiness of the sanctuary by their very presence, and are therefore excluded from the temple sphere (cf. the priest with a "defect" who performs sacrifices according to Lev 21:23), but this too is unclear, given the lack of the rhetoric of profanation in the saying. If the threat of profanation is the reason for the exclusion, then the dynamics of profanation in 2 Sam 5:8b differ markedly from those of Lev 21:17–23, where the priest with a "defect" profanes the sanctuary's holiness only if he defies the ban on his offering sacrifice, and not otherwise. In 2 Sam 5:8b, in contrast, the threat of profanation would not be situation specific, but general. At all events, the ban on the blind and the lame must have some ideological basis, and the two most likely candidates are the threat of pollution or that of profanation. In either case, a marginalizing and stigmatizing discourse would lie behind the proscription of blind and lame worshipers from the Jerusalem temple sphere.

The interdiction of Deut 23:2 (Eng. 1) appears to have a different rationale altogether. In that text, men with two types of genital damage (= "defects") are apparently prohibited from entering the temple sphere. The larger pericope of which Deut 23:2 (Eng. 1) is a part proscribes the entry of male descendants of Ammonite and Moabite immigrants for-ever, and only allows the male descendants of Edomite and Egyptian immigrants to enter in the third generation. Historical reasons are given for the ban on the Ammonite and Moabite, as well as the less severe treatment of the Egyptian; Edom's relationship to Israel according to the ancestral epic is used to justify admission of the Edomite in the third generation. However, no reason is given for the prohibition of men with two types of genital damage. Nonetheless, the text hints at the rationale for the ban by leaving out the formula it uses in other cases of unqualified interdiction: "Even the tenth generation belonging to him shall not enter the assembly of Yhwh" (vv. 3, 4 [Eng. 2, 3]). The formula is left out in v. 2 (Eng. 1) presumably because the men with genital damage cannot reproduce, and thus, it would make no sense to add such a formula to that verse. The notion that a lack of ability to reproduce should result in a ban on entering the sanctuary sphere is supported by Isa 56:3, which responds in a vigorous way to the proscription of Deut 23:2 (Eng. 1), rejecting it. In Isa 56:3, the eunuch apparently despairs of ever having cultic access because of his inability to father offspring: "Let the eunuch not say, // 'Behold – I am a dried up tree.'" Thus, at least one later writer responding to the interdiction of Deut 23:2 (Eng. 1) understood the ban to be based on a lack of reproductive ability, and that, coupled with the lack of a tenth-generation formula in Deut 23:2 (Eng. 1), suggests that inability to produce children lies behind the prohibition. This rationale for marginalizing and stigmatizing men with genital damage through exclusion from the cult is, needless to say, quite different than that of 2 Sam 5:8b, whether that text's rationale finds its basis in pollution or profanation concerns. It is also different in a number of respects from that of Lev 21:17–23.[21]

Biblical texts bear witness to a number of other stigmatizing and marginalizing strategies applied to persons with "defects." Aside from assertions of their association or possible association with profanation, with pollution, and with sterility, and the potential social ramifications of such claims, texts also stigmatize and seek to marginalize persons with "defects" through association with divine curse and punishment, vulnerability, weakness and dependence, hatred, ignorance, and bad judgment. A prime example is Deut 28:28–29, part of a list of curses that will come upon Israel should it violate Yhwh's covenant stipulations: "Yhwh shall strike you with 'madness,' blindness and bewilderment, and you shall grope at noon as a blind person gropes in the darkness. You shall not make your ways prosper, but you shall be oppressed and robbed always, without anyone to save you." The fact that blindness is listed here among divine curses intended to punish treaty violation is not insignificant for it functions to stigmatize blind persons in a number of respects.[22] Blindness as a divine punishment raises the possibility that any particular blind person is blind on account of divine disfavor.[23] Verse 29 associates blindness with victimization by enemies (and therefore, vulnerability and weakness) and with divine rejection ("without anyone to save you"). Furthermore, the grouping together of blindness with other curses such as sterility, disease, blight, drought, military defeat, lack of burial, loss of wealth and landed property, and exile ties blindness to every imaginable unwelcome condition, event, or thing, underscoring its undesirability. If blindness is intended to function emblematically here, and to evoke other "defects" as well in the mind of the reader, then all "defects" will share these negative associations of transgression, culpability, divine punishment, divine rejection, and vulnerability and weakness.[24] Several other texts associate blindness with divine punishment for transgression, either directly or indirectly. Zeph 1:17 is one such text: "I shall trouble people, // they shall go about like blind persons, // for they have sinned against Yhwh. // Their blood shall be poured out like dust, // their flesh like dung." A second text giving a punitive cast to blindness is Lam 4:14, a verse that follows immediately on a pair of verses that speak of the Babylonian depredations at the fall of Jerusalem as the result of sin. In this instance, the association is indirect, the result of the verse's placement: "They wandered blind in the streets, // polluted with blood. . . . " After having read that the disaster of 587 was the result of transgressions, the reader assumes the same for the blindness of the survivors of the Babylonian siege mentioned in the following verse. Thus, blindness, perhaps functioning in these texts as an emblematic "defect," is constructed as a negative and undesirable characteristic associated with divine curse and punishment, divine rejection, and vulnerability and weakness, therefore stigmatizing those who are afflicted with it in any number of ways.

Next, there is 2 Sam 5:6–8a, a rather obscure narrative describing David's conquest of Jerusalem. In that text, the Jebusites of Jerusalem seem to taunt David, saying that the blind and the lame will prevent his entry into the city (v. 6).[25] In v. 8a, the blind and the lame are described as "despised by David's soul," apparently on account of their disabilities.[26] Perhaps it is the weakness and vulnerability so frequently associated with physically disabled persons in the Hebrew Bible that motivates this hatred; alternatively, it may be the physical "defects" themselves that repel. Or it may be a combination of both.[27] In any case, it is obviously stigmatizing for lame and blind persons to be cast as despised, particularly by the Bible's paradigmatic hero and king. According to Deut 17:1, Yhwh abominates sacrificial animals with "defects," not unlike David's hating lame and blind persons according to 2 Sam 5:8a. Thus, an association between "defects" and hatred, both human and divine, although not frequently attested, is to be found in several texts. One wonders whether Yhwh's abominating of "defective" sacrificial animals extends to persons with "defects" as well in the minds of some biblical authors. Restrictive cultic texts such as Lev 21:17–23, Deut 23:2 (Eng. 1), and 2 Sam 5:8b, texts that seek to separate persons with "defects" from the deity's presence to a greater or lesser degree, may well assume the idea that Yhwh despises such persons, even though it is not stated explicitly.

Finally, there are the texts that associate blindness with ignorance and bad judgment. Isa 56:10 speaks of all Israel's watchmen as blind, and therefore, without knowledge; Isa 6:9–10 associates blindness with ignorance, and sightedness with knowledge and understanding. When Ps 82:5 speaks of the other gods as both walking in darkness, and ignorant and lacking understanding, it may be suggesting that they are blind, given the relationship between blindness and darkness, and blindness and ignorance, frequently witnessed in biblical texts.[28] A cuneiform text such as "Esarhaddon's Renewal of the Gods" associates blindness and deafness with ignorance in its statement that humans are unable to see and unable to hear, and therefore, ignorant, compared to the skillful, knowledgeable gods.[29] Exod 23:8 and Deut 16:19 speak of blindness metaphorically as a source of bad judgment: a bribe "blinds" (ye'awwer) the sighted/the eyes of the wise, not allowing them to judge cases justly.[30]

Association with other marginal categories of persons also serves to stigmatize persons with "defects" because such association suggests implicitly that all share the same set of devalued characteristics. Job 29:12–16 brings the blind and the lame into association with the poor, the

widow, the afflicted, the one perishing (?), and other weak and dependent
sufferers:

> I was eyes for the blind,
> feet for the lame was I.
> I was a father for the poor,
> and the lawsuit of the stranger I researched.[31]
>
> (vv. 15–16)

Another example of such an association is Ps 146:5–9, where Yhwh is said
to be an advocate for a wide variety of weak and needy persons:

> Happy is the one who has the God of Jacob as his helper,
> whose hope is in Yhwh his god,
> the maker of heavens and earth,
> the sea and all that is in them,
> who keeps faithfulness always,
> who executes justice for the oppressed,
> who provides food for the hungry.
> Yhwh frees prisoners,
> Yhwh gives sight to the blind,
> Yhwh raises up the prostrate,
> Yhwh loves the innocent,
> Yhwh watches over the resident aliens,
> the fatherless and widow he helps.
> But the way of the wicked he subverts.

In this text, the blind are associated with various persons understood
to be vulnerable, helpless, and in need of a powerful patron. Among
Yhwh's praiseworthy actions are his efforts to alleviate the downtrodden
condition of these dependent sufferers. Other biblical texts associating
"defective" persons with marginal social types include Isa 42:7, where the
blind are mentioned along with prisoners, and Isa 29:17–21, where they
are listed with the deaf, the afflicted, and the poor.

AN EXCEPTION: CIRCUMCISION

The treatment of male circumcision in the biblical text illustrates the
degree to which "defects" are constructions belonging to a particular social and cultural context. Like many "defects," circumcision is
an imposed physical alteration to the body. It might be compared to

cutting off a lip or an eyelid because it involves the removal of a naturally occurring skin covering on part of the body, exposing that which lies
beneath. However, in contrast to these alterations, which would be cast as
"defects" and would therefore have ritually and socially disabling effects
on affected individuals, circumcision is constructed as both ritually and
socially enabling and physically normative in the biblical context. In fact,
a number of texts stigmatize uncircumcised males, calling for their exclusion from the community, as if the presence of the foreskin were itself
a kind of "defect."[32] The stigmatization of the foreskin is widespread
in the biblical anthology. It is associated with disgrace (herpah) in texts
such as Gen 34:14 and Jos 5:9, not unlike "defects" in several passages
(e.g., Zeph 3:19). A number of texts allude to or speak of prohibitions on
the admission of uncircumcised alien males into Israelite ritual contexts
(e.g., Exod 12:48; Ezek 44:4–9), not unlike texts that proscribe Israelites
with "defects" from such settings (e.g., Deut 23:2 [Eng. 1]; 2 Sam 5:8b).
And a passage such as Gen 17:14 threatens uncircumcised Israelite males
with extinction of lineage on account of the fact that they have broken the covenant through neglecting circumcision.[33] Several texts treat
the Philistines, descendants of noncircumcising Aegean immigrants, as
unusual in their practice, going so far as to label them "the uncircumcised"
(e.g., 2 Sam 1:20) and to cast their foreskins as symbolic of their foreign
identity (1 Sam 18:17–27). This treatment of Philistine uncircumcision as
if it were odd and worthy of special attention underscores the normativity
of circumcision in the eyes of the biblical writers. To be circumcised is
the assumed norm; to have a foreskin is unusual and inconsistent with
expectations.

A number of texts speak of circumcision and uncircumcision
metaphorically, further developing the pejorative, disabling resonances
of the foreskin and conversely, the positive, enabling associations of its
removal. In several texts, a dysfunctional body part such as the ear or lip
is referred to as "uncircumcised." For example, in Jer 6:10, the ear of the
people is said to be uncircumcised and thus, "they are unable to hear."
Moses, referring to his lack of eloquence, calls his lips uncircumcised in
Exod 6:12, 30. Several texts speak of obedience to Yhwh as something
achieved through circumcision of the heart (Deut 10:16; Jer 4:4; cf. 9:25).
Lev 19:23 speaks of the fruit of immature fruit trees, which is off limits
to Israelites, as uncircumcised: "Three years it shall be uncircumcised

for you; it shall not be eaten." Thus, that which is physically dysfunctional, disobedient to Yhwh, and forbidden may be described as
"uncircumcised"; circumcision makes functional, improves, gives access.
The pejorative associations of metaphorical uncircumcision add depth
to the consistently negative construction of the foreskin in the biblical
context.

Circumcision as an enabling rite is richly illustrated by Exod 12:43–
49. The text is an H supplement to earlier Passover legislation, treating
the qualifications necessary to participate in the festival's central rites.
Although listing aliens, temporary workers, and all uncircumcised persons among those who may not partake of the Passover sacrifice, the text
makes provision for the participation of the uncircumcised male slave
and the uncircumcised resident alien and his household. Both may eat of
the Passover sacrifice as Israelites do if they submit to circumcision first.
"As for any male slave acquired for money, you shall circumcise him, and
then he may eat of it," says the text in v. 44. The resident alien and his
dependents are treated in v. 48: "If there resides with you a resident alien
(ger), and he would observe the Passover to Yhwh, every male belonging
to him must be circumcised. Then he may approach to observe it. He shall
be like the native of the land, but anyone who is uncircumcised shall not
eat it." Circumcision allows the uncircumcised resident alien and slave
effectively to become part of the community, and participate in rites central to the community's constitution and perpetuation. According to the
Holiness writer, the circumcised resident alien becomes, in effect, "like
the native of the land." Thus, circumcision is a fundamentally enabling
rite in a text such as Exod 12:48 for those outsiders who would choose to
embrace it. As for insiders who would neglect it, Gen 17:14 casts uncircumcision among Israelites as a covenant violation worthy of the most
severe sanction possible: extirpation of lineage. Thus, to avoid circumcis-
ing one's dependents is a stigmatizing and socially disabling act according
to Gen 17:14, one that results in classification as a covenant violator and
in the termination of one's lineage, an eventuality worse than the death
of the individual, and greatly to be feared in this cultural context.

PUNITIVE "DEFECTS" AND OTHER MUTILATIONS

The imposition of "defects" (mûmîm) and other mutilations as a vivid
form of punishment on the bodies of living and dead offenders and

enemies, as well as on iconic representations of enemy deities and rulers, is an exceedingly widespread topos in both biblical and cognate literatures. In this section of the chapter, I explore the representation of punitive "defects" and other mutilations, and consider what they are intended to accomplish. I distinguish mutilation from "defect" for two primary reasons. First, not all mutilations are to be categorized as "defects." Shaving or pulling out body hair in order to humiliate an enemy or an offender is certainly mutilating in a temporary way in this cultural context, which so values abundant hair and, in the case of a mature man, a full beard. Nevertheless, such acts do not constitute the imposition of a "defect" because the conditions they produce (e.g., a shaved head) never occur in lists of "defects," and the term "defect" (*mûm*) is never associated with them.[34] Thus, mutilation is a wider and more encompassing category than is "defect," but includes imposed or self-imposed "defects."[35] Second, the English word "mutilation," with its strongly pejorative connotations, accurately communicates the negative way in which such imposed alterations were viewed in their cultural context. Therefore, as long as we keep in mind the social and cultural specificity of notions of mutilation, the term is appropriate for use in the setting of this investigation.[36]

Living persons are subject to imposed mutilations according to any number of jurisprudential texts and writings concerned with the waging of war. An example of a biblical legal text that prescribes mutilation as a penalty is Lev 24:19–20. This passage speaks of the imposition of "defects" as just punishment for offenders who have themselves inflicted "defects" on others, as long as the penalty is proportionate ("break for break, an eye for an eye, a tooth for a tooth").[37] Mesopotamian legal texts contain similar formulations, as Hammurapi par.196 illustrates: "If an *awilu* should blind the eye of another *awilu*, they shall blind his eye."[38] They also bear witness to the imposition of "defects" as the penalty for other types of crimes. An example of this is Hammurapi par. 195: "If a child should strike his father, they shall cut off his hand."[39] As many have noted, it is the offending body part itself that is sometimes severed or mutilated as punishment for the offense.

Texts and visual representations of war and its aftermath not infrequently bear witness to the imposition of punitive mutilations on defeated enemies and vanquished rebels. A subdued enemy might be blinded or have limbs or other body parts removed, as is the case with Samson. After his capture by the Philistines, his eyes are poked out, and he is set to labor with a mill (Judg 16:21). An example of a threat to mutilate a vulnerable foe is narrated in 1 Sam 11:2. In this narrative, Nahash of Ammon seeks to maim the helpless Israelite population of Jabesh-Gilead through goug-ing out the right eye of each of them before they are rescued by Saul.[40] Treaty violators are dealt with in a similar manner. The curse of blindness will befall those Israelites who are disloyal to Yhwh's covenant, accord-ing to Deut 28:28–29. 2 Kgs 25:7 tells of the blinding of the rebellious vassal Zedekiah of Judah after his capture by agents of his overlord, the Babylonian king. An example of the infliction of a punitive mutilation that is not a "defect" on an alleged treaty violator is narrated in 2 Sam 10:4. David's emissaries to the court of his allies the Ammonites, sent as comforters at the time of the Ammonite king's death, are suspected of spying, and as a result, they are punished through the destruction of half their beards, the exposure of their genitals, and their expulsion from the Ammonite court.[41] The literature of the larger West Asian cultural context threatens potential treaty violators with punitive mutilations and speaks of numerous examples of their imposition. Esarhaddon's succes-sion treaty threatens disloyal vassals with the loss of their hands and feet, as well as blinding; similarly, the curse section of the treaty between Bir-Ga'yah and Mati''il warns the vassal Mati''il that he will be blinded and cut in two should he violate the stipulations of the treaty.[42] The Bisitun Inscription of Darius I speaks of the punishment of Fravartish, a Mede rebel: "Then I cut off his nose, his two ears, his tongue (and) blinded one eye of his. He was held in fetters at my gate. All the people could see him."[43] Ashurbanipal of Assyria boasts of mutilating captured rebels in any number of ways (e.g., cutting out their tongues, piercing their lips or chins, cutting off their heads). Sometimes, the severed or mutilated body part is identified as the source of offense against the king or patron god, as it is in some legal texts. An example is the sinful tongues of the rebels of Akkad, which Ashurbanipal claims to have cut out as just punishment for their verbal offenses.[44]

The corpses of dead foes and offenders are treated not unlike the bodies of living enemies and covenant breakers according to various texts. After Goliath is killed, his head is cut off and taken, along with his weapons, as a prize of war (1 Sam 17:51, 54). The dead bodies of Saul and his sons, killed by the Philistines on Mt. Gilboa, are stripped of their weapons, beheaded, and displayed on the wall of Beth Shean until they are rescued by the men of Jabesh-Gilead, who bury them (1 Sam 31:8–13). In 2 Sam 4:12, the hands and feet of Eshbaal's murderers are severed after their execution by David, and their corpses are hung up by the pool in Hebron. The annals of Assyrian rulers are replete with references to the mutilation and display of the corpses of defeated rebels and other enemies. Ashurbanipal cuts the head off the corpse of the Babylonian rebel Nabu-bel-shumate and displays it publicly; he also has the skins of dead Egyptian rebels stripped off and exhibited separately from their corpses.[45] Mutilation of the corpses of offenders and foes might be left to wild beasts and birds, as any number of curse formulations suggest: "Your corpse shall be food for the fowl of the heavens and for the beasts of the earth, with no one to scare them away" (Deut 28:26). The same is true of a narrative such as 2 Sam 21:1–14, which describes the killing of seven descendants of Saul on account of Saul's violation of an oath with the Gibeonites. After their execution – the form is now obscure to us – and the subsequent display of their corpses, the bodies were left unburied and exposed, and would have been consumed by birds and animals had it not been for Saul's former concubine Rizpah, the mother of several of the slain, who guarded them for an extended time period in order to preserve the integrity of the corpses.[46]

Iconic representations of deity or ruler are subject to the same kinds of abusive treatment at the hands of conquerors.[47] In fact, such mutilation of divine or royal images is a widespread topos throughout West Asia and the Mediterranean of antiquity. It is mentioned in texts of varying provenance, and material remains also bear witness to the practice. A material example is the well-known copper head of an unidentified Akkadian king found at Nineveh with left eye gouged out, ears severed, nose damaged, and beard mutilated, likely the result of Median or Babylonian agency at the time of Nineveh's fall in 612.[48] Textual examples include Ashurbanipal's mutilation of the statue of Elamite king Hallushu at the time of his conquest of Susa. Hallushu's statue's lips and mouth were maimed, and its hands were severed to pay him back for verbal and other offenses against Esarhaddon's predecessor Sennacherib.[49] Other examples include damage done to the images of Assyrian rulers on the reliefs from Nineveh after Nineveh's collapse.[50] The biblical Ark Narrative reflects this topos in its treatment of the cultic image of Dagon, the god of the Philistines, in Ashdod. In 1 Sam 5:4, Dagon's icon is found prostrate with its head and hands severed before the Ark of Yhwh, an Israelite icon brought to Dagon's temple in Ashdod as a prize of war after the Philistine defeat of Israel at Ebenezer. Unlike typical examples of the mutilation of an enemy's divine icon, which occur after victory in war and are carried out by human agency, Dagon's mutilation occurs after the Israelites are defeated, and the text hints that Yhwh himself is the agent of the maiming.[51]

What are punitive "defects" and other mutilations intended to accomplish? The texts themselves sometimes offer motives for mutilation; it is also possible to discern reasons for such acts even if no direct explanation is offered. I shall treat mutilation in legal contexts first, and then go on to mutilation in the setting of international diplomacy and war. Jurisprudential mutilations are clearly designed to function as just punishments, proportionate to the crime committed, as Lev 24:19–20 emphasizes ("as he did, thus it shall be done to him"). An eye is given for an eye, a tooth for a tooth. In cases in which the offending body part is itself to be removed (e.g., Hammurapi par. 195), the offender's body becomes a living emblem of justice imposed. Wherever a mutilated offender goes, he bears evidence of his offense, the community's measured response to it, and the power of the community's institutions to exact punishment. The backing of the community's deities for such punitive measures is also implied, even if not stated directly. The severing of particular body parts such as limbs, tongues, and lips, may also be motivated in part by a desire to strip a transgressor of agency, or to demonstrate that his power to act effectively has been lost. A mouth that has uttered offending words in the past can no longer do so once its tongue has been severed; similarly, hands that have committed crimes are neutralized once and for all with their removal.[52] The mutilation of transgressors after their execution is not dissimilar. In 2 Sam 4:9–12, the murderers of Eshbaal are condemned for their unjust act, put to death, and mutilated through the severing of their hands and feet. Their corpses are then displayed publicly. Such mutilation and display suggests not only the role of the hands and feet in the unjust murder of an innocent king, but the justice exacted by the community and its deity in response, and the inability of the offenders or their allies to do anything to prevent their punishment. The deity's role is alluded to directly in the narrative of 2 Sam 21:1–14; there, seven descendants of Saul are executed "before Yhwh" in the hill country of Gibeon for Saul's crimes against the Gibeonites (v. 9). The purpose of the executions is to appease Yhwh

and convince him to remove a famine in the land.[53] Finally, shaming of
the offender is likely also a goal of punitive mutilations in legal settings;
although this is not generally made explicit in extant texts, it is evidenced
in related materials, particularly those concerned with the conduct of war
and international diplomacy.

In the context of war and international relations, it is abundantly
clear that humiliation of the victim and the victim's family, supporters,
community, or patron (human or divine) is one primary goal of punitive mutilations.[54] When Nahash of Ammon seeks to blind the Israelite
inhabitants of Jabesh-Gilead, he does so that he "might bring disgrace
(herpah) upon all Israel" through his act (1 Sam 11:2). The humiliation of
David's emissaries by the Ammonite court – and through them, David –
seems to be a primary motive for the hostile actions of forced shaving,
exposure of the genitals, and expulsion narrated in 2 Samuel 10. Beard
mutilation in this context is so shaming that the men are not permitted
to return to Jerusalem until their beards have begun to grow back (10:5).
The offense done to the ambassadors and indirectly, to David, is great
enough that it results in a war to restore lost honor according to the text.[55]
Judith 14:18 suggests that the beheaded corpse of Holofernes is a source
of disgrace for the house of his patron, Nebuchadnezzar. Ashurbanipal's
mutilating of defeated rebels is sometimes coupled with their shaming
by other means, suggesting that mutilation itself is part of a larger effort
to dishonor them. An example is his treatment of Uaite of Arabia, who is
chained like a dog and made to guard a kennel in Nineveh after his chin
is pierced and a rope is passed through it.[56]

The shaming nature of such mutilations likely has much to do with the
fact that the victim and his supporters are powerless to prevent the abusive
act, and the victim himself must bear evidence of it on his body thereafter,
either temporarily, as in cases of shaving or depilation, or permanently,
as with most "defects," including those that would communicate most
vividly a loss of agency and power (e.g., severing a hand or a foot or the
tongue).[57] A similar observation may be made with respect to corpses
and iconic representations of deities or rulers. Their maiming brings
humiliation to the community responsible for protecting them because
that community has failed to do so on account of its own weakness. In
the case of maimed divine icons, the deities themselves whose images
are mutilated are also shown to be weak and ineffectual, incapable of

protecting their own images. The image of the beheaded, armless icon of Dagon bowing down to Yhwh's Ark in Dagon's own sanctuary sends a very clear and unambiguous message about the relative power and agency of the two gods: Yhwh is triumphant and in control; Dagon is powerless, vanquished, and without agency. Dagon cannot defend himself, and the Philistines are powerless to protect their god in his own temple. Similarly, the relief images of Assyrian rulers mutilated by Assyria's enemies are intended to tell us something about the weakness and lack of agency of Assyria, its rulers and its gods in a time when its enemies were triumphant and able to maim Assyrian images at will. The ability to mutilate or allow the mutilation of corpses also bespeaks the weakness of a vanquished foe or rebel and his patron deities, given the evident concern to protect and preserve the integrity of the human corpse, and the well-attested fear that the corpse might be subject to mutilation by birds and beasts (e.g., 2 Sam 21:10). To maim a corpse or allow it to be maimed by animals and fowl, or to mutilate the iconic representation of an enemy's god or ruler, demonstrates the weakness of the enemy and his patron deity, and leads to their humiliation.

Demonstrating the agency and power of one's patron deity is frequently attested as a motive for the imposition of punitive mutilations on enemies and rebels because the patron is typically credited with making victory possible. In 1 Sam 17:46, David threatens to kill Goliath and cut off his head "that all the land might know that Israel has a god." 2 Macc 15:35 is similar, stating that the public display of the enemy Nicanor's severed head was intended to signal the reality of Yhwh's help for Israel to all who might witness it. Parallels to this may be found in the Assyrian treatment of captured rebels whose heads are severed and displayed publicly to demonstrate the power of Assyria's deities. Esarhaddon states that he severed the heads of two rebel kings and had them displayed in order to manifest his patron's power internationally: "That the might of Assur, my lord, might be manifested to (all) peoples, I hung the heads of Sanduarri and Abdi-milkutti on the shoulders of their nobles and with singing and music . . . I paraded through the public square of Nineveh."[58] In addition to demonstrating the patron god's might and ability to act, punitive maimings also function to increase the honor of the patron and his human agents at the expense of shamed, vanquished foes. Undoubtedly such manifestations of divine power were also intended to terrify defeated populations into willing submission to their conquerors.

A third and somewhat obscure motive for mutilating enemies is witnessed in Ashurbanipal's statement that by severing the head of the rebel Nabu-bel-shumate from his corpse and by denying him burial, he "made his death greater than [it was] before."[59] It is possible that Ashurbanipal sought to disrupt the afterlife of his dead foe by cutting off his head and not allowing his corpse to be buried, and that this is what he means by saying "I made his death greater than [it was] before," but this remains uncertain. We do know, however, that Ashurbanipal did seek to degrade the afterlife of the dead kings of Elam by removing their bones from their tombs and taking them to Assyria. By doing so, he claims to have inflicted restlessness on their ghosts and to have denied them the care of a custodian in the afterlife.[60] Thus, disruption of the afterlife of Nabu-bel-shumate may well have been Ashurbanipal's intention when he severed the rebel's head from his corpse and refused it burial. This may also be a motive in biblical instances of corpse mutilation, although positive evidence for it is unfortunately lacking.

CONCLUSION

In this chapter, I examined in some detail the biblical classification that I have translated "defect" (*mûm*). Although many congenital or acquired somatic alterations are categorized as "defects" by biblical texts, not all are. Blindness, lameness, limbs of uneven length, improperly healed broken bones, a hunch in the back, a loss of distinction between the iris and the white of the eye, the loss of an eye or tooth, genital damage, two nonpolluting skin conditions, and several other physical conditions impossible to identify, constitute "defects," in contrast to other physical characteristics and conditions such as "skin disease" (*sara'at*), deafness, and muteness, which are not "defects" according to the text's classification system. Unhappily, the rationale that underlies this native system of categorization remains obscure because no single characteristic (e.g., visibility to the eye, dysfunction) can be identified that is shared by all "defects" on the one hand, but not by other conditions not classified as "defects" on the other. Most "defects," however, are visible, long lasting, or permanent, and characterized by somatic dysfunction, and several share asymmetry as a characteristic.

"Defects" are typically devalued in biblical discourse. Their negative construction is made manifest through the text's efforts to stigmatize and marginalize those who possess them. Persons with "defects" are stigmatized and assigned marginal social positions through the deployment of a number of devaluing discourses by the biblical authors (e.g., discourses of curse, profanation, hatred, and ugliness). Association with negatively constructed qualities such as vulnerability, weakness, dependence, and ignorance has a similar function, as does association with marginal categories of persons (e.g., the poor). A number of texts concerned with the cult seek to limit the sanctuary access of persons with "defects," or prohibit it entirely, thereby marginalizing them. In contrast to the many disabling somatic alterations classified as "defects," circumcision is constructed by biblical texts as emblematically enabling and even normative, demonstrating in a vivid way the degree to which the construction of "defects" is a cultural practice tied to a particular sociocultural context. "Defects" and other mutilations imposed on living enemies and offenders, corpses, and iconic representations of deities and kings as a form of punishment are ubiquitous in biblical and cognate literatures. Such punitive "defects" and mutilations appear to have had a variety of motivations, not least among them the shaming of the victim and his family, community, supporters, or divine or human patron. Needless to say, the very fact that texts portray the imposition of "defects" as a humiliating form of punishment vividly underscores the negative construction of "defects."

3

Physical Disabilities Not Classified as "Defects"

*A*LTHOUGH MANY SOMATIC CONDITIONS AND CHARACTERISTICS are categorized as "defects" (*mûmîm*) by biblical texts, others that may resemble "defects" are never classified as such. Blindness and lameness are cast as "defects," whereas deafness and muteness are apparently excluded from this classification, even though like blindness and lameness, both are physical in nature, and both are characterized by somatic dysfunction. Similarly, such nonpolluting skin conditions referred to in the biblical text as *garab* and *yallepet* appear in the list of "defects" disqualifying a priest from presenting offerings to the deity in Lev 21:17–23; in contrast, "skin disease" (*ṣaraʿat*) is never classified as a "defect" in any biblical text, although it is mentioned with some frequency throughout the biblical anthology. This chapter brings together these "defect"-like physical disabilities, as well as a number of other somatic conditions not classified as "defects," and explores their potential social ramifications, seeking to compare their representation to that of "defects." Like "defects," muteness, deafness, "skin disease" (*ṣaraʿat*), genital "flows" (*zôb*), menstruation, and parturition are frequently cast as stigmatizing, and texts often seek to marginalize persons affected by these conditions, sometimes to a significant degree. Biblical authors deploy new stigmatizing and marginalizing strategies in their representations of persons with non-"defective" physical disabilities, as well as some of the same strategies familiar from our exploration of the biblical construction of "defects." Among the new strategies deployed is association with "defective" persons. Familiar strategies include the ascription of uncleanness and curse to persons with physical disabilities not constructed as "defects," as well as the association of such persons with devalued characteristics such as weakness, vulnerability, dependence, and ignorance, and with marginal social groups such as the poor and the afflicted. Yet, interestingly, the degree of marginalization represented for persons with each non-"defective" condition varies, as do the strategies deployed by biblical authors to stigmatize and marginalize them.

DEAFNESS AND MUTENESS

In contrast to persons with "defects" (*mûmîm*) such as the blind and the lame, deaf (*ḥereš*) and mute (*'illem*) persons are subject to no evident restrictions on their access to cultic space and activities in biblical texts. No laws are attested in the biblical anthology that limit the cultic responsibilities of deaf or mute priests (cf. Lev 21:17–23), nor do any biblical texts bear witness to any ban on the entry of deaf or mute persons into the sanctuary (cf. Deut 23:2 [Eng. 1]; 2 Sam 5:8b). At first glance, it would seem from this lack of cultic restriction that the mute and deaf, although they share somatically dysfunctional conditions with the blind and the lame, are constructed quite differently from them and from others with "defects." One might even be tempted to argue that mute and deaf persons are privileged in relation to the blind and the lame: no text forbids deaf and mute worshipers from entering the sanctuary and participating in cultic rites and no passage mentions restrictions on the duties of deaf and mute priests. However, this impression is misleading in a number of ways. Although deaf and mute persons are apparently not subject to the cultic restrictions attested in several texts for persons with "defects," they are nonetheless frequently associated with such persons in biblical texts, suggesting that according to our authors, they share common characteristics, and, to some degree, a common classification and stigmatization. The mute and the deaf may not be classified as "defective," but they, as well as persons with "defects," belong to a more encompassing native category implicit in biblical texts, the name of which does not survive. In addition, a number of the stigmatizing binary discourses and associations used by the writers of biblical texts in their construction of persons with "defects" are also employed to represent the deaf and the mute. Thus, as represented in biblical texts, mute and deaf persons are often stigmatized in a number of the same ways as the blind, the lame, and others with "defects," although they do not share the same degree of marginalization, given their (apparently) unimpeded access to cult.

The deaf and the mute are frequently brought into association with "defective" persons such as the blind and the lame, suggesting that biblical writers are employing a larger schema of classification that brings together "defects" and other physical conditions not constructed as "defects." In Exod 4:11, Yhwh takes responsibility for a number of physical conditions – both "defective" and non-"defective" – that we label disabilities, including muteness, deafness, and blindness: "Who gives a human a mouth, or who makes (someone) mute, deaf, sentient or blind? Is it not I, Yhwh?"[1] The functioning or dysfunction of the eyes, tongue, and ears are the subject of this verse, which attributes to Yhwh complete control over these organs. Deafness and muteness may not be classified as "defects" by biblical authors, but this text suggests that they share with blindness a common somatic dysfunction and a common classification. The many other biblical texts that associate deafness, muteness, and "defects" such as blindness likely assume this larger, implicit classification as well. Lev 19:14 pairs the blind and the deaf in a single legal formulation, suggesting that they share a common classification based on somatic dysfunction and a common vulnerability to oppression: "Do not curse the deaf, and before the blind do not set an obstruction." In Isa 42:18, 19, the people are described as both deaf and blind, suggesting a relationship between the conditions:

> O deaf ones, listen!
> And you blind ones, look (in order to) see!
> Who is blind but my servant,
> and deaf like my messenger whom I send?[2]

Isa 43:8 is similar in its pairing of deaf and blind, ears and eyes:

> Bring forth the blind people who have eyes,
> And the deaf who have ears.

Jer 5:21 is yet another example:

> Hear this, foolish people without sense!
> They have eyes, but do not see,
> They have ears, but do not hear.

Prophetic utopian visions of a transformed future such as Isa 35:5–6 speak of the deaf, the blind, the mute, and the lame in various combinations:

> Then the eyes of the blind shall be opened,
> and the ears of the deaf be unstopped.
> Then the lame shall leap like a gazelle,
> and the tongue of the mute shout joyfully.

Isa 29:18–19 goes a step further, associating the deaf and the blind with the afflicted and the poor:

> On that day, the deaf shall hear the words of a book,
> and free of gloom and darkness,
> the eyes of the blind shall see.[3]
> The afflicted shall again rejoice in Yhwh,
> the human poor exult in the Holy One of Israel.

Although it is possible to argue from this last text that the grounds for associating these groups must be other than a common notion of physical dysfunction, the same is not true of texts such as Exod 4:11, Lev 19:14, and Isa 35:5–6, which do not mention the poor, the afflicted, or other marginal groups lacking physically disabling characteristics. Thus, the frequency with which the deaf and the mute are classified with the blind and others with "defects" (*mûmîm*) suggests an assumption shared by the writers of these texts that deafness, muteness, and "defects" such as blindness and lameness share a common characteristic – somatic dysfunction – and a common larger classification, even though deafness and muteness are not categorized as "defects."[4] The existence of this larger native class of the somatically dysfunctional, implicit in texts such as Isa 35:5–6, is confirmed by the shared morphology of the adjectives used to describe members of the class. This shared morphology also suggests the class's extent.[5] The association of the deaf, the blind, the afflicted, and the poor in Isa 29:18–19 points to yet another taxonomic operation, one likely focused primarily on weakness, vulnerability, and dependence, although these themes are not alluded to directly in the verse. Instead, the verse states that the physical dysfunction of the deaf and the blind will be transformed, just as the afflicted and the poor will become joyful. Given how other texts associate "defective" persons with the poor and the afflicted on the grounds that they share a common vulnerability and dependence (e.g.,

Job 29:15–16), the same assumption is probably operative in Isa 29:18–19
as well.

Needless to say, the somatic dysfunction shared by persons with
"defects" and others such as the mute and the deaf, as suggested in texts
such as Exod 4:11, Lev 19:14, and Isa 35:5–6, is devalued by biblical writers in
any number of ways. For example, in Isa 56:10, Israel's failed watchmen –
presumably, her prophets – are all described as "blind, knowing nothing"
and as "mute dogs, unable to bark." Thus, muteness and blindness are
used metaphorically to construct an image of prophetic inadequacy and
failure, the result of both physical dysfunction and the ignorance that
allegedly results from it.[6] The association of deafness and blindness with
ignorance is also developed in Isa 6:9–10. In this text, hearing and seeing
are correlated with understanding and knowing, whereas deafness and
blindness are linked to a lack of comprehension and knowledge:

> Go and say to this people:
> 'Hear continually, but do not understand,
> see continually, but do not know.'[7]
> Make the mind of this people unreceptive,
> its ears unresponsive,
> its eyes sealed shut.
> Lest it see with its eyes,
> and hear with its ears,
> and its mind understand,
> and it repent and be healed.

Cuneiform texts such as "Esarhaddon's Renewal of the Gods" also bear
witness to this association of deafness and blindness with ignorance and
a lack of understanding, suggesting a common topos.[8] Another example
of the pejorative treatment of physical dysfunctions such as muteness,
deafness, blindness, and one that I have already spoken of in the Introduction, is to be found in "idol" polemics such as Jer 10:5 and Ps 115:5–8.
In these texts, the muteness, lack of ability to walk, blindness and deafness of the "idols" are grounds for denigrating them as well as those who
made them and those who worship them:

> They have mouths but cannot speak,
> they have eyes but cannot see,
> they have ears, but cannot hear,
> they have a nose but cannot smell,

> their hands cannot feel,
> their feet cannot walk,
> they utter no sound in their throat.
> Like them are those who made them,
> all who trust in them.
>
> (Psalm 115:5–8)

Qualities such as the blindness, muteness, lameness, and deafness of "idols" are contrasted with the agency of Yhwh in heaven, who can do what he likes (Ps 115:3). The fact that polemicists such as the authors of Jer 10:5 and Ps 115:5–8 have chosen to focus their attack on the physical disabilities of the "idols," rather than on other qualities such as the materials out of which "idols" are manufactured, how they are made, or who made them, reveals the degree to which such somatic dysfunctions are stigmatized and devalued.[9] They become, in these passages, emblematic of what separates a living, active deity from a "false," nonexistent god.[10]

Weakness, vulnerability, and dependence, commonly associated with blind and lame persons, is also a topos in texts representing the mute and the deaf. An example is Ps 38:14–15, an individual complaint in which the petitioner compares himself to a deaf or mute person who cannot defend himself in a legal setting:

> As for me, like a deaf person I could not hear,
> and like a mute person I could not open my mouth.[11]
> I was like a man who cannot hear,
> who has no recourse to retorts.

The weakness and vulnerability of the petitioner, a common enough theme in Psalms of individual complaint, is asserted here vividly through comparison with the helplessness of deaf or mute persons before their accusers in court.[12] Such persons cannot hear the accusations against them, nor can they respond in order to refute those accusations ("no recourse to retorts"). Thus, in a text such as Ps 38:14–15, the deaf and the mute are cast as weak, vulnerable, and lacking agency. Prov 31:8 is similar in several respects to Ps 38:14–15, although it addresses one who might help the mute in court:

> Open your mouth for the mute,
> for the cause of all who are transitory (?).[13]
> Open your mouth to judge righteously,
> (for) the cause of the afflicted and poor.

In this text, the mute person is associated with other vulnerable classes of persons such as the transitory (?), the poor, and the afflicted. All are potentially subject to victimization in legal settings, and the person who might defend them is urged to do so for the sake of justice. The implication, of course, is that the mute and the others with whom they are associated by this text are weak and lack agency: They cannot defend themselves and are completely dependent on the efforts of others. As I have noted previously, the association of disabled persons with marginal groups such as the poor and the afflicted is a taxonomic move that functions to stigmatize them as marginal, weak, vulnerable, and dependent. They are further stigmatized when texts represent them as needing special protection from the strong and the able.

In addition to association with weakness, vulnerability, dependence, and ignorance, muteness and deafness are also stigmatized as curses, muteness in the biblical text, and deafness in non-Israelite West Asian sources. The self-imprecation in the oath of Ps 137:5–6 calls apparently for dysfunction of the right hand, as well as muteness, should the exiled speaker not remember Jerusalem:

> If I forget you, O Jerusalem,
> may my right hand forget (?),
> may my tongue stick to my palate,
> if I do not remember you,
> if I do not raise Jerusalem above my highest joy.[14]

Needless to say, the casting of muteness as a curse in a context such as Psalm 137 suggests its extreme undesirability and stigma. Loss of speech is placed here on the same plateau as the loss of the right hand, suggesting the degree to which the ability to speak is valued as emblematic of agency.[15] Other West Asian sources bear witness to the construction of deafness as a curse. Like blindness, deafness is mentioned several times as a imprecation in the first Hittite soldiers' oath. It is a punishment imposed by the gods of the oath on those who might violate it: "Who transgre[sses] these oaths and takes deceptive action against the king of Hatti, and sets (his) eyes upon the land of Hatti as an enemy, may these oath deities seize him and [may they] blind his army too, and further, may they deafen them."[16] Deafness and paralysis of limbs are paired curses in several *kudurru* (boundary) inscriptions from first millennium Babylon.[17]

"SKIN DISEASE" (ṢARAʿAT) AND GENITAL "FLOWS" (ZÔB)

"Skin disease" (ṣaraʿat) and genital "flows" (zôb) receive detailed treatment in the Priestly Writers' representation of cult in Leviticus 13–14 and 15, and are mentioned in any number of other texts (e.g., Num 5:1–4; 2 Sam 3:29; 2 Kgs 5:14). Although not constructed as "defects" (mûmîm) in the biblical anthology, they share with "defects," and with deafness and muteness, a significant degree of stigmatization. In contrast to most biblical constructions of human "defects," muteness and deafness, both "skin disease" and genital "flows" are cast by biblical texts as highly polluting and, therefore, significantly marginalizing for those affected.[18] According to Lev 13:46 (P) and several other texts, evidence of the presence of "skin disease" is grounds for expulsion from the community; according to Num 5:2–3 (H), "skin disease," genital "flows," and corpse contact result in such removal.[19] The severe pollution ascribed to "skin disease" and genital "flows," as well as the resulting social limitations and even isolation imposed on affected persons, are major sources of their stigma. The presence of "skin disease" and genital "flows" in curses, and the association of "skin disease" with divine punishment in several texts, also significantly stigmatize those who have these conditions. However, in stark contrast to deafness, muteness and "defects" such as blindness, biblical representations of "skin disease" and genital "flows" do not appear to stigmatize through association with qualities such as weakness, vulnerability, dependence, and ignorance, or through association with marginalized groups such as the poor and the afflicted.

The highly polluting quality of biblical constructions of "skin disease," and their stigmatizing and marginalizing effects on persons, is well illustrated by Lev 13:45–46: "As for the person afflicted with skin disease (haṣṣarûaʿ), his garments shall be torn, and as for his hair, it shall be unbound; he shall cover his upper lip and cry 'unclean, unclean.' All of the time that the affliction is in him he shall be unclean. He is unclean: he shall live alone; outside of the camp shall be his dwelling place." According to this text, the person afflicted with "skin disease" must not only take on the appearance of a mourner and dwell outside the community, but he must also warn any who might approach to stay away on account of his uncleanness.[20] In short, persons afflicted with "skin disease" are to be marginalized to the point of virtual social isolation according to this text:

they must live alone and keep others who are unaffected at a distance.[21] The degree and long-lasting nature of their pollution, the resulting social limitations and even isolation, and the ritual behaviors mandated for the afflicted by the text, function to stigmatize those with "skin disease" significantly. Although P's marginalization of the person with a genital "flow" is less severe than that of the person with "skin disease" (Lev 15:1–15, 25–30), the Holiness school demands of both the same extreme degree of removal from the community: "Command the children of Israel that they should expel from the camp every person afflicted with 'skin disease,' every person with a genital 'flow,' and anyone who has had contact with a corpse. Both male and female you shall expel; to the outside of the camp you shall remove them, that they not pollute their camps in the midst of which I dwell" (Num 5:2–3).

Like "defects," muteness, and deafness, "skin disease" and genital "flows" are constructed as imprecations in both biblical and other West Asian texts. David's curse of Joab's line in 2 Sam 3:29 begins with the pairing of these two conditions: "Let there not be cut off from the house of Joab a person with a genital "flow" (*zab*), a person with "skin disease" (*meṣora'*), a male who grasps the spindle, one who falls by the sword, and one who lacks food." Thus, "skin disease" and genital "flows" are combined with death in battle, starvation, and what is apparently gender nonconformity[22] in this list of utterly undesirable and stigmatizing events and conditions. "Skin disease" is similarly cast as an imprecation in 2 Kgs 5:27, where Elisha curses his disobedient servant Gehazi and his male line with "skin disease" forever. A polluting and socially isolating skin condition (*saharšubbu*) comparable to biblical "skin disease" (*ṣara'at*) appears as a curse in a number of Assyrian treaty contexts, not infrequently paired with blindness. In the treaty between Ashurnirari V and Mati''ilu of Arpad, both blindness and *saharšubbu* are listed among the curses.[23] The same is true of Esarhaddon's Succession Treaty.[24] The treaty of Sin-sharru-ishkun with Babylonian allies also lists this skin condition among its imprecations.[25] The presence of "skin disease" and genital "flows" in curses is stigmatizing to all who have these diseases, even to those who have not been formally cursed, given that curses represent the most undesirable things imaginable to a culture and were believed to be put into effect by a deity as a form of punishment.

Even in non-imprecatory contexts such as Num 12:10–15 and 2 Chr 26:16–21, "skin disease" is used by the deity as a penalty for transgression. Num 12:10–15 tells of the punishment of Miriam for challenging Moses' privileged position vis-à-vis Yhwh: She is struck with "skin disease," which is only removed as a result of Moses' personal intercession on her behalf.[26] In 2 Chr 26:16–21, King Uzziah of Judah's "skin disease" is explained as the direct result of his attempt to usurp the exclusive priestly privilege of incense presentation before the deity. Because of his act of sacrilege (ma'al) in the sanctuary, Uzziah is struck with a highly polluting disease that lasts for the rest of his life, cutting off entirely his access to the cult and removing him from almost all social interaction.[27] The tradition of Uzziah's "skin disease" is present in the Chronicler's source, 2 Kgs 15:5, but the Chronicler is responsible for the story of Uzziah's act of sacrilege. Clearly, "skin disease" is viewed by the Chronicler as a grievous punishment from Yhwh, and requires an equally grievous transgression in order to justify it (in this case, "sacrilege" [ma'al]), something apparently missing from the Chronicler's source in the view of the Chronicler.[28] Like biblical texts, cuneiform texts not infrequently interpret polluting skin conditions such as saḫaršubbu as divine punishments for sin.[29] Were skin afflictions such as these always understood to be punitive? Unhappily, this remains unclear. 2 Kgs 15:3–4 states that Azariah (Uzziah) "did the upright thing in the eyes of Yhwh" like his father Amaziah, although he did not remove the high places; 2 Kgs 15:5 claims that Yhwh struck him with "skin disease," but is not clear that this was the result of tolerating the high places or another transgression he might have committed. The command in Deut 24:8 to treat an outbreak of "skin disease" with great care does not hint in any way that such an outbreak is necessarily punitive, the result of sin. In short, whether "skin disease" is often understood to be a divine punishment or always understood to be so, its frequent association with transgression and curse is nonetheless stigmatizing for all afflicted persons.[30]

MENSTRUATION AND PARTURITION

Menstruation and parturition are temporary conditions, unlike most "defects," muteness and deafness, and – presumably – many cases of "skin disease" and genital "flows." In contrast to these other conditions, they affect more than a minority of the population (all/most women of childbearing age). Yet, I include the menstruant and the parturient in this discussion of biblical representations of non-"defective" physical disabilities because their conditions are physical, because of the significant degree of stigmatizing pollution ascribed to each of them, and because of the resulting limitations on their social and cultic life mandated by the text. Each is cast as a major polluter: the menstruant for 7 days, the parturient for much longer (Lev 15:19–24; 12:1–8). During the period of the menstruant's impurity, she may transmit pollution: "Anyone who touches her shall be unclean until evening. Anything upon which she lies in her menstrual impurity shall be unclean, and anything upon which she sits shall be unclean. Anyone who touches her bed shall wash his garments and bathe in water, and be unclean until evening . . . If a man lies with her, her impurity shall be upon him, and he shall be unclean seven days, and any bed upon which he lies shall be unclean" (Lev 15:19–24). The pollution of the parturient is comparable to that of the menstruant, according to Lev 12:2: "She shall be unclean as during the days of her menstruating." Thus, presumably, she, too, spreads pollution through physical contact with persons and objects. Although biblical texts are unclear about the degree of spatial separation from others demanded of the menstruant and the parturient, some evidence from other West Asian sources suggests that they were to be removed from the domicile or even the community during the time of their pollution.[31] At all events, the impurity of menstruation and parturition, even according to P, would severely limit opportunities for movement, social interactions, and sexual contact, stigmatizing affected women as worthy of avoidance (see, e.g., Lev 18:19; Ezek 18:6; 22:10; Lam 1:17). The stigma attached to the pollution of menstruation is brought into relief by texts such as Ezek 36:17, which compares the sinful way of Israel before Yhwh to the pollution of a menstruating woman, and Lam 1:17, which describes rejected Jerusalem as a menstruant in the eyes of her neighbors.[32]

Although the menstruant and the parturient of biblical texts share a significant degree of stigmatization and marginalization with persons with "skin disease," genital "flows," and other disabling conditions, there are differences between their treatment and that of the others that I now want to highlight. In contrast to the pollution of the person with "skin disease" and that of the person with a genital "flow," which has no fixed limit, might last a lifetime, and, according to Num 5:2–3, results in expulsion from the community for both, the impurity of the menstruant and the parturient is of a fixed and relatively limited duration. Furthermore, the menstruant and the parturient experience their marginalization only temporarily, and for relatively short periods of time, unlike many of the Hebrew Bible's disabled persons, whose long-lasting or permanent conditions result in long-term or permanent marginalization. Finally, neither the condition of the menstruant nor that of the parturient are stigmatized as curses by any text, in contrast to blindness, deafness, mental disability, "skin disease," or genital "flows," nor are the menstruant or the parturient associated with marginal groups such as the poor, or with devalued characteristics such as weakness, vulnerability, dependence, and ignorance, in the manner described for mute, deaf, blind, and lame persons. Perhaps most significantly, neither the menstruant nor the parturient are ever associated directly with "defective" persons or others with physical disabilities in biblical texts (e.g., the deaf, the mute, persons with "skin disease" or genital "flows"), although such persons are not infrequently brought into association with one another, as I show. Thus, even though the menstruant and the parturient are subject to the stigmatizing and marginalizing discourse of severe impurity, their treatment is distinct. Biblical texts do not deploy other stigmatizing and marginalizing discourses or associations in order to devalue them, nor do they classify them with "defective" persons or others with physical disabilities. My classification of the menstruant and the parturient among disabled persons is therefore nonnative, as none of the native categorization schemas I have discussed – implicit or explicit – includes them. Although nonnative, such a classification is justified given the physical nature of their conditions, the stigmatization and marginalization mandated by the text for them, and the discourse of severe impurity deployed to achieve stigmatization and marginalization. In short, there are several significant ways in which the treatment of the menstruant and the parturient in the text resembles that of a number of other physically disabled categories of persons, and they ought therefore to be part of this analysis. Thus, my treatment of the menstruant and the parturient here is a reflection of my decision to embrace a broad, relatively inclusive definition of disability.

Inclusion of the menstruant and the parturient among the Hebrew Bible's disabled persons also introduces a gender dimension to our discussion for a whole class of women – those of childbearing age – are stigmatized and periodically marginalized as a result of their construction as severe polluters. Even when such women are not menstruating or giving birth, their potential to pollute and the consequent need to restrict their contact with others at regular intervals is presumably never forgotten, and so their stigmatization as potential polluters is ongoing, even if their marginalization is not. One might even argue that immature girls and postmenopausal women share this stigmatization, given that they will become/once were women of childbearing age.[33] In contrast, males are not subject to such stigmatization as regular, severe polluters. Sexually mature males may pollute through emissions of semen, but such emissions result only in minor impurity, defiling the male, his partner, and anything the semen touches for 1 day (Lev 15:16–18); in addition, emissions of semen are potentially subject to voluntary control, in contrast to menstruation. Thus, unlike "skin disease," genital "flows," deafness, muteness, and most "defects," which may affect both men and women equally and are not associated with a single life stage, menstruation and parturition are both gender and life stage-specific, and are constructed in such a manner that they stigmatize and marginalize women in ways that have no parallel among men. Although menstruation and parturition are unlike most "defects," muteness and deafness, genital "flows," and "skin disease" with respect to gender and life stage of those affected, they may be compared to male genital damage, in that only one gender is at issue. However, even here, the comparison is of limited value, given the huge size of the population that would be affected by the text's efforts to stigmatize and marginalize the menstruant and the parturient, compared with the much smaller group of males with genital damage, and given the permanence of genital damage versus the periodic nature of menstrual impurity and the pollution of childbirth. Thus, a number of the characteristics of the menstruant and the parturient function to distinguish them from other persons with physical disabilities, although they share severe, stigmatizing, and marginalizing pollution in common with persons afflicted with "skin disease" and genital "flows."[34]

CONCLUSION

In this chapter, I examined a number of physical disabilities not classified as "defects" (*mûmîm*) by the biblical text, although some share qualities in common with "defects." Conditions such as muteness and deafness, like "defects," are characterized by somatic dysfunction, and "skin disease," although highly polluting, is a skin condition, as are nonpolluting skin conditions classified as "defects." Yet, the potential social ramifications of physical disabilities not classified as "defects" often differ from those of "defects," and vary among themselves. Although the deaf and the mute are not subject to the types of cultic restriction demanded by texts such as Deut 23:2 (Eng. 1) and 2 Sam 5:8b for persons with "defects," and are represented as less socially marginalized on the whole than such persons, the person with "skin disease" and the person with a genital "flow," both constructed as highly polluting in a text such as Num 5:2–3, are represented as considerably more marginal than any persons with "defects" due to the pollution attributed to them. The same is true of the menstruant or parturient during the period of her impurity. And although deaf and mute persons are stigmatized by biblical texts mainly through a combination of imprecatory discourse, and association with persons with "defects," marginal groups such as the poor and the afflicted, and devalued characteristics such as weakness, vulnerability, dependence, and ignorance, texts stigmatize and assign marginal social positions to persons with "skin disease" and genital "flows" primarily through the discourse of pollution and its resulting social limitations or isolation, as well as through the discourse of curse. Association with groups such as the poor, or devalued characteristics such as weakness and vulnerability, play no evident role in the biblical stigmatization of persons afflicted with "skin disease" and genital "flows." In the case of the menstruant and the parturient, it is through the discourse of severe pollution alone that the text stigmatizes and seeks to marginalize.

More than a few texts concerned with the representation of the deaf and the mute suggest that they share a common classification with such "defective" persons as the blind and the lame (e.g., Exod 4:11; Lev 19:14;

Isa 35:5–6; 42:18, 19; 43:8). This native categorization, implicit in our texts but never named (contrast the "defect" [*mûm*]), is likely based on a sense of a common somatic dysfunction, as suggested by the contexts in which it occurs. The existence of this class is also suggested by the shared morphology of the adjectives used to describe its members. Evidence of a second, unnamed native classification that brings together the deaf, the blind, the poor, and the afflicted, implicit in Isa 29:18–19, probably finds its basis in the notion of a shared weakness, vulnerability, and dependence.

4

&

Mental Disability

*I*N THIS CHAPTER, I EXAMINE THE REPRESENTATION OF MENTAL
disability in biblical texts, with reference to non-Israelite West Asian
materials. The technical vocabulary of mental disability used in biblical
texts, although poorly understood, constitutes a major source of evidence
for mental disability in the Hebrew Bible, and is therefore examined in
some detail. As in the previous chapters, the strategies of stigmatization and marginalization deployed by the authors of biblical and other
West Asian texts are identified and analyzed. Like "defective" and non-
"defective" physical disabilities, mental disability is represented in biblical
and related literature as a stigmatized condition frequently leading to the
marginalization of affected persons. It is cast as a covenantal curse in Deut
28:28–29, 33–34, and understood in 1 Sam 16:14 as a token of Yhwh's rejection of Saul as king. The mentally disabled are subject to the contempt of
others (e.g., 1 Sam 21:15–16 [Eng. 14–15]; 2 Kgs 9:11), and devalued characteristics such as weakness, vulnerability, dependence, and ignorance
are associated with them, just as they are with "defective" persons and
others with physical disabilities. Mentally disabled persons are associated
with persons with physical disabilities (including "defects" [*mûmîm*])
and (sometimes) with others in a number of biblical and cuneiform
texts, suggesting the presence of one or more implicit shared classification schemas that I attempt to identify and analyze.

DEFINING MENTAL DISABILITY AND IDENTIFYING
IT IN TEXTS

Mental disability is not easily defined, even in our own contemporary Western context. Those typically classified among the mentally disabled include persons with mild, moderate, and severe mental retardation; persons with autism; those with mental disturbance of some kind; and persons suffering from clinical depression and related disorders. However, definitions have shifted over time (e.g., the IQ level that constitutes mild mental retardation) and are not always productive of consensus.[1] Nonetheless, I find the general term mental disability useful for the purposes of this chapter because it encompasses a variety of mental, as opposed to physical, conditions, and roughly parallels in range of usage some of the native, Hebrew vocabulary, which is used to refer to more than one distinct condition. Although mental disability is not itself a pejorative term, it should be stated at the outset that at least some, if not all, of the Hebrew vocabulary used to identify mentally disabled persons and their characteristic behaviors is derogatory in nature, and the same is true of traditional English renderings of these terms (e.g., *mešuggaʿ* as "madman"; *petî* as "simple minded"). To preserve the sense of the Hebrew in my English renderings, while calling into question the text's pejorative labeling, I render terms such as "madness" and "foolishness," "madman" and "fool," in quotations throughout.

To speak of mental disability in the Hebrew Bible and related literature is fraught with difficulty, given our rather limited understanding of the technical vocabulary used by texts to identify persons who might suffer from a mentally disabling condition. In contrast to such physical disabilities as blindness, lameness, deafness, and muteness, mental disability in biblical and cognate texts is often not easy to identify with any precision or confidence. Although the Hebrew Bible's technical vocabulary of blindness and other physical disabilities is in general easily understood, that pertaining to mental disability is far less clear. In a text such as Exod 4:11, "blind" is contrasted with "sighted," and the ability to speak with "mute." Isa 29:18 is similar, indicating clearly that to be deaf is not to hear and to be blind is to be in darkness, without the ability to see: "On that day, the deaf shall hear the words of a book," // "and free of gloom and darkness," // "the eyes of the blind shall see." Isa 35:5–6 speaks of a utopian future in which the blind shall see, the deaf shall hear, the lame shall leap, and the mute shall cry out joyfully. After reading such texts, no reader can doubt that to be blind is not to be able to see, to be deaf is not to be able to hear, to be lame is not to be able to walk, and to be mute is not to be able to speak. The only question one might have that remains unanswered by these particular texts is whether the partially sighted person is to be classified as "blind," or the person with lameness in one leg as "lame."[2] In contrast, the technical vocabulary of mental disability is more complex and more ambiguous.

"foolishness" and "madness"

Both the native terminology of "foolishness" and that of "madness" is of interest to us as we seek to reconstruct the biblical contours of mental disability. Biblical texts frequently use terms such as *kesîl, sakal, petî,* and *'ewîl,* which are commonly translated as "fool" or "simple-minded" person; abstracts such as *kislah/kesîlût, sekel/siklût, petî/petayyût,* and *'iwwelet,* usually rendered "foolishness" or "simplicity," are derived from the same roots.[3] But do these terms ever refer to persons with mental disability? Many texts using this vocabulary associate "foolish" persons with a lack of knowledge, understanding, discipline, prudence, and good judgment. They make the wrong choices.[4] An example is 1 Sam 13:13, where Samuel describes Saul's choice to perform sacrifices in an emergency situation both as "acting foolishly" (*niskalta*) and disobeying Yhwh's commandment. Jer 4:22 speaks of the "foolishness" of the whole people of Israel:

> For my people are foolish (*'ewîl*),
> me they do not know.
> They are foolish children (*banîm sekalîm*),
> they lack understanding.
> They are skilled with respect to doing evil,
> but how to do good they do not know.

Ps 85:9 (Eng. 8) urges the people, including its righteous members, not to return to "folly." If the mind of a youth is characterized by "folly" (*'iwwelet*), the rod of discipline will drive it out (Prov 22:15). "Foolishness" is contrasted with "knowledge" in Isa 44:25; the "fool" with the "wise" person in Prov 15:7 and Eccl 7:4, 5, 6; 10:2, 12. One purpose of Solomon's words, according to Prov 1:4, is "to give prudence (*'ormah*) to the 'simple' (*petayim*), knowledge and discretion to the youth." What behaviors and characteristics constitute "foolishness"? Among those mentioned in texts, one finds being loud, simple, and not knowing anything (Prov 9:13); speaking too much (Eccl 10:14); speaking to one's disadvantage (Eccl 10:12); thinking about celebration rather than mourning (Eccl 7:4); hating knowledge (Prov 1:22); not being prudent (Prov 1:4); and not being clever (Prov 12:23). It is better, says Ecclesiastes, to hear the rebuke of the wise, than to hear the song of "fools" (Eccl 7:5). Similarly, the laughter of the "fool" is criticized (Eccl 7:6). Clearly, these texts are speaking of a wide range of persons, many if not most of whom cannot be said to suffer from mental disability. The "simple" person of Prov 1:4 can be taught prudence, and "folly" can be driven out of a youth through discipline (Prov 22:15). The terminology of "foolishness" is used to criticize persons – and the people as a whole – when their behavior does not comport with the expectations of the writers of these texts, many of whom come from a wisdom background.[5] However, some texts using terms such as these may be more relevant to us. When Proverbs speaks of the "simple minded" (*petî*) believing everything they hear or lacking basic survival skills, it may have in mind persons with mild mental retardation (e.g., Prov 14:15; 22:3).[6] The same is true of Babylonian *kudurru* (boundary) inscriptions, which frequently contain a formula listing various types of persons who might be convinced to move the marker, some because they do not know enough to understand the consequences of such an offense. Among the latter are the deaf, the blind, and the "fool" (*saklu*, cognate to Hebrew *sakal*). Thus, terms typically translated "fool" or "simple minded" *might* sometimes refer to persons with mild forms of mental retardation, although this remains unclear. Very frequently, however, it is clear that they do not. In a majority of cases, they are apparently used for persons who have a capacity to acquire knowledge and act with insight but choose not to do so. Because of this terminological ambiguity, I focus the remainder of my discussion of mental disability on vocabulary whose referents can be established with more confidence.

The biblical vocabulary of what is commonly translated "madness" is of more use to us than the terminology of "foolishness," mainly because we learn more from the texts in which it occurs. Several of these texts are rich in imagery and description, representing in some detail behaviors typically associated with forms of mental disability. A number of verbal roots and their derivatives, as well as a distinct idiom, constitute the technical terminology of "madness." Among the most important terms are verbal forms and other derivatives of the roots *hll* and *šgʿ*, as well as the idiom *šinnah ṭaʿam*. Although this set of technical terms also has its ambiguities, the texts in which the terms occur help us determine to some degree the contours of mental disability as it is constructed in biblical literature.[7] Therefore, these are the focus of much of the discussion that follows.

1 SAM 21:11–16 (ENG. 10–15)

1 Sam 21:11–16 (Eng. 10–15), a narrative in which David feigns mental disability in order to escape harm at the hands of the Philistines, is one of the richest and most important biblical texts representing behaviors associated with mental disability. The context is David's flight from Saul's court and his apparent attempt to attach himself to the retinue of Achish, the king of the Philistine city Gath[8]:

David arose and fled on that day from Saul and came to Achish, king of Gath.
    Now the servants of Achish said to him: "Is this not David, king of the land? Is it not regarding him that they sing with dances, as follows: 'Saul has killed his thousands, and David his ten thousands'?" David took these words seriously, and feared Achish, king of Gath, exceedingly. So he changed his discernment[9] in their sight, feigning "madness"[10] while under their control.[11] He drummed/made marks[12] upon the doors of the gate, and caused his spittle to run down his beard. And Achish said to his servants, "Look – You see that the man 'acts madly' (*mištaggeaʿ*). Why have you brought him to me? Do I lack 'madmen' (*mešuggaʿîm*), that you bring this one 'to act madly' (*lehištaggeaʿ*) before me? Should this one enter my household?"

We learn much from this fascinating although difficult text, and I begin my discussion with an examination of the technical vocabulary of mental disability that it deploys. The idiom that I translate "to change discernment" (*šinnah ṭaʿam*) occurs in the Hebrew Bible only here and in Ps 34:1, a text referring directly to this incident (although curiously, mentioning Abimelek instead of Achish). However, a cognate idiom (*ṭema šanû*) is more common in Akkadian texts, and is often – although not always – used to refer to mental disability of some kind.[13] The behavior described by this idiom in cuneiform literature is frequently characterized by a loss of self-control, as in Enuma elish iv 87–90, which narrates the angry response of the goddess Tiamat to the taunts of her adversary Marduk: "When Tiamat heard this, she became like one in a frenzy (and) lost her reason. Tiamat cried out loud (and) furiously, to the (very) roots her two legs shook back and forth."[14] The same may be suggested by Atra-Hasis iii 3 25, which describes the distraught reaction of a god (perhaps Enki) to the destruction wrought by the flood.[15] It is also used to depict the hysterical response of two Elamite leaders to seeing the severed head of their king on public display in Nineveh.[16] Another characteristic of behavior described by the Akkadian idiom *tema šanû* is confusion of mind.[17]

In addition to the idiom "to change discernment" (*šinnah ṭaʿam*), 1 Sam 21:14 (Eng. 13) uses the Hebrew verbal form *wayyitholel* to describe David's behavior. I render this "feigning madness," not unlike many other commentators. Other uses of the verb point to a loss of self-control, as in Jer 25:16; 51:7, and disorderly behavior, as in Nah 2:5 (Eng. 4); the notion of acting out a role ("feigning") is also typical of the particular verbal stem used (the Hitpael).[18] Most significantly, however, the text represents Achish of Gath equating the conditions and behaviors indicated by the Hebrew idiom "to change discernment" (*šinnah ṭaʿam*) and the verbal form I have translated "feigning madness" (*wayyitholel*) with derivatives of the Hebrew verb *šgʿ*, "to do with intensity, abandon," perhaps "to rave" or "to rage."[19] From Deut 28:28, we know that *šiggaʿôn*, a noun derived from the root *šgʿ*, and conventionally translated "madness," is cast as a covenantal curse; Achish uses several related words to describe David and his behavior. That the text seems to equate the conditions and behaviors described by the idiomatic expression and the derivatives of the two verbal roots occurring in 1 Sam 21:11–16 (Eng. 10–15) makes it difficult for us to draw any useful distinctions between them. David, who was described by the narrator as having "changed his discernment" (*wayšanneh ʾet-ṭaʿmô*) is also said to "feign madness" (*wayyitholel*); for Achish, David "acts madly" (*mištaggeaʿ, lehištaggeaʿ*) and is a "madman" (*mešuggaʿ*). Although these expressions refer to mental disability of some kind, they do not in themselves tell us anything very precise about the condition David feigns. In contrast, the text speaks of two specific behaviors it associates with the mentally disabled. An examination of the behaviors gives us some idea of the nature of David's feigned condition.

Allowing spittle to run down his beard is one of the two behaviors David is represented as choosing to publicly feign mental disability. Drooling is a well-known characteristic of persons who have lost muscle control on one side of the face and are therefore unable to close their lips entirely. Such a loss of muscle control is often the result of a stroke that can also cause the functional equivalent of mild, moderate, or even severe mental retardation. A stroke can come on suddenly and without warning, leaving its victim utterly changed in terms of behavior and mental function.[20] Thus, the narrative's claim that David was able to fool the Philistines into thinking he had suddenly become mentally disabled is not in itself implausible. The second behavior associated with mental disability in 1 Sam 21:11–16 (Eng. 10–15) is more difficult to pin down because at least two plausible readings are preserved in the textual tradition. Although the Masoretic text reads "he made marks upon the doors of the gate," the Septuagint preserves a different reading: "he drummed on the doors of the gate." The difference between the readings cannot be explained in any obvious way from a text-critical perspective.[21] Therefore, a look at each behavior as a potential indicator of mental disability is our best option. Of the two possibilities, drumming, a repetitive and frequently attention-seeking behavior often associated with severe mental retardation and autism, strikes me as the more plausible, particularly in a narrative context in which David is attempting to feign mental disability publicly.[22] If David is indeed drumming while drooling, he is portrayed as acting in ways indicative of severe mental retardation in a most public place – at the city or palace gate. The choice of such a place for David's activities cannot have been an accident, given his desire according to the story to fool his Philistine hosts into thinking he is no threat to them.

The idiom "to change discernment," the verbal form I translate as "feigning madness," and the terms I render "madmen" and "to act madly" can all be used according to 1 Sam 21:11–16 (Eng. 10–15) to refer to persons displaying behaviors associated with severe mental retardation. To what other conditions might they refer? It is clear from other texts that severe mental retardation can only be one possible referent of these terms. Although the idiom "to change discernment" is not used in biblical contexts other than the two that refer to David's behavior while with the Philistines (1 Sam 21:14 [Eng. 13]; Ps 34:1), the uses of its cognate in cuneiform texts suggests a wider range of meaning. The behavior of enraged, distraught, or shocked persons or gods is described using the idiom, as is that of persons subject to extreme confusion. Certainly, none of these suffers from mental retardation of any sort, yet the idiom "to change discernment" (*tema šanû*) is used to describe their behavior. In each case, the idiom seems to indicate a loss of self-control, whether it be manifest in Tiamat's rage as a result of Marduk's taunting or David's uncontrolled drooling and (perhaps) drumming. The same is true of the other terms employed to refer to severe mental retardation in 1 Sam 21:11–16 (Eng. 10–15). The verb I translate as "feigning madness" (*wayyitholel*) is used to describe drunken behavior in a text such as Jer 25:16. In this passage, the nations are to be offered Yhwh's cup of wrathful wine, with the result that "they shall drink, reel to and fro, and act madly" (*wehitholalû*). Jer 51:7 is similar:

> Babylon was a golden cup in Yhwh's hand,
> making drunk all the earth.
> From her wine the nations drank,
> therefore, the nations became mad (*yitholelû*).

It is also used of driving chariots with abandon in Nah 2:5 (Eng. 4). Clearly, drunken behavior and the wild driving of chariots are not equivalent to the behaviors of persons with severe mental retardation, although all share in common a loss – or perceived loss – of self-control.[23] Similarly, "madness" (*šigga'ôn*) in 2 Kgs 9:20, derived from the same root (*šg'*) as words I translate as "madmen" and "to act madly" in 1 Sam 21:15–16 (Eng. 14–15), means specifically to drive a chariot in a frenzied manner. It is used of Jehu, a ninth-century military usurper who becomes king of the northern Israelite tribes. Derivatives of the root are also used to describe the ecstatic behavior of prophets, which some onlookers might have associated with mental disturbance (2 Kgs 9:11; Jer 29:26; Hos 9:7).[24] Obviously, this root also refers to behaviors other than those characteristic of persons with severe mental retardation, but like David's feigned behaviors, Jehu's frenzied driving or the ecstatic behavior of prophets might also be characterized by a loss – or perceived loss – of self-control.[25] Thus, all behaviors described by the idiom "to change discernment" (*šinnah ṭa'am*) and the two verbs in question – behaviors that constitute "madness" in other words – suggest a real or perceived loss of self-control, whether

due to severe mental retardation, drunkenness, extreme anguish, rage or
shock, excessive risk taking, or some form of perceived or actual mental
disturbance. The loss of control may be temporary or permanent, and it
may have a variety of causes. However, it is the perception of an individual's loss of self-control that seems to underlie all uses of the technical
terminology of "madness" in biblical texts.

1 SAM 16:14–23

A very different representation of mental disability is found in 1 Sam
16:14–23 and several related texts (e.g., 1 Sam 18:10–16; 19:9–10; 20:30–34).
These passages speak of Saul's mental anguish and his erratic, aggressive,
and threatening behavior toward David. Although the David of 1 Sam
21:11–16 (Eng. 10–15) seeks to represent himself as no threat whatsoever
to anyone, choosing to feign what appear to be characteristic behaviors
of persons with severe mental retardation, the Saul of 1 Sam 16:14–23
and related texts is very much a threat, tormented at intervals by "an
evil spirit from Yhwh" (1 Sam 16:14–16). Saul is portrayed as capable of
speech and rational behavior when he is unaffected, readily agreeing to
the suggestion of his courtiers that a skilled musician be brought to court
to alleviate his suffering (1 Sam 16:17, 19). He even establishes a formal,
legally binding relationship with David, appointing him as his armor
bearer.[26] David's music has the desired effect, at least at first: "Whenever
the spirit of God would be upon Saul, David would take the lyre and
play, and Saul would be relieved and better (*werawaḥ leša'ûl weṭôb lô*),
the evil spirit having departed from upon him" (1 Sam 16:23). However,
according to the narrative, Saul nonetheless seeks to kill David with a
spear (1 Sam 18:10–11; 19:9–10), as well as his own son, Jonathan (1 Sam
20:33). Like many commentators, we might describe Saul's condition, as it
is represented in 1 Samuel, as a form of mental disturbance.[27] It is episodic,
and may come on suddenly and unexpectedly. Interestingly, the Hebrew
terminology used to describe Saul's condition is wholly different from
that of texts such as 1 Sam 21:11–16 (Eng. 10–15) used for David's feigned
mental disability. Saul is not said to be a "madman" (*mešugga'*) in this
text, nor is the idiom "to change discernment" used of him, nor are any
derivatives of the verb *hll* used to describe his behavior, even though this
terminology can be used to describe perceived or actual mental disability

other than severe mental retardation. In fact, no labels are used of Saul, nor is his behavior described using a distinct idiom. The evil spirit, however, is said to "terrify" him (*ûbi'atattû*) after the departure of the spirit of Yhwh. The relief experienced by Saul when David would play music is described literally in 1 Sam 16:23 as "finding space" or "respite," as if a cramped condition was somehow alleviated.[28] The text's use of the idiom "to find space" or "respite," and its notion that Saul was terrified by the evil spirit, provide for us some sense of its construction of his mental disability. It is episodic, scary, cramping in some way, and caused by an evil spirit from Yhwh. The episodic nature of Saul's mental disability and its effects on him are explained by the coming and going of the evil spirit. Finally, the text's assertion that Saul's condition comes from Yhwh is most interesting in light of Exod 4:11, where physical disabilities such as muteness, deafness, and blindness are also traced to the deity, and other texts which assert that Yhwh is responsible for conditions such as "skin disease."

STIGMATIZATION AND MARGINALIZATION

Texts stigmatize and seek to marginalize persons with mental disability using a number of the strategies familiar from the previous chapters of this investigation. Although no discourse of pollution, profanation, shame, hatred, ugliness, or "defect" is deployed by texts to devalue or assign marginal social positions to the mentally disabled, mental disability, like blindness, is cast as a covenantal curse in Deut 28:28, and understood in 1 Sam 16:14 as a token of Yhwh's rejection of Saul on account of Saul's disobedience. Denigrated characteristics such as weakness, vulnerability, dependence, and ignorance are also associated with mental disability in more than a few texts, as is contempt, even though no rhetoric of dishonor per se is used of the mentally disabled. Although lacking in extant biblical evidence, some cuneiform materials draw a connection between mentally disabled persons and other marginal social groups such as the poor, and omen collections cast the birth of a child with mental disability as an indicator of coming ruin for the male head of household. Both biblical and cuneiform texts bring mental disability into association with physical disabilities such as blindness and lameness, suggesting implicitly that these conditions share common characteristics and a common classification.

Deut 28:28–29 includes mental disability among the curses of the covenant, which will come upon those Israelites who transgress Yhwh's treaty stipulations: "Yhwh shall strike you with 'madness' (*šigga'ôn*), blindness ('*iwwarôn*) and bewilderment (*timhôn lebab*), and you shall grope at noon as a blind person gropes in the darkness.[29] You shall not make your ways prosper, but you shall be oppressed and robbed always, without anyone to save you." In v. 34, the text warns that covenant violators will become mentally disabled as a result of seeing their own ruin: "You shall become a 'madman' (*mešugga'*) on account of the vision of your eyes which you have seen." To include mental disability among the curses of the covenant is highly stigmatizing. To pair it with blindness suggests an implicit classification schema that brings together physical "defects" and mental disability. The mention of "bewilderment" (*timhôn lebab*), along with blindness and "madness," as well as the emphasis in the remainder of v. 28 on the helpless groping of the blind in broad daylight, suggests that the basis of the association of the three conditions is a sense that they share the quality of helplessness or incapacitation, as the following verse also suggests ("You shall not make your ways prosper, but you shall be oppressed and robbed always, without anyone to save you."). The text's use of two derivatives of the root *šg'* is worthy of comment, given the evidence discussed previously that this root and its derivatives can be used for severe mental retardation, as in 1 Sam 21:15–16 (Eng. 14–15), or for other conditions that might be understood to constitute mental disability of some kind by our writers (e.g., frenzied chariot driving, as in 2 Kgs 9:20; prophetic ecstasy, as in 2 Kgs 9:11; Jer 29:26; Hos 9:7). What sort of mental disability is envisioned in Deut 28:28–29, 34 with the mention of "madness" and "madman"? Whatever it is, it is clearly to be associated with helplessness, vulnerability, and the inability to take action (vv. 28–29), and is also cast as a response to seeing the ruin that will result from the manifestation of the covenant curses (v. 34). Given that "bewilderment" is listed separately as a result of the curse coming into effect, it would appear that the "madness" of Deut 28:28 is distinct in some way from it. Although "madness" in Deut 28:28 more likely describes shock, horror, or rage resulting in incapacitation than it does any kind of mental retardation, how it differs from "bewilderment," which itself suggests incapacitation as a result of shock or fear, remains unclear.

Aside from curse, mental disability is also cast as a manifestation of divine rejection in 1 Sam 16:14–23. Because Saul transgressed, Yhwh rejected him and chose David to replace him according to the text (1 Sam 16:1; cf. 13:14; 15:26, 35).[30] Once anointed by Samuel, the spirit of Yhwh rushes down on David and remains with him henceforth (16:13). In 1 Sam 16:14, we learn that the spirit of Yhwh has abandoned Saul and been replaced by an evil spirit from Yhwh: "Now the spirit of Yhwh had turned aside from Saul, and an evil spirit from Yhwh tormented him." Saul is said to fear David because he knows that Yhwh has abandoned him and is now with David (18:12). The narrator's apologetic purpose, to demonstrate Yhwh's choice of David over Saul, is well served by Saul's mental disability. It can be explained as the result of the manifestation of an evil spirit from Yhwh, clearly a token of Yhwh's rejection of Saul. Thus, as an indicator of Saul's loss of the throne, his mental disability functions in a manner not unlike his abandonment by Samuel (15:26, 35) or Yhwh's refusal to answer his desperate queries (28:6). All point to his replacement as king by another.

The association of mental disability with devalued qualities such as weakness, vulnerability, and dependence is not uncommon in extant biblical texts. In Deut 28:29, the association with weakness, vulnerability, and dependence is implicit. Deut 28:28 had spoken of three conditions to be brought on violators of the covenant by Yhwh: blindness, "madness," and bewilderment. Verse 29 focuses on blindness, stating that those who are cursed will grope in broad daylight as a blind man gropes; be victimized continually, too weak to defend themselves; and be abandoned, without a protector: "You shall not make your ways prosper, but you shall be oppressed and robbed always, without anyone to save you." Given the three conditions spoken of in v. 28, it seems fair to assume that the claim of v. 29 applies to all who are affected, not only to those blinded as a result of the curse. Thus, in my reading of Deut 28:28–29, "madness" and bewilderment, like blindness, result in weakness, vulnerability to oppression, victimization, and dependence on a stronger patron.

Another way in which the mentally disabled, or those who are alleged to be so, are devalued in biblical texts is through the lack of honor and esteem accorded them by others who interact with them. A primary example of this is the reaction of Achish of Gath to David in 1 Sam 21:11–16 (Eng. 10–15). When David feigns severe mental retardation in public, Achish responds by calling into question the judgment of his courtiers: "And Achish said to his servants, 'Look – You see that the man "acts madly" (*mištaggeaʿ*). Why have you brought him to me? Do I lack "madmen" (*mešuggaʿîm*), that you bring this one "to act madly" (*lehištaggeaʿ*) before me? Should this one enter my household?'" Such a person is simply of no interest to Achish, and he cannot imagine why his courtiers would bring David into his presence. Achish does not even find entertainment value in David's feigned behaviors. His final question – clearly rhetorical – suggests that he has no interest in admitting such a man to his retinue. The sentiment may be motivated by a desire to avoid increasing the number of his dependents, particularly those from whom little of a productive nature can be expected. It may also be motivated by the view that the affiliation of such a person with his circle would bring no honor to him, and perhaps bring dishonor. Although no explicit rhetoric of dishonor is used of David in this passage, his low status is realized through Achish's contemptuous treatment of him.[31] David, while in Gath, is certainly counted among the lightly esteemed.[32] Achish's low estimation of persons with mental disability of this sort allows David to preserve his life in a dangerous situation. By feigning behaviors associated with severe mental retardation, David makes himself irrelevant to Achish and the Philistines, and is able to escape without incident.

A second biblical text in which a person believed to have mental disability is treated with contempt by others is 2 Kgs 9:11. After the military commander Jehu is anointed king by a prophetic disciple of Elisha in a private meeting, Jehu rejoins his fellow officers, who are naturally curious to know what transpired: "As for Jehu, he came forth to the servants of his lord. They said to him, 'Is all well? Why did this "madman" (*mešuggaʿ*) come to you?' He said to them, 'You know the man and his talk.'" Jehu's fellow officers refer to the prophet disdainfully as a "madman" (*mešuggaʿ*), using the same word Achish used contemptuously of David. Jehu, attempting to keep the matter of his anointing a secret, plays to their low estimation of the prophet by dismissing the prophet's words.[33] Although the prophet displays no peculiar behaviors in the narrative in which he appears, extant texts do bear witness to a tendency to describe prophetic ecstatic behavior with derivatives of the root *šgʿ* (e.g., "madman," as in Jer 29:26; Hos 9:7). This is likely the explanation for the officers' dismissal of the prophet as a "madman." In any case, their contempt for the prophet is clear from their description of him and from Jehu's dismissive reply to their question. The prophet is anything but honored in their eyes.

Cuneiform texts also bear witness to the stigmatization of the mentally disabled and suggest their marginal social status. The omen series Shumma Izbu includes a number of omens mentioning the births of mentally disabled persons. Not surprisingly, all such births are interpreted negatively. Tablet i, number 52, reads: "If a woman gives birth to a male idiot – troubles; scattering of the house of the man."[34] Although number 53, concerning the birth of a female child with mental disability, is fragmentary, tablet iv, number 49, is not: "If a woman of the palace gives birth to a boy moron – the possessions of the king will be plundered."[35] In each case, the head of household, whether a common man or the king, suffers significantly as a result of the birth of a child with severe mental retardation by a woman in his household. Needless to say, the casting of mental disability as an omen of disaster is highly stigmatizing to those who are mentally disabled. Cuneiform texts also associate mental disability with ignorance and lack of judgment. For example, persons with mental disability, along with the deaf and the blind, are portrayed as lacking understanding and easily manipulated into transgression in Babylonian *kudurru* (boundary) inscriptions.[36] Finally, Babylonian wisdom literature speaks of the mentally disabled as having a marginal status and low rank. In "The Babylonian Theodicy," a sufferer complains that his piety has not led to reward from the gods. Instead of being well off, he is impoverished; in place of being elevated, he is diminished. Even physically and mentally disabled persons have a higher status than he does, as does the economically unproductive person.[37] This text is interesting in a number of respects. First, mental disability is associated with both low social status and poverty. This may be compared to those biblical texts that associate persons with "defects" and other physical disabilities with the poor and other marginal groups. Although no biblical text brings the mentally disabled into association with the poor or other socially marginal groups in an explicit way, "The Babylonian Theodicy" bears witness to this association in cuneiform literature.[38] Second, the mentally disabled person is categorized with the physically disabled person, the unproductive person, and, by implication, the poor, suggesting an implicit classification based perhaps on a shared poverty and low status.

CONCLUSION

Although biblical representations of mental disability are less common than those of physical disabilities, and although our understanding of the technical vocabulary of mental disability is limited, there is sufficient evidence to allow us to begin to speak of the contours of mental disability in its biblical representation. The ways in which texts employ the technical vocabulary of mental disability indicate that a number of conditions we see as distinct share a common classification. David's feigned behaviors, which suggest severe mental retardation, Jehu's frenzied chariot driving, prophetic ecstatic behavior, and extreme reactions of shock and horror in the context of disaster, are all described using derivatives of the verbal root šgʿ, traditionally translated "to be mad." The verb hll, also commonly rendered "to be mad," has a similarly broad range of application. Furthermore, these two verbs and the rare idiom šinnah ṭaʿam ("to change discernment") are equated in 1 Sam 21:11–16 (Eng. 10–15), and we know from cuneiform evidence that ṭema šanû, an Akkadian cognate of Hebrew šinnah ṭaʿam, also has a broad range of usage. What do the conditions described by this technical vocabulary have in common? All are characterized by a perception of real or apparent loss of self-control, whether the result of extreme anger, shock, or anguish; mental disturbance of some kind; drunkenness; excessive risk taking; or severe mental retardation. Interestingly, this vocabulary is absent from 1 Sam 16:14–23 and related texts, where Saul's mental disturbance is represented, although characteristics of his behavior (e.g., extreme anger, apparent loss of self-control) are not unlike those of persons described as "mad" in other biblical texts. At all events, the use of our contemporary term "mental disability," which covers a range of conditions, may be compared to the biblical use of a root such as šgʿ, which is also broad and varied in its usage, although derivatives of šgʿ are typically pejorative.

Even though mental disability is not classified as a "defect" (mûm), and discourses such as those of pollution, profanation, hatred, ugliness, and shame are not deployed directly to devalue the mentally disabled, a number of the strategies used by texts to stigmatize and assign marginal social positions to persons with physical disabilities are evidenced in biblical representations of mental disability. Mental disability is cast as a covenantal curse in Deut 28:28, and a manifestation of the deity's rejection of Saul in 1 Sam 16:14–23. It is associated with devalued qualities such as weakness, vulnerability, and dependence (e.g., Deut 28:29), as well as contempt and dishonor (e.g., 1 Sam 21:11–16 [Eng. 10–15]; 2 Kgs 9:11), although no explicit rhetoric of dishonor is used directly in these texts. Cuneiform texts associate mental disability with ignorance, poverty, and low social status, and cast the birth of a child with mental disability as an omen of disaster.

Several texts, both biblical and cuneiform, bear witness to implicit native schemas of classification, which bring the mentally disabled into association with persons with physical disabilities. A prime example is the curse of Deut 28:28–29, which speaks of "madness" (*šiggaʿôn*), blindness, and bewilderment striking violators of the covenant, leaving them weak, vulnerable to oppression, and in need of a strong patron whom they will not find. In this text, all three disabling conditions – two mental, one physical – are said to render affected persons helpless, and this shared incapacitation appears to be the basis for their common classification. Like the curse of Deut 28:28–29, "The Babylonian Theodicy" also suggests a shared, implicit classification for the physically disabled and the mentally disabled, along with the nondisabled poor and persons who are not economically productive. In this instance, the classification schema is based not on incapacity and helplessness, but on a shared low status and poverty.

5

‿

Disability in the Prophetic Utopian Vision

*V*ISIONS OF AN IDEAL FUTURE ARE NOT UNCOMMON IN BIBLICAL prophetic anthologies. Whether in response to a troubled past in which Israel has transgressed and been punished by Yhwh, often through the agency of foreign powers, or in reaction to a present characterized by the loss of central institutions such as the land, the monarchy, and the temple cult, or on account of the threat of impending disaster, prophetic utopian visions present a very different kind of reality. Mapping a world of ideal relations not infrequently characterized both by the restoration of things lost and by the creation of a novel reality never before seen, such visions give us some insight into an author's notions of what a model world might look like. In this chapter, I investigate the role of disability in the prophetic utopian vision.[1] Although disability plays no role in some utopian visions, it is central to others. Some prophetic texts speak of a utopian future of changed circumstances for disabled persons in which they are able to accomplish uncharacteristic feats such as participation in plunder during wartime or making a long, arduous journey without difficulty, or in which restrictions on their involvement in the cult are eliminated. Other passages envision the physical transformation of persons with disabilities such as blindness and deafness into persons who can see and hear, with some texts even representing disabled persons becoming persons with abilities that exceed those of the average human being. Finally, there are a number of prophetic utopian visions that lack disabled persons per se, but in which disability functions metaphorically to suggest Israel's rejection by Yhwh before his saving intervention on their behalf. Prophetic utopian texts share in common an interest in promoting Yhwh as an incomparable deity who is able to change the order of things, accomplishing profound, transformative deeds. When disabled persons are mentioned in these visions of an ideal future, they function, to a large degree, as vehicles for the display of Yhwh's agency, not unlike the disabled characters in narrative texts that I have discussed (e.g., Samson, Ahijah the prophet, Moses). Their stunning transformation or their unprecedented inclusion and empowerment, along with changes to other aspects of life as it is known, suggest Yhwh's power and preeminence. Texts that use disability metaphorically to suggest the people's rejection are also characterized by transformations wrought by Yhwh (e.g., of the rejected people's status) that enhance his own reputation for might and action. Although utopian texts function to exalt Yhwh through his saving and transformative acts, they also tend to stigmatize disabled persons in a number of ways: by eliminating their disabilities entirely in the envisioned utopia, suggesting that disabilities have no place in a model world; by suggesting that disabled persons require Yhwh's special intervention to mitigate the marginalizing effects of their disabilities, thereby allowing their inclusion; by making devaluing comparisons (e.g., of disabled persons to a desert); by the deployment of stigmatizing binary discourses (e.g., that of shame); and by associating disabled persons with other stigmatized and marginalized groups (e.g., the poor, the afflicted) and with undesirable traits and conditions to be left behind in the ideal future in some cases, to be perpetuated in others (e.g., weakness, vulnerability, immobility, dependence, feminization [of males], and divine rejection). However, one utopian text, Isa 56:3–7, foresees the full inclusion of persons with a particular disability without reinforcing their stigmatization at the same time.

THE PROPHETIC UTOPIAN VISION

I begin with Isa 2:1–4 and 11:1–9, excellent examples of the prophetic utopian vision characterized by a number of the most prominent features found in such texts. Although disability plays no role in either passage, the two texts provide a useful framework within which to consider the role of disability in the visions in which it occurs. Isa 2:1–4 reads as follows:

The word which Isaiah son of Amoz saw concerning
  Judah and Jerusalem:
"At the end of days,
the mount of the temple of Yhwh shall be established

as the highest of mountains,
exalted above the hills,
and all the nations shall flow to it.
Many peoples shall go and say,
'Come, let us ascend to the mountain of Yhwh,
to the house of the God of Jacob.
He shall teach us some of his ways, and we shall walk in his paths.'
For from Zion shall go forth the teaching,
the word of Yhwh from Jerusalem.
He shall judge between nations and reprove many peoples.
They shall beat their swords into mattocks,
their spears into pruning hooks.
Nation shall not lift up sword against nation,
nor shall they learn war anymore.

In this vision attributed by the text to Isaiah of Jerusalem (eighth c. BCE), set at the "end of days" (an idiom for an unspecified future time), Jerusalem and Yhwh's temple there are exalted, the nations become Yhwh worshipers and make pilgrimage to his temple, Yhwh passes judgment on the peoples, and universal peace is established.[2] Isa 11:1–9, a text the provenance and date of which continue to be debated, goes further.[3] It not only speaks of a future, ideal Davidic monarch who will judge the poor and the afflicted justly and slay the wicked, but also envisions the utter transformation of animal life as we know it:

The wolf shall dwell with the lamb,
the leopard shall lie down with the kid,
the calf, young lion and fatling together,
and a young child shall lead them.
The cow and the bear shall graze,
their young shall lie down together,
the lion shall eat straw like the steer.

(vv. 6–7)

Just as war is replaced by universal peace in Isa 2:1–4, carnivores are transformed into herbivores, aggressive animals into docile beasts in Isa 11:6–8. Harm and destruction are therefore excluded from Yhwh's holy mountain (v. 9). Each passage shares a setting in the future ("the end of days" in 2:2; a completely unspecified time in 11:1); each is characterized by transformation of life as it is known (e.g., universal peace and the universal worship of Yhwh in 2:3–4; the complete alteration of animal behavior and the consequent abolishment of violence in 11:6–9); and each suggests that Yhwh is the agent who brings these changes about (2:4; 11:2, 9).

Some of the transformations envisioned in these two passages are not implausible (e.g., the emergence of a just Davidic king). Some are extraordinary, although not utterly inconceivable (e.g., universal peace or the embrace of Yhwh by all nations). However, some go beyond anything anyone could realistically imagine (e.g., the transformation of carnivores into herbivores). All of these changes are emblematic of Yhwh's incomparable power: nothing whatever is too much for him according to these texts. Interestingly, the two texts are characterized by a significant ethnocentric coloring, even given their manifest universal concerns. Jerusalem, its temple, and its god become a magnet for the nations and the source of instruction in Isa 2:2–4; Yhwh's holy mountain is the site of the transformation of animal life envisioned in 11:6–8. Such a parochial orientation is not uncommon in the ideal future of the utopian visions, with their central focus on Israel and its destiny.

A UTOPIAN FUTURE OF CHANGED CIRCUMSTANCES
FOR DISABLED PERSONS

Several prophetic utopian visions describe Yhwh acting to change the circumstances of persons with disabilities in order to include them in his scenario of salvation and to express his incomparable capabilities. In the case of Jer 31:7–9 and Isa 33:17–24, Yhwh acts to mitigate the physical limitations imposed on disabled persons by their disabilities; in the case of Isa 56:3–7, Yhwh eliminates the cultic proscription of the eunuch, allowing him access to the sanctuary.[4]

Jer 31:7–9 is part of the so-called "Book of Consolation" (Jer 30:1–31:40), a collection of mainly positive, future-oriented oracles of Yhwh concerning Israel and Judah embedded in the Book of Jeremiah.[5] Responding in large part to the exile of Judah's elite to Babylon during the sixth century BCE, restoration is a primary theme of this collection, which speaks of both southern and northern exiles. Aspects of restoration include the return of both Judean and Israelite exiles to their land (30:10; 31:4–6, 8–9); reestablishment of the Davidic monarchy (30:9); readoption of the people by Yhwh (30:22; 31:1, 33); and the rebuilding of Jerusalem (30:18;

31:38–40). Jer 31:7–9 is concerned specifically with the return of northern exiles to their land. The setting is evidently in the near future ("I am about to bring[6]"):

> For thus says Yhwh:
> "Cry out joyfully for Jacob,
> cry shrilly over the chief of the nations,
> make known, praise, and say:
> 'Deliver your people, Yhwh,
> the remnant of Israel.'
> I am about to bring them from the land of the north,
> I shall gather them from the ends of the earth,
> among them the blind and lame,
> the pregnant and bearing woman, together.
> They shall return here as a great assembly,
> with weeping they shall come,
> I shall conduct them compassionately.
> I shall bring them to streams of water,
> on a level way on which they shall not stumble.
> For I have become a father to Israel,
> Ephraim is my firstborn son.

Among the northern exiles returning to their land are four examples of persons for whom it is evidently not customary to travel great distances due to their physical limitations: the blind, the lame, the pregnant woman, and the woman giving birth. The presence of such vulnerable, atypical travelers among the vast assembly brought by Yhwh from the north is intended to suggest Yhwh's ability to make even their travel possible. On account of his paternal compassion, even the blind, the lame, and pregnant and bearing women will have a relatively easy journey, well watered, on a flat roadway traversed without difficulty ("they shall not stumble"). In this text, there is no radical transformation of the blind, the lame, and the others who travel with difficulty; rather, through Yhwh's initiative, even they are to be included among the returnees. In short, Yhwh has changed the circumstances in which those who normally travel with difficulty find themselves, allowing them to journey a great distance with relative ease. The trouble-free journey envisioned for the blind and the lame, similar to that imagined for pregnant and bearing women, is intended to exalt Yhwh, who leaves no one behind. The weakness, immobility, vulnerability, and dependence of blind and lame persons is suggested by the text through the association of the blind and the lame with other nonambulatory or semiambulatory types, and by the exceptional circumstances that allow them to travel in this one particular instance. In fact, an implicit class of persons lacking easy mobility is suggested by this passage, a class in which the blind and the lame are brought together with pregnant and bearing women. Although the text presumably speaks of both male and female disabled persons in its vision of a return of the whole of the northern exile, the effect of classifying blind and lame males with two groups of nonambulatory or semiambulatory women, as well as with blind and lame females – as opposed to classifying them with other groups of men or mixed-gender groups that might have trouble traveling (e.g., those who are ill) – is not insignificant. For such a classification suggests the feminization of blind and lame men on account of their nonambulatory or semiambulatory status. Lack of easy mobility is gendered feminine in this particular text because of the groups making up the nonambulatory or semiambulatory class. Like women at their weakest, blind and lame men will also be able to make the arduous journey only on account of Yhwh's intervention.

A second text that envisions changed circumstances for persons with disabilities is Isa 33:17–24. As with the other passages under consideration, this text evidently refers to an idealized future time "when your eyes shall see the king in his beauty," an ambiguous reference that may suggest Yhwh or a future Davidic king. At this time, the land will be rid of foreign oppressors and Jerusalem will be secure and rest easy as a result of Yhwh's intervention:

> For Yhwh is our judge,
> Yhwh is our ruler,
> Yhwh is our king.
> He is the one who shall deliver us . . .
> Then the blind shall divide much spoil,[7]
> the lame shall seize plunder.
> No dweller shall say, "I am sick,"
> the people who dwell in her shall be pardoned of iniquity.

Similar to the blind and the lame of Jer 31:7–9, and in contrast to disabled persons mentioned in several other utopian visions, the blind and the lame of Isa 33:23 are apparently not physically transformed themselves. Rather, it is their situation and status that are transformed, allowing them to perform acts that were evidently impossible before Yhwh's intervention. Alluding obliquely to a military victory over enemies, the text asserts that in the utopian future, blind and lame males will be able to pillage the vanquished as other warriors routinely do. (By mentioning participation in plunder, the text apparently refers to blind and lame males, given the typical gendering of such activity as masculine.[8]) As in Jer 31:7–9, where the blind and the lame are able to travel a great distance on account of Yhwh's intervention on their behalf, Isa 33:23 foresees a future in which disabled persons are in effect normalized as part of Yhwh's saving activity. Although their conditions remain – they are still the blind and the lame – the effects of those conditions are mitigated to the point where the blind and the lame can take part in uncharacteristic acts normally expected of others without disabilities but not of them.[9] In short, the blind and the lame of the future utopia are represented as active agents not unlike persons without disabilities. In the case of Isa 33:23, I would even venture that Yhwh has restored the masculinity of blind and lame males who can now participate in pillage like other males. Far from being dependent on nondisabled persons, blind and lame plunderers act as providers by bringing back booty to their families.[10] Texts that portray normalized disabled persons nonetheless function both to stigmatize disability and to exalt Yhwh's incomparable abilities at the same time. Disability is stigmatized by the suggestion that disabled persons lack agency and, with respect to males specifically, that they need Yhwh's special intervention in order to mitigate the marginalizing effects of their physical conditions, thereby allowing them to participate in regular, gendered activities such as dividing and bringing home the spoils of war, activities that function to constitute masculinity in this culture. Yhwh, for his part, is exalted by the claim that it is he who makes the normalization of disabled persons possible in a future time of salvation.

A third text that describes a change in the circumstances of persons with a disability is Isa 56:3–7. I quote vv. 4–5:

> For thus says Yhwh,
> to the eunuchs who observe my Sabbaths,
> and choose that which I delight in,

and grasp onto my covenant.
I shall give to them in my house and within my walls
a memorial monument
better than sons and daughters.
An everlasting name I shall give to them,
which shall not be cut off.

This text, which envisions a temple cult into which the pious eunuch is admitted and assigned a position of privilege just as he is, differs from the two previously discussed examples in some significant ways. Although it shares a utopian orientation with Jer 31:7–9 and Isa 33:17–24, and although one of its functions is surely to exalt Yhwh on account of his ability to transform the order of things, Isa 56:3–7 does not envision the normalization of the eunuch through efforts by Yhwh to mitigate any marginalizing effects of his physical disability. No such effects are suggested by the text. Rather, it is the cultic proscription of the eunuch, based on a broad reading of Deut 23:2 (Eng. 1), that is to be eliminated in the future utopia, allowing the eunuch to participate fully in the rites of Yhwh's temple, even if he cannot sire children. Unlike Jer 31:7–9 and Isa 33:17–24, Isa 56:3–7 does not stigmatize the eunuch's disability by suggesting that he is weak, vulnerable, immobile, dependent, or, in the case of males, feminized, or that he requires Yhwh's special intervention to make his disability less marginalizing. According to Isa 56:3–7, it is not the eunuch's disability per se that Yhwh addresses, but rather the ban on his entry into the temple and participation in its rites. In short, the text rejects any stigma that might be associated with the eunuch, and any degree of cultic exclusion that he might experience, as wholly illegitimate and unwarranted, in contrast to Jer 31:7–9 and Isa 33:17–24, which not only envision the inclusion of disabled persons in utopian scenarios, but also reinforce their stigmatization at the same time.

A UTOPIAN FUTURE IN WHICH DISABILITY DISAPPEARS

A number of prophetic utopian texts describe Yhwh's elimination of disability at the time of his future intervention. I focus on two such texts, Isa 35:4–10 and 29:17–21.

Isa 35:4–10, a text often attributed to Second Isaiah that may well be directly dependent on Jer 31:7–9,[11] describes the imminent coming of Yhwh to deliver his people and return them to their land:

> Say to the panic-stricken:
> "Be strong, fear not!
> Behold, your god shall come with vengeance,
> the recompense of god.
> He himself shall come and deliver you."
> Then the eyes of the blind shall be opened,
> and the ears of the deaf be unstopped.
> Then the lame shall leap (*yedalleg*) like a gazelle,
> and the tongue of the mute shout joyfully.
> For water bursts forth in the desert,
> and streams in the wilderness.
> The parched ground shall become a pool,
> and the thirsty ground springs of water.
> In the habitation of jackels . . .
> (there shall be) grass, reeds and rushes.[12]
> There shall be a highway there,
> it shall be called "a holy way."
> The unclean shall not pass over it . . .
> And (even) fools shall not go astray.
> There shall be no lion there,
> no violent beast shall ascend on it.
> They shall not be found there,
> but the redeemed shall go (on it).
> The ransomed of Yhwh shall return,
> they shall come to Zion with a joyful cry.
> Eternal joy shall be on their heads,
> rejoicing and joy shall overtake (them),
> suffering and groaning shall flee.

As in Jer 31:7–9, the focus of Isa 35:4–10 is the return of exiles to their land on a path provided by Yhwh. Similarly, persons with disabilities are counted among the returnees. However, in the case of Isa 35:4–10, a transformation of such persons is envisioned, rather than simply a change in their circumstances that allows them to travel easily. In Isa 35:5–6, the blind become sighted, the deaf acquire hearing, the lame are able to leap like a gazelle, and the mute shout joyfully. Yhwh's transformation of persons with disabilities into persons with the ability to see, hear, move freely, and speak/shout is paralleled by equally profound changes in the landscape: desert land becomes exceptionally well watered; the highway back to Zion is easy for all to navigate – even fools – and kept free of violent predators. Such transformations, similar to the changes in circumstances narrated in Jer 31:7–8, underscore Yhwh's power to act and accomplish profound change. The impossible becomes possible because of the agency of Yhwh.

Yet, the nature of the changes brought about by Yhwh is worthy of some further exploration, for in at least one instance, there is more to the transformations than one might realize at first blush. The lame who are able to leap as a gazelle does have acquired more than simply average human agility; their abilities now exceed those of other nonlame persons. It is also interesting to note that leaping like a gazelle is precisely the simile used of the male lover of the Song of Songs, whose agility is characteristic of his beauty:

> The sound of my lover,
> behold he comes,
> leaping (*medalleg*) upon the mountains,
> bounding in the hills.
> My lover is like a gazelle . . .[13]
>
> (2:8–9)

Thus, Isa 35:6 may imply not only that the lame shall become extremely agile as a result of Yhwh's intervention; the text may also be suggesting that what was ugly shall become beautiful, given the association of "defects" (*mûmîm*) with ugliness elsewhere, and that of the agility of the gazelle with male beauty in Song of Songs 2:8–9.[14]

The parallel drawn in Isa 35:4–10 between disabled persons who lose their disabilities and the desert that loses its aridity, becoming well watered and productive of grass, reeds, and rushes, is most revealing. Both transformations are the result of Yhwh's intervention, and it is difficult not to notice that the author is implicitly comparing disabled persons to a desert, thereby stigmatizing them in yet another way. For just as a desert is arid, unproductive, and limited with respect to the life it supports, the author appears to be suggesting something comparable for the blind, the lame, the deaf, and the mute through his implicit comparison. Like a desert, persons with disabilities lack certain essential characteristics of life; they are somehow incomplete in an analogous way. Unhappily, because the comparison is implicit, it is not easy to pinpoint the author's views of disability's shortcomings. However, it seems clear that by comparing disabled persons to a desert, and by envisioning the elimination of both desert and disability in the utopian future, the text underscores the undesirability of both. Yhwh's future utopia of joyous restoration will have no place for suffering, arid desert, or disability.

Isa 29:17–21 is a second example of a vision of the immediate future in which both landscape and persons are transformed, presumably by Yhwh's actions. Like a number of texts discussed, this passage is generally attributed to Isaiah of Jerusalem:

> In a little while yet,
> shall not Lebanon return to garden land,
> and garden land be thought of as forest?
> On that day, the deaf shall hear the words of a book,
> and free of gloom and darkness,
> the eyes of the blind shall see.[15]
> The afflicted shall again rejoice in Yhwh,
> the human poor exult in the Holy One of Israel.
> For the ruthless shall disappear,
> the scoffer come to an end,
> all who are watchful to do evil shall be cut off . . .

In this passage, as in Isa 35:4–10, deaf and blind are transformed into persons who are able to hear and see in the imminent utopia.[16] However, here, their transformation is paralleled both by that of the landscape and by that of the poor and the afflicted, who will now be able to rejoice in Yhwh free of their oppressors. Although the meaning of v. 17b, which describes the topographical aspects of the utopian transformation, is not entirely clear and continues to be debated, it seems evident that the changes wrought on the landscape must be positive in some way, given that the other transformations are cast as improvements over the status quo.[17] The newfound ability to hear and see attributed to the deaf and blind is compared implicitly to the improved situation of the poor and the afflicted, thereby underscoring in yet another way the negative construction of the disabilities of deaf and blind persons. Just as the poor and the afflicted are freed of their oppressors, so the deaf and the blind are freed of their disabilities. The listing of the deaf and blind with the poor and the afflicted also suggests a common classification that I have noted in other texts, a classification likely based on a shared vulnerability and weakness.

DISABILITY AS METAPHOR FOR DIVINE REJECTION

In contrast to the preceding texts that speak of the fate of disabled persons in Yhwh's future utopia, several texts use disability metaphorically to suggest the people's temporary rejection by Yhwh before he acts to save them. Mic 4:6–7 and Zeph 3:19 are two such passages.

Mic 4:6–7 and its close parallel, Zeph 3:19, are both set at a future time when Yhwh will intervene decisively in the affairs of Judeans.[18] Mic 4:6–7 reads as follows:

> "At that time," oracle of Yhwh,
> "I shall gather in the limping one,
> and bring in the one which was driven away,
> and those I treated injuriously.
> I shall turn the lame one into a remnant,
> and the rejected one (?) into a numerous people."[19]
> And Yhwh shall rule over them on Mt. Zion,
> from now until eternity.

As more than a few commentators and translators have noted, this text appears to be employing metaphoric language to describe Judeans as sheep whom Yhwh, their shepherd, has previously rejected but will now gather in after an apparent change of heart.[20] The rejected "sheep," described as "limping," "driven away," and "those I treated injuriously," are not only gathered in, but will be transformed into a "remnant" and a "numerous people" under Yhwh's eternal rule, clearly changes betokening the deity's reconciliation with Judah. Zeph 3:19 presents the same core material, but with some interesting differences:

> I shall save the limping one (*haṣole'ah*),
> and bring in the one which was driven away (*hanniddaḥah*).
> I shall turn their shame (*boštam*) into praise and reputation
> (*šem*) in all the land.[21]

Similar to Mic 4:6–7, Zeph 3:19 is characterized by shepherding metaphors, including the people in the figure of a limping sheep and one that is driven away. The two texts include transformation of the people's condition as part of Yhwh's saving intervention. In Mic 4:6–7, the formerly rejected are embraced, and their acceptance is suggested by their increase in population (they become "a numerous people"). In Zeph 3:19, those formerly rejected are also embraced, but here their acceptance is indicated differently: the shame of those who have been rejected, not mentioned in Mic 4:6–7, will be transformed into praise and reputation in all the land.

In both Mic 4:6–7 and Zeph 3:19, disability is emblematic of rejection. The limping sheep is closely associated with the one that was driven away and, in Mic 4:6, with those that have been treated injuriously by the deity; all have been rejected by Yhwh before he reverses himself and gathers them back in. Mic 4:6–7 adds the notion of small numbers as indicative of rejection (this is implied by the statement that they will become a numerous people); Zeph 3:19 suggests that such rejection is shameful, thereby associating disability with shame. The figure of the rejected, limping sheep as a metaphor for Yhwh's people before their restoration in both Mic 4:6–7 and Zeph 3:19 is worthy of additional scrutiny, because lameness among sacrificial animals such as the sheep is constructed as a "defect" (*mûm*) in a number of biblical texts that have been discussed (e.g., Deut 15:21). Such "defective" sacrificial animals are generally unacceptable for sacrifice, and some are even described as "ugly" (Deut 15:21; 17:1) and as "abomination(s) of Yhwh" (Deut 17:1).[22] A highly stigmatizing discourse of rejection and inferiority is characteristic of texts that describe such animals (e.g., "their destruction [*mošḥatam*] is in them; a 'defect' [*mûm*] is in them; they shall not be accepted for you" [Lev 22:25; cf. Mal 1:14]). Thus, the figure of a lame sacrificial animal, like an animal "driven away" by its shepherd, functions effectively to communicate the deity's evident rejection of his people before he changes his mind and acts to deliver them. When salvation comes, the rejected "sheep" are gathered in. Metaphor is abandoned in Mic 4:7, and the people are spoken of directly. They are transformed into a "numerous nation" over which Yhwh will rule forever. In Zeph 3:19, the transition from metaphor to direct discussion of the people's fate is more subtle (implied by the statement that Yhwh will turn their shame into praise and reputation in all the land). This is likely the reason that the clarifying gloss in v. 20 was added after v. 19:

"At that time, I shall bring you,
at that time, I shall gather you.
For I shall make you renowned and an object of praise
among all the nations of the earth,
when I restore your fortunes in your sight,"
says Yhwh.[23]

Thus, disability functions figuratively in Mic 4:6–7 and Zeph 3:19 to suggest Yhwh's rejection of his people. Similar to other utopian texts in which transformations occur, Mic 4:6–7 and Zeph 3:19 describe radical change, but in these texts, it is not the circumstances of disabled persons that is transformed, nor is disability itself eliminated by Yhwh. Here, with disability as a metaphor for Yhwh's rejection of his people, it is the shame of a rejected people that is changed into praise and reputation (Zeph 3:19) or their numbers multiplied, with Yhwh as their ruler in Jerusalem (Mic 4:7). Such transformations, like those which Yhwh accomplishes in other utopian visions, function to underscore his greatness and power: It is only on account of his saving acts that his rejected, dispersed, and depleted/shamed people might return to their land and be increased/honored. Needless to say, disability itself is stigmatized in these texts by its association with divine rejection and, in the case of Zeph 3:19, with shame.

CONCLUSION

The prophetic utopian visions map a model set of relations and conditions, and thereby provide us with a glimpse of what an ideal world might look like to the authors of our texts. Although the details might differ from text to text, the return of exiles to their land and the reestablishment of Israel's relationship with Yhwh on a positive footing are common themes found in many of the visions. Other themes include military victory over enemies, the removal of domestic oppressors, the establishment of universal peace, the attachment of nonresident foreigners to Yhwh and Jerusalem, the emergence of an ideal (Davidic) ruler, and various transformations of the natural world. Disability plays a central role in more than a few of these utopian visions. In some texts, the circumstances of disabled persons are changed by Yhwh in order to allow them to participate in the return of exiles to their land, in the military defeat of enemies and its aftermath, or in the temple cult of the ideal future. Other passages envision a physical transformation of disabled persons into persons with abilities that might even exceed those of average people at the time when Yhwh acts to deliver Israel. Still other texts lack disabled persons per se, but use disability metaphorically to suggest the people's state of rejection before Yhwh's salvific, transformative intervention. Each passage makes use of disability as a vehicle to exalt Yhwh as an incomparable god, whose agency will allow disabled persons to participate in his utopian plan, and who can even act to eliminate disability entirely should he so choose. Although utopian texts consistently exalt Yhwh, they often stigmatize disabled persons at the same time. They may eliminate disabilities in the ideal future, suggesting they have no place in a utopia; they may suggest that disabled persons depend on Yhwh's special efforts to mitigate the marginalizing effects of their physical conditions in order for them to be normalized; they may devalue disabled persons through stigmatizing comparisons (e.g., to a desert); they may make use of stigmatizing binary discourses (e.g., that of shame); and they may associate disabled persons with other stigmatized and marginalized groups (e.g., the poor, the afflicted) and with devalued characteristics and conditions such as weakness, vulnerability, immobility, dependence, feminization [of males], and divine rejection, some of which are to be eliminated in the utopia, while others persist. In contrast, at least one utopian text, Isa 56:3–7, envisions the full inclusion of persons with a particular disability without stigmatizing them at the same time.

6

Nonsomatic Parallels to Bodily Wholeness and "Defect"

SOMATIC "DEFECTS" (*MÛMÎM*) AND THEIR OPPOSITE, BODILY
wholeness, have been of considerable interest to this investigation
thus far. In chapter 1, I explored the relationship of physical "defects" and
ugliness, on the one hand, and a lack of "defects" and beauty, on the other.
The focus of chapter 2 is the disabling dimensions of corporeal "defects."
In this chapter, I investigate nonsomatic parallels to bodily wholeness
and "defect." I begin with two insightful claims of Mary Douglas: (1) that
wholeness and completeness are paradigmatic in biblical thought and
characteristic of the quality of holiness, and (2) that there is a symmetrical relationship between the "defects" of sacrificial animals and those
of priests. For Douglas, that which is holy is whole and complete, and
somatic perfection characterizes both the priests serving in the temple
and the sacrifices brought to the deity: "The sanctity of cognitive boundaries is made known by valuing the integrity of the physical forms. The
perfect physical specimens point to the perfectly bounded temple, altar,
and sanctuary." Douglas argued that "defective" sacrificial animals and
priests are excluded from the cult because they lack the quality of wholeness required for admission.[1] Although Douglas erred in some of her
assumptions about the biblical cult as represented in the P and H materials of Leviticus (e.g., that bodily wholeness is required of all persons
entering the sanctuary and of all sacrifices), the major elements of her
thesis may be both supported and elaborated by turning to evidence she
did not consider: nonbodily analogues to whole and "defective" sacrificial
animals and priests.[2] More important, for our purposes, an investigation
into nonsomatic parallels to bodily wholeness and "defect" demonstrates
the degree to which the notion of the "defective" and its analogues are

evidenced in biblical thought, and the extent to which texts consistently devalue and seek to marginalize that which is cast as "defective" or lacking in wholeness. Just as priests with "defects" are prohibited from offering sacrifices in Leviticus 21 and are stigmatized and partially marginalized as a result by that text, and just as "defective" sacrificial animals are excluded from the cult with few exceptions, so stones understood to lack whole-ness and completeness may not be used to build either the altar of burnt offerings or the temple building according to several texts (Exod 20:25; Deut 27:5–6; Jos 8:30–31; 1 Kgs 6:7).[3]

THE STONES OF THE ALTAR

Exod 20:24–25, a section of a discrete legal collection called the Book of the Covenant, contains legislation concerning the building of an altar for burnt offerings to Yhwh.[4] Two types of altar are possible according to this pericope: either an altar of earth (v. 24) or an altar of stones (v. 25).[5] Regarding the stone altar, the text has this to say: "And if you make an altar of stones for me, you shall not build it of finished, quarried stone (*gazît*). For were you to wield your tool upon it, you would profane it (*teḥaleleha*)."[6] If finished ashlar blocks are proscribed for the altar, what kind of stone is permitted? The text seems to suggest indirectly that a stone altar may only be built of field stones, stones that by definition are not worked with a tool. Deut 27:5–6, which recasts the law in Exod 20:25, attempts to clarify this point by referring directly to the permitted stones: "You shall build there an altar to Yhwh your god, an altar of stones.[7] You shall not wield upon them any iron (tool). With 'full' stones (*'abanîm šelemôt*) you shall build the altar of Yhwh your god, and offer up upon it whole burnt offerings to Yhwh your god." Field stones, the stones permitted for building the altar, are referred to as "full" or "whole" stones by Deut 27:6. Jos 8:30–31, which refers directly to the legislation in Deut 27:5–6, uses the same expression to describe the stones of the altar: "Then Joshua built an altar to Yhwh, god of Israel on Mount Ebal as Moses, servant of Yhwh commanded the children of Israel, (and) as it is written in the book of the Torah of Moses: an altar of 'full' stones (*'abanîm šelemôt*) upon which no one has wielded an iron (tool)." Thus, the permitted field stones, not mentioned directly by Exod 20:25, are referred to as "full" or "whole" stones by Deut 27:5–6 and Jos 8:30–31.

Exod 20:25 suggests that stone altered by human agency through the use of a tool is profaned or made common, and therefore unfit for building an altar to Yhwh. To claim that working stone with a tool profanes the stone suggests that unworked stone is holy, the opposite of that which is profane or common.[8] Furthermore, Exod 20:25 implies that the altar itself, because it is made of holy stones, is a holy cultic item, not unlike other items of the sanctuary, its priests, and the sanctuary itself according to a number of biblical texts.[9] To profane the stones means that they lose their quality of holiness and become common material, inappropriate for use in the sanctuary. Thus, Exod 20:25 provides a motive for the exclusive use of field stones for the building of the altar: to preserve the altar's holiness. Deut 27:5 reworks the condition in Exod 20:25 regarding the wielding of a tool on the stones into a commandment and adds the specification that it is an iron tool that is in question. However, Deut 27:5 says nothing explicitly about the profaning effect of working the stones with a tool, although it may well assume it. If Deut 27:5–6 does not seek to preserve the holiness of the altar stones, and by extension, the altar itself, it is unclear what its motive is for requiring unfinished stones for the altar.

The use of the term "full" or "whole" stones ('abanîm šelemôt) in Deut 27:6 for field stones untouched by a tool is striking, given the range of the Hebrew root šlm, from which the adjective šelemah (plural, šelemôt), "whole" or "full," is derived. The root is polyvalent, suggesting completeness, wholeness, balance, and that which is in order.[10] Derivatives of the root are used to describe the payment of vows (= completion), soundness and safety, peace, friendly relations between parties, and fair weights and measures. Thus, the "full" field stones may be understood as whole and in order, the opposite – apparently – of finished ashlar blocks (gazît), which, the text implies, would be somehow incomplete, out of order, and, according to Exod 20:25, profaned or made common. Stones worked with a tool, proscribed by Exod 20:25 and Deut 27:5–6 for building the altar of burnt offerings, are thus analogous to sacrificial animals and priests with "defects" (mûmîm), in that the stones, the animals, and the priests all lack the quality of wholeness or completeness. Although the idiom used of the altar stones (šelemah, "full" or "whole," derived from the root šlm) differs from those used of sacrificial animals (tamîm/temîmah, "whole," non-"defective," derived from the root tmm) and, by implication, priests, the meaning appears to be the same.[11] The term *šelemah*, "full" or "whole," parallels the terms *tamîm/temîmah*, "whole" or non-"defective," in its usage, and is evidently the term used of inanimate objects such as stones, whereas *tamîm/temîmah* are used of the bodies of living creatures such as sacrificial animals.[12] Clearly, Mary Douglas's idea that wholeness and completeness are paradigmatic biblical concepts gains further support from the example of the altar in Exod 20:25, Deut 27:5–6, and Jos 8:30–31. Furthermore, her association of holiness with wholeness and completeness is more broadly attested than she initially suggested because the permitted stones of Exod 20:25 are evidently both holy and "whole."

THE STONES OF THE TEMPLE

The term "full" or "whole" stone is also used of the temple building in 1 Kgs 6:7: "As for the temple, when it was built, it was built of 'full' stone (*'eben šelemah*) from the quarry; neither hammers, pick(s), nor any (other) iron tool was heard in the temple when it was built."[13] This description of the building of the temple shares much in common with Deut 27:5–6 and Jos 8:31. Like these texts, it refers to a requirement to use only "full" or "whole" stone, and notes that no iron tool was used at the time the temple was erected. However, unlike Deut 27:5–6, Jos 8:30–31, and Exod 20:25, 1 Kgs 6:7 does not refer to the building of an altar for burnt offerings, but to the erection of the temple building in Jerusalem. 1 Kgs 6:7 therefore appears to reflect an extension of the principle of the altar laws to cover the temple building as well, as the two allusions to Deut 27:5–6 in its formulation suggest. (The allusions are evident in the mention of only "full" or "whole" stone used as the building material, and in the avoidance of the use of iron tools when the building was erected.) Similar to the altar, the temple itself was to be built of "full" or "whole" stones without the use of iron tools. Interestingly, according to 1 Kgs 6:7, unfinished *quarried* stone qualifies as "full" or "whole" stone, although the stone was quarried, like finished ashlar blocks, and not gathered from the ground, as are field stones. Apparently, as long as the stone remains unfinished, it is considered "whole" or "full" according to 1 Kgs 6:7, and therefore acceptable. Thus, 1 Kgs 6:7 evidently bears witness to an expansion of the category "full" or "whole" stone to include unfinished quarried stone blocks in addition to field stones.[14] Furthermore, the blanket proscription of the use of iron tools on stone in Deut 27:5–6 is possibly modified to some extent in 1 Kgs 6:7. The text says that iron tools were not heard at the site of the temple when the building was erected, suggesting that the stones remained unfinished, although nothing is said of the use of such tools at the quarry, where iron tools or wooden wedges were routinely used to remove the rough-hewn stone blocks.[15] Thus, it is possible that the text is suggesting that stone cut from the quarry with iron tools could still be considered "full" or "whole" stone as long as iron tools were not used at the building site to finish the rough-hewn blocks.

NONSOMATIC ANALOGUES TO STIGMATIZATION
AND MARGINALIZATION

Stones that are not "full," that lack wholeness, are, as I argue, the analogues of "defective" sacrificial animals and priests. Thus, their exclusion from use in the construction of the altar of burnt offerings according to Exod 20:25, Deut 27:5–6, and Jos 8:30–31, and in the building of the temple in 1 Kgs 6:7, is analogous to the stigmatization and marginalization of priests and sacrifices with "defects" (*mûmîm*). Just as sacrificial animals with "defects" are stigmatized as inferior by being labeled "ugly" or "abomination(s) of Yhwh" and excluded with few exceptions from all forms of sacrifice according to biblical texts, so altar stones not understood as "full" or "whole" are cast as inferior in Exod 20:25 by their categorization as "profane" or "common," and by their rejection from sanctuary use. Just as priests with "defects" are both stigmatized and partially marginalized by Leviticus 21 through exclusion from offering sacrifices to Yhwh and through the threat to the sanctuary's holiness that they pose should they offer such sacrifice, so finished ashlar is, by implication, cast as undesirable for the building of the temple and, therefore, excluded from the construction process according to 1 Kgs 6:7.

A lack of holiness characterizes both stones worked with a tool according to Exod 20:25 and certain "defective" sacrificial animals according to Deuteronomy 15.[16] (The evidence is ambiguous with respect to priests with "defects.") "Defective" male firstlings, unlike "whole" male firstlings that are normally sanctified to Yhwh (Deut 15:19), clearly lack holiness according to Deut 15:22, which states that they may be eaten outside the sanctuary by the clean and unclean alike.[17] Thus, firstlings with "defects" are profane or common according to Deut 15:22, not unlike the stone that has been worked with a tool according to Exod 20:25. If there is a difference between them, it is that the stones lose their holiness as a result of having been worked with a tool, while the "defective" firstlings were never sanctified in the first place.[18] The status of "defective" priests in Leviticus 21, in contrast, is ambiguous with respect to holiness, given that they still have access to the most holy foods according to Lev 21:22, those foods reserved for priestly males alone. It may be that "defective" priests have lost their priestly sanctification according to Leviticus 21, just as "defective" firstlings lack holiness according to Deut 15:22, and altar stones worked with a tool are profaned (Exod 20:25), but the "defective" priest's continued access to the most holy offerings suggests otherwise.[19] Thus, the treatment of the worked altar stones of Exod 20:25 with respect to holiness likely parallels more closely the treatment of "defective" firstlings of Deut 15:21–22 than it does that of "defective" priests in Leviticus 21. In both the case of the altar stones and the case of the firstlings, expected holiness is clearly absent, either lost or never established in the first place. A lack of holiness characterizing items that should possess it is stigmatizing. Although some exceptional forms of profanation are licit in biblical representations of the cult, most are illicit and subject to punishments ranging from fines to death (e.g., profanation of the Sabbath, of Yhwh's name, of the holy foods, or of the priest).[20] Thus, profanation of that which is holy is generally an undesirable, stigmatizing thing, and the profanation of the altar stones in Exod 20:25 is no exception to this pattern. Similarly, the removal of "defective," unsanctified firstlings from the cult in Deut 15:21–22, and their consumption even by persons who are unclean, suggests their inferiority to firstlings without "defects" and their rejection by the deity.

There is an irony in constructing ashlar blocks as undesirable for altar and temple building in the texts under consideration. In contrast to field stones, a commonplace building material of minimal value used even by persons of very modest means to construct houses and other nonofficial structures, ashlar was extremely expensive to produce, a token of wealth, used in official building projects, the stone par excellence of kings. It is described as "beautiful" in texts such as 1 Kgs 5:31 (Eng. 17); 7:9, 11, texts that claim ashlar was used in the building of the temple in Jerusalem (in contrast to 1 Kgs 6:7).[21] The wealthy are said to live in houses made of ashlar in Amos 5:11. Archeological evidence of the use of ashlar for official building projects at sites such as Iron II Samaria, Dan, Megiddo, and Jerusalem is abundant.[22] Also, we know that ashlar could be used to construct altars for burnt offerings in ancient Israel (e.g., the altar for burnt offerings from Beersheba) and that incense altars could be made from blocks of limestone.[23] There is also archeological evidence that ashlar was used in the construction of sanctuaries (e.g., the Tel Dan "*bamah*").[24] So why should the texts in question stigmatize a building material that was actually used for constructing altars and sanctuaries and that otherwise has such strongly positive associations (e.g., with beauty and wealth)? The reasons, alas, remain obscure, although the very fact of such devaluing and rejection of ashlar in texts such as Exod 20:25, Deut 27:5–6, and 1 Kgs 6:7 brings into relief the arbitrary nature of operations that stigmatize and, conversely, moves that ascribe value and other positive characteristics, something I highlight in chapter 1, my investigation of biblical constructions of beauty and ugliness. There is nothing inherent in finished ashlar blocks that should lead to their construction as deficient in fullness or wholeness, as profaned, and as disqualified from use in constructing the altar or the temple building.

CONCLUSION

In this chapter, I sought to demonstrate that somatic "defects" and wholeness, central to any study of biblical disabilities, are paralleled by nonbodily analogues. The stones of the altar of burnt offerings are to be "full" or "whole" according to Deut 27:6, likewise, the stones of the temple, according to 1 Kgs 6:7. Such "full" or "whole" stones are analogous to the "whole" or non-"defective" bodies of sacrificial animals and priests discussed in texts such as Leviticus 21–22. The technical vocabulary used to describe the wholeness of stones differs from that used with respect to the wholeness of the bodies of sacrificial animals or priests, but the meaning appears to be the same. Furthermore, the efforts of texts to stigmatize and marginalize "defective" sacrificial animals and priests are paralleled closely by the devaluing and disqualification of altar and building stones not understood to be "whole" or "full." Shared strategies to devalue, disqualify, and proscribe include the withholding or stripping of holiness from items expected to possess it (e.g., sacrificial animals, altar stones), the rejection of those items, and the demand for their removal from the sanctuary sphere. This investigation of nonsomatic parallels to bodily wholeness and "defect" provides additional support for Mary Douglas's idea that wholeness and completeness are paradigmatic biblical concepts; it also suggests that her association of holiness with wholeness is more broadly attested than she initially realized. Most important, however, a study of nonsomatic parallels to bodily wholeness and "defect" demonstrates the extent to which the idea of the "defective" and its analogues are evidenced in biblical thought and the degree to which "defective" persons, animals, and things are cast as inferior and assigned a marginal status by biblical texts. Just as altar stones worked with a tool are profaned and, therefore, to be rejected from sanctuary use, so "defective," sacrificial animals might be described as ugly abominations, cast as profane, and disqualified from use in sacrifice, as in Deut 15:21–22 and 17:1. Similarly, Lev 21:23 stigmatizes and partially marginalizes "defective" priests, disqualifying them from offering sacrifices, the most highly esteemed ritual activity assigned to priests, and casting them as a greater threat to the holiness of the sanctuary than their non-"defective" fellows.

Exegetical Perpetuations, Elaborations, and Transformations: The Case of Qumran

*T*HIS FINAL CHAPTER EXPLORES SOME OF THE WAYS IN WHICH disability is represented in Jewish exegetical texts from the period of the Second Temple (515 BCE–70 CE). My specific focus is those texts produced by ancient Jewish biblical interpreters and found among the Dead Sea Scrolls that perpetuate, elaborate on, or transform earlier biblical notions of disability and earlier biblical models of classification.[1] Such an investigation illustrates well the widely evidenced and oft-remarked tendency of ancient interpreters of biblical materials to reconfigure texts in such a way as to infuse new life into them, allowing them to address the needs of later audiences.[2] Biblical materials are reworked to achieve a variety of ends: ambiguous passages are clarified through elaboration, contradictory texts are harmonized, implicit associations are made explicit, and spare narrative is amplified. The common biblical tendency to produce representations of disability that stigmatize and seek to marginalize is also evidenced in ancient Jewish exegetical recastings of or allusions to scriptural passages. In some cases, interpreters produce representations of disability not unlike the representations familiar from earlier biblical texts. In other instances, exegetes offer representations of disability that can only be characterized as more devaluing and potentially marginalizing than the older biblical models from which they draw. Examples of the latter tendency include the casting of blindness as a polluting condition in the Temple Scroll; the direct association of the "deafness" and "blindness" of transgressors with the "Spirit of Wrong" (*rûaḥ ʿawlah*) in 1QS 4:11; and the proscription on the entry of groups such as the deaf, the mute, and the mentally disabled into the community's assembly according to several texts. This chapter is divided into three parts. In the first section, I consider the treatment of "defects" (*mûmîm*) in the Dead Sea Scrolls. This will be followed by an investigation into the representation of disabled persons who are not classed as "defective" in biblical texts (e.g., the deaf and the mute, the person afflicted with "skin disease" [*ṣara'at*], the menstruant and the parturient, the person with mental disability). I conclude the chapter with a discussion of implicit and explicit classifications evidenced in Qumran literature, and how they compare to their biblical antecedents.[3]

"DEFECTS" IN THE DEAD SEA SCROLLS

"Defects" (*mûmîm*) such as blindness and lameness are mentioned with some frequency in materials from Qumran. Some texts among the Dead Sea Scrolls perpetuate biblical notions of "defect," whereas others elaborate on or reconfigure them, producing novel representations. I focus on examples of each interpretive tendency in the following discussion. In some of the passages I discuss, the "defect" in question is literal (e.g., blindness as a physical condition); in other passages, it is metaphorical or figurative (e.g., blindness as a spiritual state).

Perhaps the most frequently attested case of the perpetuation of a biblical idea concerning "defects" without significant elaboration is the association of blindness with ignorance and with bad judgment, including transgressive acts. In 4Q166 2:1–6 (4Q pHos^a), a text interpreting the book of Hosea for the era in which the interpreter lives, Hos 2:10 (Eng. 8) is understood to refer to Judeans outside the sect who have forgotten "the god of justice" and rejected his commandments: "And to those who lead them astray they have listened and have honored them, and like gods they reverence them in their blindness."[4] Similarly, 4Q245 2:3, a fragmentary Aramaic text related to the Daniel tradition, ties the people's straying to their "blindness."[5] Yhwh's chosen are those whose eyes he has uncovered that they might know "hidden things" (*nistarôt*) according to 4Q268 1:7 (4QD^c), implying that before this they were ignorant, "blind" to the "truth." The Damascus Document speaks of a leaderless, penitent remnant of Israel as having been "like blind persons and like those who grope the way for twenty years" until Yhwh raised for them a Teacher of Righteousness "to direct them on the way of his heart" (CD 1:8–11); it also refers to the "blindness of Israel" throughout the ages, as recounted in the

Book of Jubilees (CD 16:2–4). In 4Q271 3:7–9 (4QD^f), Deut 27:18, "Cursed be the one who leads astray a blind person in the road," is interpreted metaphorically to apply to a bride's father who might mislead a potential son-in-law who is himself ill informed about his bride's "defects" (*mûmîm*).[6] In each example, blindness is associated with ignorance; in some, it is tied to bad judgment, and even transgression. Like the Judean watchmen of Isa 56:10, who are described as "blind, knowing nothing," Judeans who are ignorant of the "truth" as the writers of these texts understand it, are characterized as blind, as are the ill informed with respect to personal matters such as marriage. Just as Judeans who do not "see" transgress, and cannot repent and save themselves according to Isa 6:9–11, so too does the blindness of the people lead to sin according to a variety of Qumran texts. In these examples, both biblical and Qumranic, the blindness in question is figurative rather than literal. Nonetheless, such an association of blindness with ignorance, bad judgment, and transgression stigmatizes blind persons, just as the association of the metaphorical foreskin with dysfunction as in Jer 6:10 and with disobedience as in Deut 10:16 stigmatizes persons who are uncircumcised.

A number of Qumran texts modify or transform biblical notions of "defect," often with the result of increasing the stigmatization and potential marginalization of "defective" persons. One example of this is the association made by 1QS 4:11 of blindness with the "Spirit of Wrong" (*rûaḥ 'awlah*). In this text, a long list of qualities is said to belong to this Spirit, including stiffness of neck (= stubbornness), a reviling tongue, abominable acts, wickedness, falsehood, and pride. The punishment of those who walk in the "Spirit of Wrong" will be "a multitude of strokes by the hand of all the angels of destruction for eternal destruction..." (1QS 4:11–12). Thus, blindness is brought into association not only with a substantial selection of negative qualities, but with the antithesis of the deity himself (the "Spirit of Wrong," "the ways of darkness") and with destruction at the hands of God's angelic minions. Although blindness is a metaphorical indicator of ignorance and often, transgression, as it is elsewhere in the Dead Sea Scrolls and in earlier biblical and non-Israelite West Asian literatures, it is treated in a novel way in this passage. It is associated with a number of preeminently negative qualities such as wickedness and falsehood, with opposition to the deity, and with destruction in a hell-like place. Needless to say, such associations increase the stigma of blindness, representing it in novel and unprecedented ways.

A second example of the modification of biblical notions of "defect" is the representation of the blind as polluters in 11Q19 (11QT[a]) 45:12–14, the Temple Scroll: "As for any blind persons, they shall not enter into it [the city of the sanctuary[7]] all their days.[8] They shall not pollute the city in the midst of which I dwell for I, Yhwh, dwell in the midst of the children of Israel forever." Here, blindness is cast as a source of pollution, and the blind are proscribed permanently from entering the sanctuary city, conceived as holy in the Temple Scroll and therefore to be protected from pollution. Chapter 45:7–18 of the Temple Scroll, the pericope of which the regulation under discussion constitutes a part, concerns a number of different polluters and prescribes their ritual treatment. Among the polluters, in addition to the blind, are men who have had a nocturnal emission of semen, men who have had an emission of semen during sexual intercourse, men recovering from a genital "flow," persons who have had contact with dead bodies, and persons with "skin disease" (sara'at). Interestingly, the other polluters mentioned in this passage may enter the city or the sanctuary when they have been cleansed of their impurities, but the blind are banned permanently and without exception. There is simply no possibility, suggests the text, that they can be purified.[9]

Antecedents to the Temple Scroll's treatment of the blind may be found in a number of biblical texts, some of which are echoed in 11Q19 45:12–14. It is clear that the Temple Scroll alludes to Num 5:3 in its statement that the blind "shall not pollute the city in the midst of which I dwell" (welo' yetamme'û 'et ha'îr 'ašer 'anî šoken betôkah).[10] In Num 5:3, the person with "skin disease," the person with a genital "flow," and the person unclean as a result of corpse contact are to be expelled from the desert camp: "They shall not pollute their camps in the midst of which I dwell" (welo' yetamme'û 'et mahanêhem 'ašer 'anî šoken betôkam). The formulations of Num 5:3 and the Temple Scroll are virtually identical, the only change being the substitution of the city for the camps and the consequent change in pronoun. By alluding to Num 5:3 in this manner, the Temple Scroll suggests that blindness is a major source of pollution not unlike "skin disease," genital "flows," and corpse contact, and should be treated accordingly. A second biblical source for the Temple Scroll's interdiction is Isa 52:1, which speaks innovatively of Jerusalem as a holy city and bans the entry into it of "the uncircumcised who are unclean" (or, possibly, "the uncircumcised and the unclean").[11] In either reading, unclean persons may not enter the sanctuary city, and this appears to be a scriptural basis for the Temple Scroll's construction of Jerusalem as holy and in need of protection from pollution. A third biblical text used to formulate the Temple Scroll's proscription of the blind is evidently 2 Sam 5:8b: "Anyone blind or lame shall not enter the house." Allusion is made to this saying through the adoption of its "he shall not enter" (*lo' yabô'*) rhetoric. Its apparent proscription of the entry of blind and lame persons into the temple sphere (the "house") is transformed by the Temple Scroll into an interdiction on the entry of the blind into the holy city. What might be implicit in 2 Sam 5:8b – that the blind and the lame are polluters and therefore banned from entering the temple – is made explicit in the Temple Scroll's banning of the polluting blind from entering the sanctuary city, perhaps under the influence of Mal 1:6–14, which explicitly constructs "defects" in sacrificial animals as polluting.

"Defects" (*mûmîm*) are not constructed as polluting in most biblical texts, nor are persons with "defects" generally prohibited from entering holy space (e.g., the sanctuary sphere) or living in the community. For example, in Leviticus 21, the priest with a "defect" remains in the sanctuary sphere and continues to eat holy and most holy foods, although he may not offer sacrifices to Yhwh. Possible exceptions to this biblical pattern are 2 Sam 5:8b and Mal 1:6–14. The former proscribes the entry of blind and lame persons into the sanctuary sphere for reasons that are unclear, although pollution is one distinct possibility; the latter suggests fairly clearly that "defective" sacrificial animals are polluting, but says nothing about human "defects." 11Q19 45:12–14, although it draws exegetically on a number of biblical texts, modifies biblical precedent regarding the treatment of "defects," casting blindness as polluting in an unambiguous way, and prohibiting the blind from entering the holy space of the sanctuary city. Although no other "defects" are mentioned in this passage, it may be that blindness is intended as a synecdoche, suggesting all human "defects."[12] If this is the case, the Temple Scroll is profoundly innovative, constructing all "defects" as polluting and therefore grounds for exclusion from the city of the Temple. The text may also be suggesting that exclusion from the city means exclusion from the community because it alludes directly to Num 5:3, which concerns the expulsion of serious polluters from the desert camp (= the community). Needless to say, the casting of blindness – or all "defects," if the blind are intended to be a synecdoche – as polluting, with the result that affected persons should be permanently removed from the sanctuary city, would increase both the stigmatization and the marginalization of those who are excluded. Pollution now becomes an established characteristic of blind persons (and perhaps all persons with "defects"), cutting them off forever from the sanctuary and its many benefits, as well as life in Jerusalem, the sanctuary city.

A third example of biblical "defect" treated in a novel manner is 4QMMT B 49–54, a statement of legal policy apparently concerned with blind priests and deaf priests who have access nonetheless to the holy foods.[13] According to this text, these priests should not have such access because they do not know what to do with respect to purity regulations, not having seen and not having heard, and are therefore in a position to err in ignorance. The text is evidently responding to a more permissive position that allows blind priests and deaf priests to have access to the holy foods. That position must be based mainly on Lev 21:22, a verse that states that priests with "defects," although they cannot offer sacrifices at the altar, are nonetheless able to eat the holy and most holy foods: "The food of his god, from the most holy offerings and the holy offerings, he may eat." Leviticus 21 places no restrictions whatsoever on priests with non-"defective" disabilities such as deafness. 4QMMT B 49–54, alluding indirectly to Lev 21:22, takes a less tolerant stance: blind priests and deaf priests, because of their inability to make purity judgments, may not eat holy foods, which must be consumed in a state of purity. Although 4QMMT does not construct blind persons as polluters, in contrast to the Temple Scroll, 4QMMT's restriction functions nonetheless to increase the stigma that blind priests must bear on account of their disability. It also seeks to marginalize them in significant new ways. Where priests with "defects" (including blindness) in Leviticus 21 were stigmatized and partially marginalized by the proscription on their participation in rites of sacrifice and stigmatized by their potential to profane the sanctuary should they make offerings in defiance of the ban, blind priests according to 4QMMT should also lose their access to the holy foods, increasing both their stigmatization and their marginalization. Not only can they not sacrifice with their peers; 4QMMT implies that they cannot dine with them, or with sighted members of their own households, who would presumably have access to holy (although not most holy) foods, as Lev 22:10–13 suggests.

Several other exegetical texts from Qumran seek to increase the marginalization and stigmatization of persons with "defects" by demanding their exclusion from the community's army and assembly. In the War Scroll, the eschatological war camp is off limits to men with several types of "defect" and unclean men, as well as women and children: "No child or woman shall enter into their camps when they leave Jerusalem to go to war until they return. And as for any lame man or blind man or limping man[14] or a man who has a permanent 'defect'[15] in his flesh or a man stricken with uncleanness in his flesh – all these shall not go with them for war. All of them shall be men freely offering themselves for war and 'perfect' with respect both to spirit and flesh. . . . And any man who is not clean from his 'fount' on the day of the battle shall not go down with them, for the holy angels are together with their armies" (1QM 7:4–6). The War Scroll excludes both polluted men and men with permanent "defects" from the eschatological war camp, and requires that all those who would participate in the war be physically and spiritually "perfect" or "whole" (temîmê rûaḥ ûbaśar). Unlike the Temple Scroll, the blind (and others with "defects") are not constructed as polluters by this text; the text, in fact, continues to distinguish polluters from those with "defects." Although biblical texts such as Num 5:3 exclude polluted persons from the desert camp and texts such as 1 Sam 21:5–6 (Eng. 4–5) suggest that warriors routinely avoid pollution, the interdiction of potential warriors with "defects" in the War Scroll is an innovative development not found in biblical sources. 1QM 7:4 appears to draw mainly on Leviticus 21 to construct its proscription.[16] This text, which speaks of the prohibition of "defective" priests from offering sacrifice, evidently served as a model for both the rhetoric of "defect" (mûm) and the form of 1QM 7:4 (a list of "defective" persons). However, the War Scroll has transformed Leviticus 21, reworking its restriction on the cultic activities of "defective" priests into a general prohibition on the entry of all men with permanent "defects" into the war camp.

Why are "defective" warriors disqualified from participating in the eschatological war? The text is not entirely clear in this regard. However, the mention of the presence of the holy angels with the armies in 7:6 as the reason why men polluted by a seminal emission cannot participate probably also applies to others mentioned previously who are excluded. Such a reading is clear in 1QS^a 2:8–9 and 4Q 266 8 i 6–9 (4QD^a), both of which ban various classes of persons from the communal assembly on account of the presence of the holy angels. Exclusion of persons with "defects" on account of the presence of holy beings suggests innovation because in most biblical texts concerned with "defective" persons in general, and priests in particular, these are nonetheless able to enter holy places and, in the case of priests, eat holy and most holy foods. (2 Sam 5:8b is the exception, as previously discussed.) In 1QM, "defects" have evidently been recast as utterly incompatible with holy space, holy items, and holy beings such as angels, not unlike impurities. Because the War Scroll maintains the distinction between that which is "defective" and that which is polluting, in contrast to the Temple Scroll, it seems likely that according to 1QM, "defective" warriors are a threat to the holy angels because their presence would profane the angels' holiness, just as polluters are a threat because their presence would pollute. Where Lev 21:23 constructs the threat "defective" priests pose to holiness as situational – they are only a threat to the holiness of the sanctuary if they defy the ban and offer sacrifices – the War Scroll understands warriors with "defects" to pose a general threat to holiness, and therefore, they are to be excluded from the eschatological army.

1QS^a 2:3–11 is similar to 1QM 7:4–6 in a number of respects, although it concerns entry into the assembly rather than the war camp. According to this text, "any man stricken with any human uncleanness shall not enter the assembly of God.[17] Any man stricken with these shall not take office in the midst of the congregation. And anyone stricken in his flesh – damaged with respect to feet or hands, lame or blind, or deaf or mute, or stricken with a 'defect' in his flesh that the eyes can see . . . these shall not station themselves in the midst of the congregation of the men of name, for the angels of holiness are (in) their (congreg)ation." This text, which excludes not only the polluted and – apparently – the "defective" from the assembly, but also the mute and the deaf, is not unlike the War Scroll in its maintenance of a distinction between that which is "defective" and that which is polluting, and in its explanation for these exclusions – the presence of the holy angels. However, in contrast to 1QM 7:4–6, which uses Leviticus 21 as its major source, 1QS^a 2:3–11 clearly draws on Deut

23:2 (Eng. 1) in addition to Leviticus 21.[18] The focus of Deut 23:2 (Eng. 1) – men with damaged genitals excluded from Yhwh's assembly – is here expanded to include a variety of "defects" having nothing to do with genital damage, plus deafness and muteness, and various sources of pollution.[19] All persons afflicted with these conditions are to be excluded from the community's congregation, with which the assembly of Yhwh in Deut 23:2 (Eng. 1) has been identified. The influence of Leviticus 21 may be discerned in the list of "defective" persons excluded from the assembly and in the rhetoric of "defect" (*mûm*) itself. Aside from what may be a general proscription of persons with "defects" from the community's assembly (cf. Deut 23:2 [Eng. 1], which only bans men with genital damage), as well as the deaf and the mute, another innovative aspect of this text is the implied contrast between visible and nonvisible "defects," which I shall discuss.

Several texts introduce novel constructions of "defects" not attested in biblical sources. A contrast between permanent and temporary "defects" is implied in 1QM 7:4, which mentions "a man who has a permanent 'defect' (*mûm 'ôlam*) in his flesh" among those to be excluded from the army that will fight the forces of darkness at the time of the future eschatological war. The concept of permanent "defect" implies the existence of a companion notion of temporary "defect." The text seems to suggest that only those with permanent "defects" are to be excluded from the eschatological army. Unhappily, it is unclear what might count as a temporary "defect," in contrast to a permanent one. Perhaps sores that routinely heal, or a temporary limp caused by a minor injury, would be so counted. A second novel construction of "defects" evidenced among the Dead Sea Scrolls but not present in biblical texts is the implied contrast between visible "defects" and those not readily apparent to the eye, as suggested by 1QS^a 2:6–7: ". . . stricken with a 'defect' in his flesh that the eyes can see." Although the text does not mention nonvisible "defects," it implies a notion of such by its explicit mention of visible "defects." Presumably, the "defects" that the eye cannot see are covered by clothing. These might include the types of genital damage that play such a significant role in texts such as Leviticus 21 and Deut 23:2 (Eng. 1). A third novel construction of "defects" is attested in 4Q271 3:7–9, which states that a father must inform his future son-in-law of his daughter's "defects" (*mûmîm*). Are these "defects" to be understood as physical in nature or figurative? The passage understands blindness metaphorically in its interpretation of Deut 27:18, as discussed, suggesting that a figurative interpretation of the daughter's "defects" is not out of order. In addition, much of the rest of the fragment concerns female sexual transgressions, possibly understood by the text as figurative "defects." Thus, it seems likely that the daughter's "defects" are to be understood metaphorically as transgressions. Conveniently, 1QM 7:4 bears witness to a notion of spiritual wholeness, alongside physical wholeness, which would be the antitype of spiritual or figurative "defect."[20] In short, 4Q271 and 1QM evidently attest to a pairing of spiritual or figurative wholeness and "defect" that parallels the contrast between somatic wholeness and "defect." This spiritualizing or figurative elaboration of the "whole"/"defective" contrast in texts from Qumran might be compared to the earlier, biblical elaboration of the opposition "whole"/"defective" in the form of nonsomatic parallels to bodily wholeness and "defect" (e.g., with respect to the stones of altar and temple).

NON-"DEFECTIVE" DISABILITIES IN QUMRAN LITERATURE

In addition to its varied treatments of "defects" (*mûmîm*), the literature from Qumran is rich in representations of what I have been calling non-"defective" disabilities. As was the case with "defects," non-"defective" disabilities in the Dead Sea Scrolls are represented both in ways that perpetuate biblical notions of disability and in innovative ways that modify biblical ideas, sometimes radically. If one can speak of a general tendency in the exegesis of the Qumran corpus with respect to the representation of persons with non-"defective" disabilities, it is to attempt to increase both their stigmatization and their marginalization using a variety of strategies.

Various texts perpetuate biblical notions of non-"defective" disabilities. As with blindness, deafness is treated metaphorically, and associated with ignorance, bad judgment, and even transgression. It was not until Yhwh's chosen "opened their ears and heard deep things" that they could understand that which would come upon them before it comes to pass; before this, they were "deaf" and lacked understanding (4Q266 2 i 5–6; 4Q268 1:7). The association of literal deafness with ignorance is present in 4QMMT B 52–54, a passage concerned to restrict the access of deaf and blind priests to the holy foods. The deaf "have not heard law(s) and statute(s) and purity regulations, and have not heard the statutes of Israel." Therefore, they "do not know what to do" with respect to purity requirements, and the text assumes that they cannot learn. Other examples of the perpetuation of biblical notions of non-"defective" disabilities include the Temple Scroll's call for the expulsion of persons with "skin disease" (ṣaraʿat) and genital "flows" (zôb) from the community, following Lev 13:46 in the case of "skin disease," and Num 5:3 in the case of both "skin disease" and genital "flows" (11Q19 45:15–18). The idea that such persons must be physically separated from others reproduces an older biblical understanding without significant modification. Finally, the use of the term "madman" (mešuggaʿ) to designate a person with mental disability in 4Q266 8 i 7 (= CD 15:15) is familiar from earlier biblical usage (e.g., 1 Sam 21:16 [Eng. 15]).

Yet, the vast majority of Qumran texts treating non-"defective" disabilities modify biblical notions of disability, sometimes in profound ways, often with the evident intent of increasing the stigmatization and marginalization of affected persons. Deafness, like blindness, is associated with the "Spirit of Wrong" (rûaḥ ʿawlah) and various negative qualities, including abominable acts, wickedness, and falsehood, thereby increasing its stigma (1QS 4:11). Where deafness is often associated with ignorance in biblical materials, deafness in 1QS is tied to a variety of the most undesirable human qualities, as well as to the antithesis of the deity (the "Spirit of Wrong") and eternal punishment at the hand of Yhwh's angelic servants. Thus, deafness is more profoundly stigmatized in 1QS than it is in any biblical text.

4QMMT B 52–54 stigmatizes and seeks to marginalize deaf priests, like their blind brethren, in new ways. It not only associates their deafness with ignorance, but insists that they cannot have access to the holy foods on account of their inability to hear purity rules and know how to act with respect to purity. This text's restriction on deaf priests' access to holy foods is even more striking than its similar restriction on blind priests, given that Leviticus 21, the biblical basis for the position of opponents against which the 4QMMT writer is reacting, has no concern whatsoever with deaf priests, only priests with "defects." Where 4QMMT augments biblical restrictions on the activities of blind priests, it establishes a new limitation (no access to holy foods) on deaf priests whose behavior is entirely unregulated in biblical texts. Thus, 4QMMT stigmatizes deaf priests as unworthy of access to the priestly prerogative of the holy foods, and seeks to marginalize them to the extent that they cannot share meals with other priests or their own families.

The menstruant and the parturient, although serious polluters, are not subject to removal from the community according to biblical texts such as Lev 12:1–8 and 15:19–24, in contrast to the treatment of the person with "skin disease" in Lev 13:46, and both the person with "skin disease" and the person with a genital "flow" in Num 5:3. However, the Temple Scroll (11Q19 48:14–17) calls for the expulsion of both the parturient and the menstruant from the community for the period of their pollution, not unlike the treatment of persons with "skin disease" and genital "flows" in the same passage. All such polluters are assigned to special loci in every city. According to 11Q19 46:16–18, three places east of Jerusalem are to receive that city's polluters, including men who have had an emission of semen, the most minor type of polluter according to biblical texts such as Lev 15:16–17, and not subject to removal from the community. These two passages suggest that according to the Temple Scroll, menstruant, parturient, and even a man who has had an emission of semen are now to be treated in the same manner as the person with "skin disease" and the person with a genital "flow." In short, all polluters are to be entirely removed from social intercourse with the nonpolluted, thereby increasing their marginalization and the stigma they bear on account of pollution. Their removal is a result of the Temple Scroll's casting of the whole of the Temple city as holy space in need of protection from any sort of pollution.

Mental disability is also represented in the Qumran literature in novel ways. Although it is clear that terms such as "simple" person (*petî*) and "fool" (*'ewîl*), occurring most frequently in biblical Wisdom literature, do not refer in the main to persons with mental disability in the biblical context, the terms are used in 4Q266 8 i 6–7 (= CD 15:15), along with "madman" (*mešugga'*), a term used of mental disability in biblical texts, evidently to designate specific classes of the mentally disabled. These classes of persons with mental disability, along with others such as the deaf, the lame, and the blind, are to be excluded from the community's assembly. Thus, a rather vague set of biblical terms associated with "foolishness," terms that are rarely if ever used of persons with mental disability in the biblical text, and never in conjunction with the vocabulary of "madness" (root *šgʿ*), come to be used, in association with the biblical term "madman" (*mešuggaʿ*), to refer to different types of mentally disabled persons. Although the differences between the classes of the mentally disabled in 4Q266 remain unclear, the establishment of the classes themselves through the use of both the vocabulary of "foolishness" and that of "madness" in tandem is a departure from biblical usage. From the context, it would seem that these terms refer to persons with mental retardation of some kind. Some other texts from Qumran also seem to use the "foolishness" terminology of the Hebrew Bible in just this way. CD 13:6–7 speaks of a priest who is "simple" (*petî*) who must nonetheless deal with cases of "skin disease": "And (even) if he is a 'simple' person, he himself shall separate him, for the judgment is theirs." The text implies that under normal circumstances, anyone classified as "simple" would not be given such a responsibility. 1QSᵃ 1:19–22 speaks of severe restrictions on the responsibilities of the "simple" person. He should not assume any office in the assembly having to do with legal matters or other communal responsibilities, nor should he serve in the army. He should only do work of which he is capable. These restrictions suggest that the text has a mentally disabled person in mind. Although a number of Qumran texts make use of the vocabulary of "foolishness" in innovative ways, other texts among the Dead Sea Scrolls continue to use this vocabulary in ways familiar from biblical Wisdom texts such as Proverbs (e.g., "simple" persons can be made to understand and gain prudence, as in 1QH 5:2; 10:9; 4Q381 1:2, not a usage suggestive of mental disability).

Perhaps the most interesting texts among the Dead Sea Scrolls that treat non-"defective" disabilities are 1QSᵃ 2:3–11 and 4Q266 8 i 6–9. Both texts, which I mentioned previously in my discussion of the treatment of "defects," speak of classes of persons who may not enter the congregation on account of the presence of the holy angels. In addition to polluters and persons with visible "defects," 1QSᵃ also proscribes the admission of the deaf, the mute, and the old man who stumbles and cannot support himself physically in the midst of the assembly. 4Q266 bans what appear to be various classes of persons with mental disability (including the "madman" [*mešuggaʿ*]), as well as those unable to see, the lame, the limping, the deaf, and the young child. In each text, persons with non-"defective" physical and mental disabilities are excluded from the communal assembly. Each text appears to draw on and reconfigure Deut 23:2 (Eng. 1), which concerns the proscription of men with genital damage from entering the assembly of Yhwh, understood in these Qumran texts to refer to the community's congregation. Each text expands the narrowly tailored prohibition of Deut 23:2 (Eng. 1) to include not only other "defects," but non-"defective" disabilities as well, with interesting implications. Where biblical texts placed no restrictions on the access of deaf, mute, and mentally disabled persons into cultic and other communal settings, the Qumran texts in question forbid them access to the communal assembly on the grounds that holy angels are present there. This suggests that the entry of deaf, mute, and mentally disabled persons into the assembly is somehow threatening to the continuing presence of these divine beings. In my previous discussion, I noted that such a ban on the entry of persons with "defects" suggests an understanding of "defects" as incompatible with the holy in all contexts – not simply in certain situations, as Lev 21:23 suggests – not unlike impurities, which are always a threat to holiness. I suggested that because "defects" and impurities continue to be distinguished in texts such as 1QM and 1QS[a], the presence of persons with "defects" likely threatens to profane holiness rather than to pollute. Could it be that non-"defective" disabilities such as muteness, deafness, and mental disability are constructed similarly in 1QS[a] and 4Q266 as agents of profanation threatening to holiness?[21] Although this is impossible to demonstrate, at minimum we can say that the presence of the holy angels is clearly the reason given for the exclusion of persons with these conditions; that such persons must threaten the presence of the holy angels in some way; and that holiness is typically threatened either by profanation or pollution.[22]

IMPLICIT AND EXPLICIT CLASSIFICATIONS

The Dead Sea Scrolls bear witness to the perpetuation of biblical taxonomic schemas, to a number of interesting modifications or possible modifications to biblical classifications, and to the genesis of wholly new schemas of classification, both implicit and explicit. The "defect" class, the single native category of disability mentioned explicitly in the biblical text, continues to be carefully distinguished from the polluter class in a number of important texts devoted to classification. In the War Scroll, "a man

stricken with uncleanness in his flesh" forms a separate category of disqualified warrior from "any lame man or blind man or limping man or
a man who has a permanent 'defect' in his flesh" (1QM 7:4–5). Similarly,
in 1QSᵃ 2:3–11, "any man stricken with any human uncleanness" is distinguished from "anyone stricken in his flesh – damaged with respect to
feet or hands, lame or blind, or deaf or mute, or stricken with a 'defect' in
his flesh that the eyes can see." However, the Temple Scroll departs from
this practice, blurring the distinction between the "defect" class and the
polluter class by casting the blind (and perhaps others with "defects,"
if the blind are to be understood as a synecdoche) as intrinsic polluters
(11Q19 45:12–14). What may be implicit in the ban on the blind and the
lame entering the sanctuary in 2 Sam 5:8b – that they are polluters –
is made explicit in 11Q19 45:12–14, possibly under the influence of Mal
1:6–14, which casts the "defects" of sacrificial animals as polluting. Other
evident modifications of the "defect" class include the previously discussed introduction of distinctions between permanent and temporary
"defects" (1QM 7:4), visible and invisible "defects" (1QSᵃ 2:6–7), and the
novel notion of the spiritual or figurative "defect" (4Q271 3:8) and its
accompanying idea of spiritual wholeness (1QM 7:4). Finally, a possible
reconfiguring of the "defect" class may be evidenced in 1QSᵃ. This text
may broaden the definition of what constitutes a "defect" by adding the
deaf and mute to the "defect" class: ". . . anyone stricken in his flesh –
damaged with respect to feet or hands, lame or blind, or deaf or mute,
or stricken with a 'defect' in his flesh that the eyes can see. . . ." It may
be that "stricken in his flesh" in this context means specifically "having
a defect" and that all examples that follow are to be viewed as "defective," including the deaf and the mute. Such an understanding is suggested by the observation that the deaf and the mute in the list of 1QSᵃ
are both preceded and followed by "defective" persons. However, this
conclusion must remain only a tantalizing possibility because we have
no unambiguous evidence for such an expansion of the "defect" class to
absorb formerly non-"defective" physical disabilities such as deafness and
muteness.[23]

Not only does 1QSᵃ appear to broaden the "defect" class; it also introduces an explicit, larger, nonbiblical classification – persons who are
"stricken" (*menuggaʿ*) – that brings together all those in that text who
are denied entry into the community's assembly because they constitute

a threat to the presence of the holy angels.[24] Referring both to "any man stricken with any human uncleanness" and to any who are "stricken in his flesh" with a physical disability, the text states that "if one of these (persons) has a matter to speak of to the holy council, they shall seek it from him, but to the midst of the council the man shall not come, for he is stricken" (*kî menugga' hû'*). It is clear from the text that the person in question might be any of those previously listed, meaning either an unclean person; one afflicted with a condition such as lameness, blindness, deafness, or muteness; or the stumbling old man. All those who are "stricken" are evidently a threat to the presence of the holy angels, likely on account of their potential either to pollute or to profane holiness. 1QM 7:4 may reflect a similar notion of the "stricken" as a class, constituted by those with "defects" and those who are unclean, although the text is not explicit in this regard.[25]

As in the biblical text, Qumran sources bear witness to implicit classifications that bring together various types of disabilities. 4Q266 8 i 6–9 is a primary example. In this passage, what are evidently four types of mental disability, the inability to see, lameness, a limping condition, and deafness are all grounds for exclusion from the community's assembly on account of the presence of the holy angels. By listing these various disabilities together, the text is suggesting the existence of a single, implicit class to which the listed disabilities belong. This implicit class is distinct from the "stricken" class of 1QS[a] because persons with mental disability are included, and polluted persons are not. The implicit class of 4Q266 also includes the immature boy. How innovative is the implicit class of 4Q266, and on what shared characteristics is it based? Earlier biblical texts sometimes bring together "defects" and mental disability (e.g., Deut 28:28), or "defects" and non-"defective" physical disabilities (e.g., Exod 4:11; Lev 19:14; Isa 35:5–6), suggesting implicit, larger classes constituted by more than one disability. The members of these classes may be believed to share a common somatic dysfunction, as is evident in Exod 4:11; or weakness, vulnerability, and even helplessness, as Lev 19:14 or Deut 28:28 suggest. They may be joined by groups believed to share the same characteristics, groups such as the poor and the afflicted (e.g., Isa 29:18–19). The class of 4Q266 does not appear to be constituted on the basis of physical dysfunction because the disabilities of 4Q266 are not exclusively physical, nor can a convincing argument be made that the immature youth is constructed as somatically dysfunctional. Could a shared weakness, vulnerability, or incapacitation be the basis for the text's exclusion? This is a possibility, given that all categories of persons mentioned by the text could be understood by the text as weak and vulnerable, if not incapacitated. However, if so, why would this shared weakness threaten the presence of the holy angels? Typically, as I have mentioned, holiness is threatened by either pollution or profanation. I have already suggested that profanation may be the source of the threat, although this cannot be demonstrated. Furthermore, it is quite unclear why the presence of the young child would threaten to profane holiness. Thus, even though 4Q266 suggests an implicit class that combines persons with various types of disability and the immature youth, the basis for constituting this class, as well as the reason why its members are understood to pose a threat to holiness, remain unclear to me.

CONCLUSION

Texts from Qumran bear witness to the perpetuation, modification, and even the transformation of biblical ideas about disability and biblical models of classification. Some texts perpetuate biblical representations of disability. Examples include passages that speak of the "deafness" of transgressors, those that associate blindness with ignorance and bad judgment, and those that maintain the common biblical distinction between "defects" and impurities. Other materials are more innovative, modifying or radically transforming biblical notions. Examples of this include the blurring of the common biblical distinction between "defects" and impurities in the Temple Scroll, which casts blindness (and possibly, other "defects") as polluting; the emergence of nonbiblical contrasts such as permanent/temporary "defect," visible/nonvisible "defect," and somatic/spiritual "defect"; and the possible classification of deafness and muteness as "defects" in 1QS^a. Other examples of modification and transformation include the notion that at least some "defects" and other disabilities are generally incompatible with the holy, as witnessed in the War Scroll, 1QS^a, and 4Q266; the use of a novel combination of the biblical vocabulary of "foolishness" and that of "madness" to designate classes of persons with mental disability in 4Q266; and the emergence of new, nonbiblical classes (e.g., the "stricken" of 1QS^a).

In many instances, the novel representations of disability in the Dead Sea Scrolls seek to increase the degree of stigmatization and marginalization of persons with disabilities. The "deafness" and "blindness" of transgressors are associated with the "Spirit of Wrong" (*rûaḥ 'awlah*) and various characteristics of the antithesis of the deity in 1QS 4:11. By casting the blind (and possibly others with "defects") as polluters, the Temple Scroll seeks to add both to their stigma and to their marginalization; its call for the expulsion of all polluters from the Temple city, including the menstruant and the parturient, as if they had "skin disease," has a similar effect. 4QMMT seeks to increase both the stigmatization and the marginalization of deaf and blind priests by denying them access to the holy foods, and texts such as 1QSᵃ and 4Q266 do the same for groups such as the deaf, the mute, and the mentally disabled by prohibiting them from entering the community assembly, and casting them as a threat to the presence of the holy angels there.

Conclusion

*T*HROUGHOUT THIS INVESTIGATION, I HAVE SOUGHT TO RECON-
struct the ways in which disability is represented in biblical texts,
with reference to its representation in cuneiform and other non-Israelite
West Asian literatures for comparative purposes. I have also compared
biblical representations of disability to those of the Dead Sea Scrolls
in order to develop a perspective on how ancient Jewish exegetes both
perpetuate and modify earlier biblical representations of disability. A
central goal of my treatment has been to investigate the ways in which
the authors of our texts frequently stigmatize and seek to marginalize
disabled persons through their representations, thereby contributing to
social differentiation and inequality. I have also endeavored to recover
the contours of ancient patterns of classification, and to investigate the
degree to which biblical and other taxonomic categories evidenced in the
texts under consideration overlap with contemporary, Euro-American
notions of disability. In this conclusion, I address each of these issues. I
also consider the evidence for a hierarchy of stigmatization in the biblical text, and for varying perspectives on the etiology of disability and
the deity's attitude toward disabled persons. In addition, I attempt to
identify some possible native explanations for why the authors of biblical
texts seek so frequently to stigmatize and marginalize disabled persons.
Finally, I consider the gender dimensions of biblical representations of
disability.

Representations of disability in the Hebrew Bible and the other West
Asian literary corpora under consideration in this investigation share a
number of common characteristics. Like biblical representations of disability, more than a few cuneiform and other non-Israelite West Asian

texts cast conditions such as blindness, deafness, mental disability, and polluting skin diseases as curses (e.g., the Aqhat epic, the treaty of Ashurnirari V and Mati''il of Arpad), and the association of blindness and deafness with ignorance is a topos shared by both cuneiform literature and texts of the Hebrew Bible (e.g., "Esarhaddon's Renewal of the Gods"). In fact, the association of the mentally disabled, the deaf, the blind, and others allegedly lacking understanding in Babylonian *kudurru* (boundary) inscriptions resembles similar biblical classifications based on ascribed ignorance. However, there are also differences between the corpora. No biblical text explicitly associates mental disability with poverty in the way cuneiform texts do (e.g., "The Babylonian Theodicy"), and there is nothing in the biblical anthology quite like the cuneiform use of terms such as *akû* and *lillu* as synonyms for "poor," although biblical texts commonly associate the blind, the lame, and others with physical disabilities with the poor. All told, the representations of disability in the non-Israelite West Asian texts that I have compared to biblical materials resemble biblical representations more than they differ from them, although some notable differences are evident.

Like cuneiform and other non-Israelite West Asian representations of disability, representations of disability in the Dead Sea Scrolls are characterized by a mixture of features shared with biblical representations and distinct characteristics. A primary characteristic common both to Qumranic and biblical representations of disability is the association of blindness and deafness with ignorance and bad judgment. In addition, some other biblical patterns of treatment are perpetuated by some texts from Qumran (e.g., the expulsion of persons with "skin disease" from the community, or the maintenance of the common biblical distinction between impurities and "defects" [*mûmîm*]). In general, however, representations of disability from the Qumran corpus tend to modify those of the biblical anthology in innovative ways, ascribing greater stigma to persons with disabilities and seeking to increase their marginalization. The Temple Scroll blurs the distinction between "defect" and impurity, casting blindness (and possibly other "defects") as polluting. This results in the permanent exclusion of blind persons (and possibly others with "defects") from the sanctuary city according to this text. Metaphoric deafness and blindness are associated with the "Spirit of Wrong" and the "ways of darkness" in 1QS 4:11, significantly increasing the stigma of physical blindness and deafness. The Temple Scroll demands the expulsion of the menstruant and the parturient, along with all other polluters, from the sanctuary city, separating them from the community to a degree unknown in biblical sources. Several texts proscribe the entry of deaf, mute, and/or mentally disabled persons into the community assembly, casting them as a threat to the continued presence of the holy angels (4Q266, 1QS[a]), an innovation that goes well beyond anything biblical both in terms of the groups excluded, and in terms of the text's casting of deaf, mute, and/or mentally disabled persons as incompatible with holiness. Texts from Qumran also bear witness to the development of other novel, nonbiblical ideas pertaining to disabilities (e.g., the notion of spiritual wholeness and "defect"), which might be compared to the earlier, biblical elaboration of the contrast "whole"/"defective" in the form of nonsomatic parallels to bodily wholeness and "defect."

I have spoken at length of the strategies used by the writers of biblical texts to stigmatize and to assign marginal social positions to persons with disabilities, thereby casting them as inferior. Binary discourses are deployed to devalue disabled persons and, in some cases, restrict their social intercourse and their cultic opportunities, by casting them as "defective," profaning of holiness, cursed, shamed, hated, polluting, and – implicitly – ugly. A second, and exceedingly common, strategy marshaled by our authors is the association of disabled categories of persons such as the blind and the deaf with other stigmatized and socially marginal types such as the poor, the widow, the fatherless, the alien, and, in the case of persons with non-"defective" disabilities, those cast as "defective"; with devalued personal characteristics such as weakness, vulnerability, dependence, ineffectuality, ignorance, and bad judgment; with ideas such as contempt and divine rejection; and, in the case of males, with categories of women, suggesting their feminization. In addition to these strategies, the biblical text may also stigmatize through implicit comparison (e.g., of disabled persons to a desert) and through constructing a utopian future that has no place whatsoever for disabilities.

Some categories of disabled persons are stigmatized through the application of several of the strategies mentioned previously, whereas others are devalued through the operation of one or two strategies alone. Several examples serve to illustrate the range of ways in which biblical texts stigmatize persons with disabilities. Blind persons are cast as "defective," and blindness is not infrequently listed among curses. The blind are often associated with the poor, the afflicted, and other marginal types, and with characteristics such as ignorance, weakness, and dependency. In one utopian, prophetic text (Jer 31:7–9), blind (and lame) males are feminized through classification with pregnant and bearing women. Although generally not the case in biblical texts, blindness (and lameness) may well be cast as polluting in 2 Sam 5:8b. Deafness and muteness are never cast as "defects" by biblical texts, in contrast to blindness, but deaf and mute persons are frequently associated with the blind and others with "defects," stigmatizing them as a result. In addition, the mute and deaf are stigmatized through association with the poor, and with qualities such as ignorance and helplessness. Muteness occurs as a self-imprecation in Psalm 137. In contrast to the blind, the deaf, and the mute, persons with "skin disease" (ṣaraʿat) are constructed as major polluters in the biblical text, and their pollution is the main source of their stigma. Persons with "skin disease" are also devalued by the frequent casting of their condition as a curse or as divine punishment for transgression. However, unlike the blind, the mute, and the deaf, persons with "skin disease" are never stigmatized through association with groups such as the poor or the "defective," or with devalued personal characteristics such as weakness and dependency. Finally, the menstruant is stigmatized almost entirely as a result of her construction as a serious polluter. Texts do not associate her with groups such as the poor or the alien, or with devalued qualities such as vulnerability and helplessness. This may be compared to the treatment of the person with "skin disease," although that individual's condition is also frequently cast as a curse. Thus, a variety of strategies are marshaled by the authors of biblical texts in order to stigmatize persons with disabilities, and patterns of stigmatization may be discerned by comparing the combinations of strategies deployed to stigmatize various disabled groups.

Social marginalization, at least in theory, may be a result of the text's deployment of one or several stigmatizing strategies. Major polluters such as persons with "skin disease" are to be entirely cut off not only from the cult and its benefits, but also from life in the community according to various biblical texts. The menstruant is also subject to restriction on her movements and her social intercourse, although the degree to which she is to be marginalized according to texts such as Leviticus 15 remains unclear. Priests with "defects" such as blindness and lameness may not present offerings to Yhwh according to Leviticus 21, nor may men with genital damage enter the "assembly" according to Deut 23:2 (Eng. 1). 2 Sam 5:8b appears to ban the blind and the lame (and perhaps others with "defects") from entering the sanctuary sphere, possibly because the text constructs such persons as polluters or profaners of holiness. The casting of persons with disabilities as despised, rejected by Yhwh, shamed, or cursed in biblical texts, could well have had the effect of causing others to avoid contact with them, leading to their social marginalization. Texts from Qumran tend on the whole to elaborate on biblical models of the marginalization of persons with disabilities, seeking to increase marginalization for those whom biblical texts seek to marginalize.

Are we justified in speaking of a hierarchy of stigmatization evidenced in the biblical text? On the one hand, it is certainly the case that some disabilities are subjected to a larger number of stigmatizing strategies than are others. For example, multiple stigmatizing strategies are used by biblical authors to cast blind persons as inferior, while fewer are deployed to devalue the deaf. However, the number of devaluing strategies marshaled cannot be used alone to determine degrees of stigmatization. Although persons with "skin disease" are only subjected to a few stigmatizing strategies in the biblical text, the severe pollution ascribed to them is highly denigrating in and of itself, and has greater implications for social marginalization than do many of the strategies deployed to stigmatize a group such as the blind. Furthermore, it seems likely that to be cast as cursed, as are those with "skin disease," would increase stigmatization significantly, given that curses represent that which the ancients most dread. In short, any hierarchy of stigmatization that we might reconstruct would have to take into account the number of devaluing strategies deployed for each disability, the severity of the stigma attached to the particular strategies deployed, and the ramifications of those strategies with respect to social marginalization. As an example, one might compare the text's treatment of the deaf, the blind, the mentally disabled, and the person with "skin disease." Given that deaf persons in biblical texts are never subject to discourses of pollution or profanation, in contrast to the person with "skin disease" or the blind, and given that deafness is never explicitly cast as a curse in biblical sources, it seems justified to conclude that deafness is a less stigmatized disability in biblical sources than are blindness and "skin disease," even if it is subject to a larger number of stigmatizing strategies than is "skin disease." Like deaf persons, persons with mental disability are subject to a number of stigmatizing strategies, but are never cast as polluting or profaning of holiness in biblical texts. However, in contrast to deaf persons, and similar to persons with "skin disease" and the blind, their condition is represented as a curse. Thus, mental disability appears to be more stigmatized than deafness in the biblical text, although less denigrated than blindness and "skin disease."

Classification has been a central theme of this investigation. Throughout the study, I have sought to identify the various taxonomic categories – both explicit and implicit – evidenced in biblical texts, in the cuneiform and other non-Israelite West Asian materials I have considered, and in exegetical texts from Qumran. One goal in doing so was to determine the degree to which native classifications overlap with broad, contemporary, Euro-American ideas of disability. Although I have found no evidence pointing to the existence of a single, native classification comparable in its contours and comprehensiveness to any contemporary, Western notion of disability, I have found many examples of what we would call disabilities or disabled categories of persons classified together by texts on the basis of an alleged shared characteristic. These characteristics, most of which are implicit in the texts and all of which are constructed negatively, include somatic dysfunction, weakness and vulnerability, incapacitation, ignorance, and immobility, among others. Some of these implicit classes may be made up exclusively of persons with disabilities, whereas others include persons we would not classify as disabled. Each text stigmatizes the categories of persons or the disabilities it brings together, and some seek to marginalize those they classify.

Many examples of such classifications could be mentioned here, but four examples must suffice. A text such as Isa 35:5–6 seems to classify the blind, deaf, lame, and mute together on the basis of the perception of a shared somatic dysfunction; Deut 28:28–29 associates blindness and mental disability as curses, evidently on account of the helplessness they are believed to engender. Babylonian *kudurru* (boundary) inscriptions list deaf persons, blind persons, and persons with mental disability together, creating a class of persons cast as ignorant, who are assumed to be easily manipulated into committing transgressions. Finally, several texts from the Qumran corpus generate classes of persons, including persons with disabilities, who are constructed as a threat to holiness (specifically, the holy angels), and are therefore barred from entering the communal assembly. In 4Q266, these include what appear to be various classes of persons with mental disability, those unable to see, the lame and the limping, the deaf, and the young child. Thus, although biblical and other texts of interest to this study do not bear witness to a single, implicit classification that parallels any contemporary, Western notion of disability, let alone such an explicit classification, more than a few texts bring together disabilities of various sorts (e.g., "defects" with mental disability, "defects" with non-"defective" physical disabilities). The basis for the association of the various disabilities does not appear to be an underlying notion of shared disability per se, but rather something else (e.g., shared somatic dysfunction, ignorance, helplessness, a shared threat to holiness).[1]

Disability's etiology is not infrequently traced to divine agency. In Exod 4:11, Yhwh himself claims that he is responsible for disabilities such as blindness, deafness, and muteness, as well as the ability to speak, see, or hear. Many of the texts that treat disabilities suggest that they are the result of divine disfavor, and some cast disability explicitly as a punishment for sin. The evil spirit that torments Saul is said to have come from Yhwh, and it functions in the narrative to underscore Yhwh's rejection of Saul (1 Sam 16:14). King Uzziah's attempt to usurp the priestly privilege of incense presentation results in Yhwh striking him with "skin disease" for the rest of his life (2 Chr 26:16–21). Curses, which are brought into effect by deities, commonly include blindness, deafness, mental disability, skin diseases, and other disabling conditions among their various punishments (e.g., Deut 28:28; 2 Sam 3:29; Esarhaddon's Succession Treaty).

Do all disabilities have a divine origin, or is there evidence that some might have been understood as the result of accidental causes or natural, physical developments? The minibiography of Meribbaal (Mephiboshet), son of Jonathan, seems to suggest the possibility that at least some biblical writers could view disability as the consequence of an accident rather than the result of divine agency.[2] In 2 Sam 4:4, we are told of the circumstances that led to Meribbaal's lameness. As a 5-year-old child, he was dropped by his nurse as they hurried to flee after hearing of the deaths of Meribbaal's father, Jonathan, and grandfather, Saul, in battle. Neither 2 Sam 4:4, nor any other part of the Meribbaal minibiography that mentions his inability to walk, suggests that Meribbaal's lameness was the result of anything other than an accidental fall in childhood. Furthermore, according to 1 Kgs 14:4, the prophet Ahijah of Shiloh became blind as a result of old age, a natural, physical development.[3] Nowhere does this text suggest that Ahijah's blindness was caused by Yhwh's agency, although the narrative uses Ahijah's disability to bring Yhwh's superior knowledge into relief, as I have discussed. Thus, it may be that the viewpoint of Exod 4:11, that all disabilities are the result of divine action, represents only one of a number of perspectives in the biblical anthology on the etiology of disability. Whether disabilities are explained as the result of divine initiative, accidents, or natural processes, they are frequently stigmatized in biblical representation, given their various negative associations and the range of discourses typically deployed by biblical authors to devalue them.

How does the deity of the Hebrew Bible regard persons with disabilities? According to texts such as Psalm 146, Yhwh is an advocate for disabled persons, just as he is for other categories of persons represented as weak and marginal (e.g., v. 8: "Yhwh gives sight to the blind"). In addition, various prophetic utopian visions portray an ideal future in which Yhwh acts decisively to normalize disabled persons by mitigating the marginalizing effects of their physical conditions, or to eliminate disability altogether. Although these texts tend indirectly to stigmatize disabled persons, they suggest nonetheless that Yhwh takes an interest in them and is willing to act to improve their lot. One text, Isa 56:4–5, rejecting the restriction of Deut 23:2 (Eng. 1), provides a more successful challenge to the stigmatization of disability by portraying a Yhwh who accepts the eunuch unequivocally in his sanctuary, assigning him a privileged place among his worshipers. Other texts in the biblical anthology present a different perspective. Lev 21:17–23 suggests that Yhwh does not desire to have his offerings, which must themselves be without "defect" (*mûm*), presented by priests who are not physically "whole," nor may a high priest with a "defect" approach the tabernacle curtain. 2 Sam 5:8b goes further, evidently prohibiting the blind and the lame (and possibly others with "defects") from entering the sanctuary; Deut 23:2 (Eng. 1) excludes men with genital damage from entering the "assembly of Yhwh," likely a reference to the sanctuary. Given Yhwh's abominating of sacrificial animals with "defects" in Deut 17:1, it may be the case that in at least some circles, if not many, Yhwh was believed to abominate persons with "defects" as well.[4] "Defective" persons may well have been understood by some writers to be ugly and repellent, and therefore unfit to enter the presence of a deity who is believed to esteem the beautiful and the "whole." Texts from Qumran that exclude "defective" persons and others with disabilities from the communal assembly on account of the presence of the holy angels also suggest an incompatibility between that which is holy and divine, on the one hand, and persons with disabilities, on the other. In short, the texts of the Hebrew Bible and the biblical tradition present a variety of views on Yhwh's attitude toward disabled persons; some are favorable, others much less so. Yhwh's views, as represented in these texts, reflect a range of culturally specific attitudes characteristic of the text's authors.

What might have motivated biblical authors to seek so frequently to stigmatize and marginalize persons with disabilities? Needless to say, this is a very difficult question to answer because the motives of authors are rarely if ever discernible in texts and can only be guessed. It is far easier to show the ways in which authors, through their representations, seek to denigrate and marginalize disabled persons than it is to identify their reasons for so doing. However, several texts hint at possible native explanations for the devaluing of persons with disabilities, and these are worthy of our consideration. First, there is the likely association of human "defects" (mûmîm) with ugliness and abomination, as suggested by the biblical treatment of the "defects" of sacrificial animals. Such an association could have motivated at least some biblical authors to stigmatize and seek to marginalize persons with "defects." A second possible motivation is to be found in "idol" polemics such as Jer 10:5, which suggests indirectly that persons with both "defective" and non-"defective" physical disabilities lack human characteristics considered fundamental by the author of the text, quintessential qualities of the living such as the ability to walk, speak, see, and hear. The implication is that persons who lack these fundamental qualities are somehow less than fully human, just as the denigrated "idols" of the polemic, which lack the same characteristics, are not real gods. Also, just as the disabilities of the "idols" are the basis for denigrating and dismissing them in Jer 10:5, so too, by implication, are human disabilities the basis for denigrating and marginalizing persons who are disabled. A second text, Isa 35:4–10, also suggests implicitly that persons with physical disabilities such as the blind, the lame, the deaf, and the mute, lack certain fundamental, positively constructed characteristics of the living; like a desert, to which they are implicitly compared, they are somehow incomplete, unfruitful, and not entirely alive.[5] Thus, the stigmatizing and potentially marginalizing treatment of persons with disabilities in so many biblical texts may have been motivated in whole or in part by the idea that such persons are ugly and worthy of abomination, that they are somehow less than fully human, that they lack certain fundamental characteristics of the living.[6]

The gender dimensions of the biblical representation of disability are worthy of our serious consideration, given that some contemporary disability theorists understand the feminization of disabled bodies as a common stigmatizing strategy in Euro-American discourse.[7] To what degree does the evidence under consideration in this study also reflect such a strategy? As I have discussed, there is some evidence for the feminizing of disabled men in biblical texts. Jer 31:7–9 feminizes blind and lame males through association with nonambulatory or semiambulatory women; Isa 33:23 envisions an ideal future when blind and lame men are normalized by Yhwh, pillaging the vanquished as other males do, and thereby reclaiming their masculinity. Yet, aside from these two texts, biblical materials representing disabled males do not typically associate them with women or things feminine. Even a text such as Deut 23:2 (Eng. 1), which deals with males who have lost their reproductive capacity as a result of genital damage, does not feminize them in any way. These men are implicitly compared with aliens and (evidently) others with lineage issues in the larger pericope of Deut 23:2–9 (Eng. 1–8), not with women.[8] Far more common than association with women or that which is constructed as feminine is the association of disabled categories of persons, such as the blind, the lame, and the deaf, with marginal groups, such as the poor, the afflicted, and the alien, on account of a perception of shared vulnerability and weakness. Thus, feminization, although attested in the biblical anthology as a strategy to stigmatize disabled males, is a seldom attested strategy at best, in contrast to what one might find in Euro-American discourses, and in contrast to much more frequent associations with the alien, the poor or the afflicted. Such a finding underscores the necessity of many more studies focusing on disability in non-Western and pre-modern contexts if we hope to develop comparative, cross-cultural, and transhistorical perspectives on disability.

Notes

1. I use "defect" in this study only to translate the Hebrew technical term *mûm*. I never use it to refer generally to conditions that might be understood to depart from a perceived physical or mental norm. In like manner, I use "defective" (e.g., "defective persons," "defective bodies") only to refer to persons/bodies with "defects" (*mûmim*).

2. Exceptions include L. Holden, *Forms of Deformity* (Sheffield, UK: JSOT Press, 1991); H. Avalos, *Illness and Health Care in the Ancient Near East: The Role of the Temple in Greece, Mesopotamia, and Israel* (Atlanta: Scholars Press, 1995); C. Fontaine, "Disabilities and Illness in the Bible: A Feminist Perspective," in *A Feminist Companion to the Hebrew Bible in the New Testament* (ed. A. Brenner; Sheffield, UK: Sheffield Academic Press, 1996), 286–300; S. J. Melcher, "Visualizing the Perfect Cult: The Priestly Rationale for Exclusion," in *Human Disability and the Service of God: Reassessing Religious Practice* (ed. N. L. Eiesland and D. E. Saliers; Nashville, TN: Abingdon Press, 1998), 55–71; J. L. Berquist, *Controlling Corporeality: The Body and the Household in Ancient Israel* (New Brunswick, NJ: Rutgers University Press, 2002); J. Schipper, "Reconsidering the Imagery of Disability in 2 Samuel 5:8b," *Catholic Biblical Quarterly* 67 (2005):422–434; idem., *Disability Studies and the Hebrew Bible: Figuring Mephibosheth in the David Story* (New York: T. & T. Clark, 2006); and J. H. W. Dorman, "The Blemished Body: Deformity and Disability in the Qumran Scrolls" (Ph.D. dissertation, University of Groningen, Groningen, The Netherlands, 2007), who treats Leviticus 21:16–23 in some detail. (The last two items came to my attention as I was completing the final form of this manuscript for publication.) A number of other disability-related studies are soon to appear (e.g., H. Avalos, S. Melcher, and J. Schipper, eds., "This Abled Body: Rethinking Disabilities in Biblical Studies" *Semeia*, in press; R. Raphael, *Biblical Corpora: Representations of Disability in Hebrew Biblical Literature* [New York: T. & T. Clark, in press]). J. Z. Abrams, *Judaism and Disability: Portrayals in Ancient Texts from the Tanach through the Bavli* (Washington, DC: Gallaudet University Press, 1998), is a work by a specialist in rabbinics with

limited biblical training, and includes discussion of some biblical texts in their own context.

3. As in J. Milgrom, *Leviticus 17–22* (New York: Doubleday, 2000), 1821–1832 on Lev 21:17–23.

4. On disability as a "key defining social category" not unlike race, class, and gender, see the discussion of C. J. Kudlick, "Disability History: Why We Need Another 'Other,'" *The American Historical Review* 108 (2003):764. Kudlick could also have mentioned sexuality as a "key defining social category."

5. On the difficulty of defining disability, see the discussions of S. Wendell, *The Rejected Body: Feminist Philosophical Reflections on Disability* (New York: Routledge, 1996), 11–33; Kudlick, ibid., 767; and A. Bérubé's introduction to S. Linton, *Claiming Disability: Knowledge and Identity* (New York: New York University Press, 1998), vii. Bérubé describes disability as "the most labile and pliable of categories," comparing illness. Linton, ibid., 12, notes the tendency toward broad definition among scholars in disability studies. Wendell's discussion compares the varied definitions. For the broader understanding of disability, see also P. K. Longmore and L. Umansky, eds., *The New Disability History: American Perspectives* (New York and London: New York University Press, 2001), 4–5. On the notion of shared stigmatization or, more positively, "a common social and political experience," see Longmore and Umansky, ibid., 12; Linton, ibid., 12; and R. Garland Thomson, *Extraordinary Bodies: Figuring Physical Disability in American Culture and Literature* (New York: Columbia University Press, 1997), 15, among others. Garland Thomson makes an argument for disability as a form of "ethnicity" on account of shared social inferiority among disabled persons (ibid., 6). Some of the scholars mentioned previously focus on contemporary America; others work on the nineteenth and twentieth centuries. A helpful survey of various contemporary "models" for the study of disability may be found in Schipper, *Disability Studies*, 15–24. See also B. M. Altman, "Disability Definitions, Models, Classification Schemes, and Applications," in *Handbook of Disability Studies* (ed. G. L. Albrecht et al.; Thousand Oaks, CA: Sage, 2001), 97–122.

On stigma and stigmatization, the classic work is E. Goffman, *Stigma: Notes on the Management of Spoiled Identity* (Englewood Cliffs, NJ: Prentice Hall, 1963), which has exercised a significant influence on contemporary social scientific approaches to disability, as Garland Thomson notes (ibid., 30). (I have found Garland Thomson's assessment of Goffman's theory to be most helpful [ibid., 30–32]). B. Major and C. P. Eccleston, "Stigma and Social Exclusion," in *Social Psychology of Inclusion and Exclusion* (ed. D. Abrams et al.; New York: Psychology Press, 2005), 63–87, is a recent contribution of note which surveys current and classic literature on stigma in social psychology. For Major and Eccleston, stigmatized individuals "are systematically devalued and excluded from a broad array of social relationships and social domains" ("Stigma and Social Exclusion," 64). Melcher, "Visualizing the Perfect Cult," 57–59, makes extensive use of Goffman's theorizing in her investigation.

6. I borrow the expression "natural and timeless" from D. C. Baynton, "Disability and the Justification of Inequality in American History," in *New Disability History*, 52. See Longmore and Umansky, *New Disability History*, 12, on disability as a

social construction. On disability and inequality, see, e.g., Kudlick, ibid., 765; Garland Thomson, ibid., 5–9; and Baynton, ibid., 52: "It may well be that all social hierarchies have drawn on culturally constructed and socially sanctioned notions of disability."

7. Garland Thomson, ibid., 5, describes disability as "another culture-bound, phys-ically justified difference to consider along with race, gender, class, ethnicity, and sexuality." She goes on to point out that although physical differences exist, "their sociopolitical meanings and consequences are entirely culturally determined" (ibid., 7). Longmore and Umansky, ibid., 19, point out that although disability is socially constructed, there is interplay between condition and construction, between difference as a social product and difference as a physical/mental fact: "Throughout the history of what we have come to call 'disability,' physiological states and social contexts have acted on one another." Wendell, *The Rejected Body*, 44–45, strives to balance acknowledgment of "the hard physical realities that are faced by persons with disabilities" with acknowledgment of the role of "cultural representation." Some scholars in disability studies prefer to distinguish between impairment, a physical phenomenon, and disability, a social phenomenon. On this, see, e.g., the discussion and critique of Schipper, *Disability Studies*, 17–18.

8. Among the "defects" are blindness, lameness, genital damage, and broken or crushed limbs. Note that mental disability, deafness, and muteness are not cat-egorized as "defects" (*mûmîm*) in biblical discourse. On this, see further the discussion in chapter 2.

9. The context suggests that *kebad peh ûkbad lašôn* in Exod 4:10 refers to impeded speech of some kind. A variety of disabilities, both "defects" and non-"defects," are also brought together in so-called idol polemics such as Jer 10:5 and Ps 115:5–8. On these, see my upcoming discussion.

10. This means that medical questions, such as the clinical identification of biblical "skin disease" (*ṣaraʿat*), will not generally be of interest in this investigation, nor is my focus the inherently limiting characteristics of disabilities. Although I acknowledge that disabilities may impose limits on affected persons apart from the ways in which cultures might cast them, I am far more interested in disability as a cultural product. The one context where clinical identification will be of interest is chapter 4. There, I shall examine the opaque technical vocabulary of mental disability, and expend some effort to identify to what conditions each term of interest refers. I do this because no discussion of the representation of mental disability in the Hebrew Bible is possible without an attempt to determine the meaning of the text's technical vocabulary.

11. "Gender: A Useful Category of Historical Analysis," in *Gender and the Politics of History* (New York: Columbia University Press, 1988), 44–45.

12. The occasional material datum from archeology is relevant (e.g., models of deformed feet or other body parts possibly brought to sanctuaries as votive gifts by disabled petitioners or their supporters). On the examples from Horvat Qitmit, see Z. Zevit, *The Religions of Ancient Israel: A Synthesis of Parallactic Approaches* (New York: Continuum, 2001), 146. Unhappily, archeological data relevant to this investigation are few and far between, much in contrast to the study of disability

in Greco-Roman contexts, where a plethora of material remains, including vase illustrations and miniature sculptures, abound. On this, see, e.g., R. Garland, *The Eye of the Beholder: Deformity and Disability in the Greco-Roman World* (Ithaca, NY: Cornell University Press, 1995), 105–122, with photographs. For a brief survey of relevant material remains from ancient West Asia, see Schipper, *Disability Studies*, 62–64, with citations.

13. An exception to the last point is the possibility of comparing earlier biblical constructions of disability to later materials from the Second Temple period, something I pursue in chapter 7, focusing specifically on the representation of disability in the Dead Sea Scrolls.

14. On the representation of the past, see, e.g., the discussions of S. Weitzman, "Plotting Antiochus's Persecution," *Journal of Biblical Literature* 123 (2004):219–234, esp. 221–222; and R. S. Hendel, "The Exodus in Biblical Memory," *Journal of Biblical Literature* 120 (2001):601–622. Studies focusing on representations of biblical ritual include S. M. Olyan, *Rites and Rank: Hierarchy in Biblical Representations of Cult* (Princeton, NJ: Princeton University Press, 2000); idem., *Biblical Mourning: Ritual and Social Dimensions* (Oxford, UK: Oxford University Press, 2004); and W. Gilders, *Blood Ritual in the Hebrew Bible: Meaning and Power* (Baltimore: The Johns Hopkins University Press, 2004). The literature on biblical gender representations is large and varied. Examples of note include C. Meyers, *Discovering Eve: Ancient Israelite Women in Context* (New York: Oxford University Press, 1988); T. Frymer-Kensky, *In the Wake of the Goddesses: Women, Culture, and the Biblical Transformation of Pagan Myth* (New York: Free Press, 1992); A. Brenner, *The Intercourse of Knowledge: On Gendering Desire & 'Sexuality' in the Hebrew Bible* (Leiden, The Netherlands: Brill, 1997); and S. Ackerman, *Warrior, Dancer, Seductress, Queen: Women in Judges and Biblical Israel* (New York: Doubleday, 1998). On the cultural turn in the practice of history in the American academy, see, e.g., L. Hunt, ed., *The New Cultural History* (Berkeley: University of California Press, 1989); V. E. Bonnell and L. Hunt, eds., *Beyond the Cultural Turn: New Directions in the Study of Society and Culture* (Berkeley: University of California Press, 1999); and "Review Essays: Beyond the Cultural Turn" in the *American Historical Review* 107 (2002):1475–1520, as well as H. White's classic collection of essays, *The Content of the Form: Narrative Discourse and Historical Representation* (Baltimore: The Johns Hopkins University Press, 1987).

15. Ibid, 209.

16. Scott, *Gender and the Politics of History*, 45, 59–60; J. Z. Smith, "Fences and Neighbors: Some Contours of Early Judaism," in *Imagining Religion: From Babylon to Jonestown* (Chicago: University of Chicago Press, 1982), 8; B. Lincoln, *Discourse and the Construction of Society: Comparative Studies of Myth, Ritual, and Classification* (New York: Oxford University Press, 1989), 140.

17. "Classification," in *Guide to the Study of Religion* (ed. W. Braun and R. T. McCutcheon; London: Cassell, 2000), 38.

18. *Rites and Rank.*

19. Note that an absence of "defects" (*mûmîm*) does not necessarily result in categorization as beautiful. On this, see my discussion in chapter 1. All translations from the ancient languages are my own unless otherwise noted.

20. Cf. Melcher, who understands such priests as "in a partial sense...devalued" ("Visualizing the Perfect Cult," 59). I believe they are stigmatized as inferior; what is partial is their marginalization.

21. The stranger in question is referred to literally as "(one) I did not know." It is not clear from the context whether a foreigner is meant, or simply someone who is not a local.

22. The text suggests that before Job's own calamities, he embodied a number of the ideals commonly ascribed in the Hebrew Bible to the mature, free male, especially the king: divine favor, wealth, honor, agency, independence, and the ability to intimidate others and exercise power over them. In fact, Job compares himself to a king in 29:25.

23. On this, see my upcoming discussion. Although S. Vargon notes the biblical text's association of disabled persons with weakness (citing Lev 19:14 and Deut 27:18) and with other vulnerable groups (citing Ps 146:8–9 and Job 29:15–16), he claims (apologetically?) that disabled persons were not regarded as inferior: "In the sphere of personal relationships, one having a deformity is regarded as a weak (though not inferior) person, whom we are instructed to protect and to whom we should accord special treatment" ("The Blind and the Lame," *Vetus Testamentum* 46 [1996], 501). Obviously, my position on the issue of ascribed inferiority is very different from Vargon's. Curiously, Vargon does not develop his observation that the text associates disabled persons with weakness and with other vulnerable groups, nor does he speak of classification as an operation in the text.

24. See similarly Isa 6:9–10; Ps 38:14; cf. Ps 82:5. The reading "his watchmen" (*sopayw*) follows the qere and 1QIsa[a].

25. For example, L. W. King, *Babylonian Boundary-Stones and Memorial-Tablets in the British Museum* (London: British Museum, 1912), iv 3 5–7, for the text in Akkadian with English translation.

26. W. G. Lambert, *Babylonian Wisdom Literature* (Oxford, UK: Clarendon Press, 1960), 18, n. 1.

27. On the social and political dimensions of these polemics, see especially N. B. Levtow, "Images of Others: Icon Parodies and Iconic Politics in Ancient Israel" (Ph.D. dissertation, Brown University, Providence, RI, 2006), a revised version of which is to be published in the series Biblical and Judaic Studies from the University of California, San Diego (Eisenbrauns).

28. Fontaine has noted the way in which disabled persons function in biblical narrative and poetic texts as "objects of divine action," serving "as marvelous plot-devices that show off the power of God" to heal ("Disabilities and Illness in the Bible," 293–294). Although I agree with her that emphasizing Yhwh's power and agency is the central concern of these texts, it is not the case that healing is always, or even often, Yhwh's aim, as the following examples demonstrate. It may be that Fontaine's characterization is overly influenced by the examples from the gospels that she discusses, where healing is a central focus.

29. The blinding and fettering of male prisoners of war and their subjection to humiliating labor with a hand mill was not atypical in the West Asian context, as K. van der Toorn has shown ("Judges XVI 21 in the Light of the Akkadian Sources,"

Vetus Testamentum 36 [1986]:248–253). Blinding and fettering were intended to prevent the prisoner's escape.

30. In Judg 16:26, the blind Samson is led by the hand by a youth and must ask the youth to help him touch the temple pillars so that he might lean on them. These details bring his apparent dependence and lack of agency into relief.

31. On the prophet as divine mouthpiece, see, e.g., Jer 23:16–18, 21–22.

32. On the expression *kebad peh ûkbad lašôn*, see n. 9. As is often noted, Exod 4:10 is a typical example of the common topos of deficiency found in call narratives. This topos is also found in texts such as Judg 6:15; 1 Sam 9:21; Isa 6:5; and Jer 1:6. In Jer 1:6, the issue, as in Exod 4:10, is the prophet's ability to speak, but here, the prophet protests that he cannot speak because he is "only a youth." Physical disability is only one of a number of possible deficiencies manifest in texts attesting to this topos. On *piqqeaḥ* as "sentient" or "percipient," meaning both "sighted" and "hearing" in this context, see the argument of W. H. C. Propp, *Exodus 1–18* (New York: Doubleday, 1999), 212.

33. The challenge is not entirely effective in the case of Yhwh granting special protection to the poor. On the one hand, Yhwh's concern for the poor is demonstrated through his actions, thereby raising their status; on the other, the vulnerability, weakness, and dependence of the poor are brought into relief by Yhwh's special advocacy. The same is true of Yhwh's concern for other dependent sufferers such as the resident alien, the widow, and the fatherless. In contrast, to claim that the poor possess honor based on wisdom rather than wealth (Sir 10:30) challenges their stigmatization more successfully because to make such a claim does not affirm the weakness of the poor or any other stigmatized characteristic commonly attributed to them in the biblical text. On the textual issues of Sir 10:30, see P. W. Skehan and A. A. di Lella, *The Wisdom of Ben Sira* (New York: Doubleday, 1987), 232.

34. The formula occurs in Exod 22:20–23 (Eng. 21–24); Deut 10:18; 14:29; 24:17, 19–21; 26:12, 13; 27:19; Isa 1:17; Jer 49:11; Mal 3:5; Ps 68:6 (Eng. 5); 146:9, among many other passages. Sometimes, only the fatherless and widow are mentioned (e.g., Isa 1:17; Jer 49:11); in Deuteronomic contexts, the Levite may be added to the formula (e.g., Deut 14:29; 26:12). The notion that such persons are entitled to the protection of the powerful is a common topos in ancient West Asian literatures (see, e.g., Hammurapi's epilogue [M. T. Roth, *Law Collections from Mesopotamia and Asia Minor* (Atlanta: Scholars Press, 1995), 133], and the Kirta epic from Ugarit [*CAT* 1.16 VI 45–50]. The poor and other dependent sufferers may be added to the list, as in the Kirta epic).

35. As with texts claiming that Yhwh grants special protection to the poor, the widow, and other vulnerable persons, the two laws protecting persons with disabilities, as well as a text such as Ps 146:8, suggest both Yhwh's special concern for such persons and their status as weak, vulnerable, and dependent. Thus, texts such as these are not entirely effective as challenges to the stigmatization of disabled persons, given that they affirm their weakness, dependency, and vulnerability. On the paucity of mitigating narratives in literary representations of disability in modern Western literature, see the comments of Garland Thomson, *Extraordinary Bodies,* 10–11.

Why there are so few passages like Lev 19:14, Deut 27:18, and Ps 146:8, given the many texts challenging the stigmatization of the widow, the orphan, and the resident alien, and, to a lesser degree, the poor and the afflicted, is not an easy question to answer. A text such as Job 29:12–15 suggests that these persons (including the blind and the lame) share a common weakness, vulnerability, and dependence, and that treating them justly and generously is the appropriate and expected response of the powerful. Psalm 146 suggests that Yhwh himself has a special concern for such persons, including the blind. Given this, it is perhaps surprising that blind, lame, and deaf persons do not typically appear in the most commonly attested versions of the formulaic list of dependent/protected persons. The widow, the fatherless, and the resident alien are frequently listed together; occasionally, they are joined by the poor, the afflicted, and even the Levite (in Deuteronomy). However, persons with disabilities are usually not present. At the very least, it seems fair to say that although disabled persons such as the blind, lame, and deaf are sometimes brought into association with the poor, the widow, and other persons cast as vulnerable and dependent, the most commonly attested version of the formulaic list of dependent sufferers, for whatever reason, includes only the widow, the fatherless, and the resident alien. It may be that these particular persons have come to represent all who are cast as vulnerable and dependent for the writers of the texts in which the formula occurs.

36. On the debate over the date of Isa 56:3–7, see Olyan, *Rites and Rank*, 90, and 164, n. 114. It is unclear what entry into the assembly means in Deut 23:2–9 (Eng. 1–8), but the text's earliest extant interpreters understand the expression to mean entry into the Jerusalem Temple for the purpose of worship (Lam 1:10; Isa 56:3–7; Ezek 44:7, 9). The *mamzer* of Deut 23:3 (Eng. 2) remains obscure.

37. The substitution of the eunuch in Isa 56:3–7 for the two categories of men with damaged genitals mentioned in Deut 23:2 (Eng. 1; *kerût šopkah* and *peṣûaʿ dakka'*) reflects an exegetically expansive understanding of Deut 23:2 (Eng. 1) that must have been current at the time Isa 56:3–7 was composed. On the substitution, see further ibid., 164, n. 116.

38. I discuss the use of Yhwh's authoritative voice in this passage in ibid., 92, although my focus there is the treatment of the alien rather than that of the eunuch.

39. On the memorial monument and the notion of an everlasting name, see the discussion of J. Blenkinsopp, *Isaiah 56–66* (New York: Doubleday, 2003), 139–140. On the "name" with the sense of "the sum of a person's deeds and accomplishments, means and reputation" as well as "descendants," see A. S. van der Woude, "*šem* name," *TLOT* 3:1356–1357. Texts suggest that descendants normally invoke (keep in memory) the name of the dead (e.g., 2 Sam 18:18). Obviously, I understand *yad wašem* as a hendiadys construction.

40. On the modern, Euro-American focus of much scholarship in disability history, see the comments of Kudlick, "Disability History," 765, 790. Monographic works in Classics include Garland, *The Eye of the Beholder*, and M. L. Rose, *The Staff of Oedipus: Transforming Disability in Ancient Greece* (Ann Arbor: University of Michigan Press, 2003). For disability in rabbinic literature, see T. C. Marx, *Disability in Jewish Law* (London and New York: Routledge, 2002) and Abrams, *Judaism and Disability*.

1. CONSTRUCTIONS OF BEAUTY AND UGLINESS

1. J. L. Berquist's brief reconstruction of biblical notions of beauty from a social constructionist perspective came to my attention as I was preparing the final text of this study for publication (*Controlling Corporeality: The Body and the Household in Ancient Israel* [New Brunswick, NJ: Rutgers University Press, 2003], 22–26). Berquist's treatment focuses more on the Song of Songs than does mine, although there is some overlap. In contrast to my treatment in this chapter, Berquist does not consider ugliness, nor does he explore the relationship of beauty and somatic wholeness in any depth. In addition, his understanding of wholeness is not the biblical text's understanding (e.g., he claims that "a whole body contains all its parts and functions," and suggests directly that deafness is a "defect," when it is never classified as such; on the classification of deafness, see my discussion in chapter 3).

2. 1 Sam 9:1–10:16; compare 8; 10:17–27.

3. The expression *baḥûr waṭôb* is likely a hendiadys construction, and this assumption is reflected in my translation. On *ṭôb* with the meaning "handsome," see the upcoming discussion.

4. Where MT reads *'admonî 'im yepeh mar'eh*, LXX reads *purrakes meta kallous ofthalmon*. Both may in fact be expansions on a Vorlage mentioning only David's youth as the object of Goliath's hostility. See further the discussion of P. K. McCarter, Jr., *I Samuel* (Garden City, NY: Doubleday, 1980), 275.

5. "Fat" in these passages is most likely a reference to plumpness rather than obesity. Obesity is apparently described using the expression "very fat" (*barî' me'od*), as in Judg 3:17.

6. This verse follows on a description of Absalom's outstanding beauty in the previous verse. Thus, the context suggests that Absalom's thick, heavy hair is an example of his beauty.

7. On mourning and debasement, see further S. M. Olyan, *Biblical Mourning: Ritual and Social Dimensions* (Oxford, UK: Oxford University Press, 2004), 137–139 and passim. For beard and hair manipulation associated with mourning rites, see, e.g., Isa 15:2; Jer 41:5; Ezra 9:3. In 2 Sam 10:4, beard manipulation in a mourning context is distorted forcibly and grotesquely in order to humiliate. Isa 7:20 alludes to shameful rites of shaving beard, head, and pubic hair of male prisoners. Several texts allude to degrading attacks on beard or head hair by others, coupled with physical beatings (e.g., Isa 50:6; Neh 13:25).

8. Note also the mention of "the gazelle of Israel" in 2 Sam 1:19, an allusion either to Saul or Jonathan.

9. A beautiful male singing voice is also mentioned in *CAT* 1.3 I 20–22 (*yšr ġzr ṭb ql 'l b'l b ṣrrt ṣpn*).

10. I understand the mention of twin-bearing ewes in 6:6 (cf. 4:2) to suggest the desirability of symmetrical teeth. A concave navel is suggested by "a round goblet" (*'aggan hassahar*).

11. Texts concerned with "defects" in sacrificial animals often contrast "defective" offerings with those that are "whole" (*tamîm* or *temîmah*) or non-"defective" (e.g., Lev 22:19–22). Mary Douglas's early work emphasized the contrast between the "whole" and the "defective," bringing into relief the notion of wholeness or

completeness as paradigmatic in biblical thought and characteristic of such qualities as holiness. Her identification of a symmetrical relationship between notions of animal and priestly "defect" has influenced the thinking of biblical scholars, including my own (*Purity and Danger: An Analysis of the Concepts of Pollution and Taboo* [1966; Boston: Ark, 1984, reprinted], 50–52; eadem., "Deciphering a Meal," *Daedalus* 101 [1972]:76–77).

12. On the challenges involved in identifying conditions such as *ḥarum* and *śarûaʿ*, see, e.g., J. Milgrom, *Leviticus 17–22* (New York: Doubleday, 2000), 1825–1828.

13. I shall have much more to say about "defects" in chapter 2.

14. If that is how we ought to understand Hebrew *dal* in this context. The usual meaning is "poor," "needy," or "lowly" (e.g., Jer 39:10; Judg 6:15), which can hardly make sense here.

15. It is not clear in Gen 34:14 whether the disgrace is the result of allowing a sister to marry an uncircumcised man or whether the foreskin itself is disgraceful. In either case, the man's lack of circumcision is constructed as an unappealing physical characteristic in this passage. On this, see further S. M. Olyan, *Rites and Rank: Hierarchy in Biblical Representations of Cult* (Princeton, NJ: Princeton University Press, 2000), 65 and 152, nn. 11 and 12. Elsewhere, the words "uncircumcised" (*ʿarel*) and "foreskin" (*ʿorlah*) are used idiomatically of physical and moral dysfunction, illustrating well the depth of the negative construction of a lack of circumcision in the biblical context (e.g., Exod 6:12, 30; Deut 10:16; Jer 4:4; 6:10).

16. The morphological form of the adjective "bald" (*qereaḥ*) is shared by a number of other adjectives that denote physical disabilities, both "defective" and non-"defective" (e.g., *ʿiwwer*, "blind," and *ʾillem*, "mute"). On this form, see further my discussion in n. 5, chapter 3.

17. It has also been taken by some as an indirect comment on Saul, whose extreme height was emphasized in the narratives describing the origins of his choice as king. On this, see McCarter, *1 Samuel*, 277–278, for discussion.

18. Evidence for a Hellenistic date for Ecclesiastes is convincingly marshaled by M. V. Fox in *A Time to Tear Down and a Time to Build Up: A Rereading of Ecclesiastes* (Grand Rapids, MI: Eerdmans, 1999), 6–7.

19. For comparable examples from the Septuagint and the gospels, see the discussion of D. Kellermann, "*śemoʾl*," *TDOT* 14:141. Fox, *Proverbs 1–9* (New York: Doubleday, 2000), 330, explains the addition in Prov 4:27 as intended in part to make the imagery "more familiar to the Greek reader." See also his comments on p. 338.

20. The word *ṭôb* is as easily translated "beautiful" as it is "handsome." Its use in the Hebrew Bible with the meaning "beautiful" or "handsome" is paralleled in other West Asian literary materials, including the Baal Cycle from Ugarit (*CAT* 1.3 I 20) and the Epic of Gilgamesh (xi.256). The Ugaritic vocabulary of beauty is not dissimilar to that of the Hebrew Bible, with *ṭb*, *tp* (likely from *yph*), *nʿm*, and *ysm/ysmsm* used in such texts as *CAT* 1.3 I 19–20 and 1.96:2–3, for the most part to describe deities such as Baal. Akkadian usage also has some parallels to Hebrew usage, with *ṭabu*, *banû*, and *damqu* used of beautiful persons and deities, e.g., Gilgamesh xi.256 *ṭabu . . . zumuršu* (A. R. George, *The Babylonian Gilgamesh Epic. Introduction, Critical Edition and Cuneiform Texts* [2 vols.; Oxford, UK:

Oxford University Press, 2003], 1:718, for the text in Akkadian; 719, for English translation).

21. C. Dohmen, "r "," TDOT 13:564.

22. McCarter, I Samuel, 173: "The quality is to be interpreted as a physical symptom of special divine favor."

23. The verb form, although possibly corrupt, appears to be derived from the root yph. The king's beauty is also a theme in Isa 33:17. On the king as a human rather than a divine figure in Isa 33:17, see the discussion of Blenkinsopp, Isaiah 1–39 (New York: Doubleday, 2000), 445.

24. Other examples of attractive heroes or heroines favored by Yhwh include Joseph (Gen 39:5–6), Esther (Esther 2:7), and the newborn Moses (Exod 2:2), all listed by McCarter, ibid., 173. 1 Sam 16:7 is no exception to this pattern. Although Yhwh urges Samuel to look beyond height and physical appearance in the choice of a king, the man he ends up choosing (David) is nonetheless described as possessing physically attractive attributes (1 Sam 16:12).

25. The text goes on to mention the servant's apparent illness in v. 3. On this, see Blenkinsopp, Isaiah 40–55 (New York: Doubleday, 2000), 352–353.

26. On the wisdom tradition, see, conveniently, Fox, Proverbs 1–9, 6–12, 17–27.

27. The Greek text of Sir 9:8 states explicitly that "by the beauty of a woman, many have been deceived" (en kallei gunaikos polloi eplanethesan). The Hebrew text of Sir 9:8–9 is explicit that female beauty is at issue in v. 8 ('ešet ḥen, yopî), although v. 9 states only that "through a woman, many are destroyed." Nonetheless, the thrust of v. 8 makes it clear that the beauty of a woman is at issue in v. 9 as well.

28. I choose my words carefully as I do not wish to give the impression that I believe contemporary Westerners all embrace the same notions of beauty and ugliness. Clearly, this is not the case, even in a single society such as that of the United States, where alternative discourses of beauty and ugliness have always existed, shaped often by ethnicity, class, and race. Nonetheless, a dominant discourse of beauty and ugliness, created and disseminated through mass advertising and television programming, does exist and is nearly impossible to avoid. That discourse esteems youth, thinness, agility, and athleticism, among other qualities, and devalues their antitypes.

2. PHYSICAL DISABILITIES CLASSIFIED AS "DEFECTS"

1. Non-"defective" human beings are typically described in the biblical text as "having no 'defect'" (e.g., 2 Sam 14:25 lo' hayah bô mûm; Song of Songs 4:7 mûm 'ên bak; Dan 1:4 'ên bahem kol mum), whereas non-"defective" sacrificial animals are characterized using a different idiom: "whole" or "perfect" (e.g., Lev 22:19 tamîm; f. temîmah). The reasons for this variation remain unclear, although J. Milgrom argues that H, like D, reserves the term tamîm for moral perfection only (Leviticus 23–27 [New York: Doubleday, 2000], 2441). As I note in chapter 1, n. 11, it was Mary Douglas who initially emphasized the "whole"/"defective" contrast, and brought into relief the idea of wholeness or completeness as paradigmatic in biblical thought and characteristic of qualities such as holiness. Her insight that a symmetrical relationship exists between the "defects" of priests and those

of sacrificial animals has exercised considerable influence on the work of biblical scholars, my own included (*Purity and Danger: An Analysis of the Concepts of Pollution and Taboo* [1966; Boston: Ark, 1984, reprinted], 50–52; eadem., "Deciphering a Meal," *Daedalus* 101 [1972]:76–77).

2. On the "Holiness Code" (Leviticus 17–26), the larger Holiness Source of which it is a part, and the circles that produced it, see, e.g., I. Knohl, *The Sanctuary of Silence: The Priestly Torah and the Holiness School* (Minneapolis, MN: Fortress, 1995) and J. Milgrom, *Leviticus 17–22* (New York: Doubleday, 2000), 1319–1443.

3. Elite ritual actions claimed for priests exclusively by certain biblical texts include blood manipulation, fat burning, and the offering of incense (Num 16:1–17:5 [Eng. 16:1–40]; Ezek 44:7, 15; 2 Chr 26:16–21). The former two are rites included in the notion of approaching the altar of burnt offerings to sacrifice to the deity. The presentation of incense is a separate ritual act not mentioned in this text. The text's silence may suggest that offering incense is still open to priests with "defects," not unlike their continued access to the exclusive most holy foods, although this seems unlikely to me, given the proscription's apparent focus on priests approaching the deity. (For the holy and most holy foods, see v. 22 and the upcoming discussion.) On the elite rites and privileges that constitute priestly status, see further S. M. Olyan, *Rites and Rank: Hierarchy in Biblical Representations of Cult* (Princeton, NJ: Princeton University Press, 2000), 27–35. For priestly blood manipulation, in particular, see W. K. Gilders, *Blood Ritual in the Hebrew Bible: Meaning and Power* (Baltimore: The Johns Hopkins University Press, 2004).

4. The fourth term in the list, *śarûaʿ*, likely means a limb of extended length, given the apparent meaning of the root, "to extend," as indicated by Isa 28:20 *hiśtareaʿ*, "to stretch oneself out." The sixth term, *gibben*, is rendered "hunchbacked" in the LXX (*kurtos*). This may be correct, given the meaning of the apparently related word *gabnunnîm*, "many peaked," with reference to mountains, in Ps 68:17 (Eng. 16). The eighth term *teballul beʿênô*, most likely means "a mixing in his eye," and probably refers to an indistinct iris, a condition not uncommon among blind persons. The well-established meaning of the root *bll* ("to mix" or "mingle") suggests something like this. The term *garab* must refer to a skin condition (or a set of skin conditions) that is nonpolluting because the affected priest may remain in the sanctuary and eat holy and most foods. Its pairing with "boils" and other skin problems in Deut 28:27, and the meaning of the Akkadian cognate *garabu* suggest a skin condition, as Milgrom has noted (*Leviticus 17–22*, 1828). Cf. *ṣaraʿat*, "skin disease," which is highly polluting, and is therefore classified differently from *garab*. A second nonpolluting skin condition may be meant by the term *yallepet*. That *merôaḥ ʾašek* refers to some kind of genital damage is indicated by the meaning of cognates of *ʾešek* in Ugaritic (*ʾušk*) and Akkadian (*išku*): "testicle" (as noted by Milgrom, *Leviticus 17–22*, 1828). The other terms in the list remain obscure in meaning. For a discussion of comparable notions of "defect" in cuneiform materials, see K. van der Toorn, *Sin and Sanction in Israel and Mesopotamia: A Comparative Study* (Assen, The Netherlands: van Gorcum, 1985), 29–30.

5. See the cultic interpretation of Deut 23:2–9 (Eng. 1–8) in Lam 1:10, Isa 56:3–5, and Ezek 44:7, 9, all texts of the sixth and fifth centuries BCE. In Neh 13:1–3, the marriage

interpretation of the idiom "to enter the assembly" is evidenced for the first time. That Deut 23:2–9 (Eng. 1–8) antedates the exile is suggested by the allusion to it in a text such as Lam 1:10.

6. I understand Isa 56:3–5 to suggest that the eunuch, like the alien of v. 7, has access to Yhwh's sanctuary for worship, given the mention of a memorial monument for the eunuch in the temple. The dating of Isa 56:3–8 is difficult to determine, although a late sixth- or fifth-century date seems likely. On the problem and various solutions that have been proposed, see *Rites and Rank*, 90 and 164, n. 114.

7. This argument is developed in detail in my article "'Anyone Blind or Lame Shall Not Enter the House': On the Interpretation of Second Samuel 5:8b," *Catholic Biblical Quarterly* 60 (1998):218–227. The word *bayit* ("house") is commonly used of temples, and the idiom *ba' 'el* ("enter into") also suggests that the "house" is a temple, given that the idiom itself and others like it (*ba' be-, ba' le-, ba' lipnê, ba'*) are frequently used to describe the entry of priests as well as worshipers and others (e.g., aliens) into the sanctuary sphere (e.g., Exod 28:29, 30, 35; Lev 12:4; 16:17, 23; Isa 56:7; Ezek 44:9, 27; 46:8, 9; Lam 1:10; and probably Deut 23:2–9 [Eng. 1–8]; see also H. D. Preuss, "*bô',*" *TDOT* 2:22–24). The general reference to "anyone blind or lame" suggests the persons of concern are worshipers rather than priests (priests are not named specifically); furthermore, the popular nature of the adage (at least according to its presentation) also suggests a general exclusion, given that the qualifications for priestly service would not be of much concern to the average person. Thus, I cannot accept the argument of A. R. Ceresko that the blind and lame of 2 Sam 5:8b refer to specific individuals (Meribbaal/Mephiboshet and Zedekiah) who may not enter the palace (= be king) ("The Identity of 'the Blind and the Lame' ['iwwer upisseaḥ] in 2 Samuel 5:8b," *Catholic Biblical Quarterly* 63 [2001]:23–30). Although *bayit* can mean "palace" or "dynasty" as easily as "temple," the combination of *bayit* with the verbal idiom *ba' 'el* suggests that *bayit* means "temple" rather than "palace" in this context. (Forms of the verb *ba'* are occasionally used of the physical entry of visitors into a palace complex [e.g., Esther 6:4] or the admission of a person into a royal household [1 Sam 21:16 (Eng. 15)], but I am not aware of an example of a form of the verb *ba'* + a word for palace meaning "to assume kingship" or "to rule.") Furthermore, the general nature of the formulation ("anyone blind or lame" or "a blind or lame person") militates against seeing specific individuals as the referents (compare *'iwwer 'ô pisseaḥ* in Lev 21:18, *peṣûaʿ dakka' ûkerût šopkah* in Deut 23:2 [Eng. 1], or *'arel weṭame'* in Isa 52:1, all surely general in their reference), as does the larger contextual discussion in 2 Sam 5:8a in which the saying is embedded. One might also note that LXX and Vulgate understand "house" in 2 Sam 5:8b as a reference to the temple rather than the palace. J. Schipper elaborates on Ceresko's argument in a recent article ("Reconsidering the Imagery of Disability in 2 Samuel 5:8b," *Catholic Biblical Quarterly* 67 [2005]:422–434). Like Ceresko, he chooses to ignore the philological evidence that suggests the idiom usually refers to temple access, although the philological evidence is more significant for determining the meaning of the adage than any data Ceresko or Schipper marshal to defend their views. S. Vargon has also argued unconvincingly against understanding *bayit* as a reference to the sanctuary: "This explanation, presupposing a prohibition of entry to the

Temple by cripples, is unlikely; indeed, such a prohibition was in fact unknown."
Instead, he asserts, on the basis of 2 Sam 5:9, that "the house" referred to in 5:8b is
the palace ("The Blind and the Lame," *Vetus Testamentum* 46 [1996], 500). Like
Ceresko and Schipper, Vargon ignores the evidence of the common idiomatic use
of the verb *ba'* + preposition + term for sanctuary. Instead, he makes much of
the fact that a general proscription on the entry of blind and lame persons into
the temple is otherwise unattested in extant biblical texts (see similarly Schipper,
ibid., 422, n. 2). However, this says nothing about the meaning of the adage of 2
Sam 5:8b, which appears to reflect a viewpoint regarding the worthiness of the
blind and lame to enter sanctuary space different from that of H (Lev 21:17–23)
and other sources. There are, in fact, more than a few prohibitions attested in
one biblical source or legal collection that have no parallel in other biblical texts
(e.g., the proscriptions of Lev 18:22 and 20:13, which occur only in the "Holiness
Code").

8. Aversion to the exposure of the genitalia is widely evidenced in biblical texts (e.g.,
   Gen 9:23; Exod 20:26; 28:42–43; 2 Sam 10:4–5; Isa 20:4).

9. No vocabulary distinguishing congenital from acquired "defects" is evidenced in
   our texts.

10. This is in contrast to Qumran, where the distinction between a permanent and a
    temporary "defect" is suggested by the presence of the term *mûm 'ôlam* in 1QM
    7:4. It is not clear how long-lasting skin conditions such as *garab* were believed
    to be; other "defects" that can be identified appear to be permanent. Note that
    mutilation of a beard or of hair is never listed among "defects," probably because
    these are reversible over a relatively short period of time.

11. In favor of such an interpretation, one might observe that "blind or lame" stand
    at the head of the list in Lev 21:17–23, perhaps suggesting that they might be used
    alone to stand in for the list as a whole. Other texts concerned with "defective"
    sacrificial animals mention blindness and lameness among emblematic "defects"
    or other disqualifying conditions (e.g., Deut 15:21; Mal 1:8, 13; "Anyone Blind or
    Lame," 225). One might also mention that blindness and lameness are "defects"
    affecting the top (head) and bottom (feet) of the body, and may therefore be
    intended to be inclusive where they stand alone, as David Konstan and William
    Gilders have reminded me (oral communications). Biblical texts often use inclu-
    sive idioms such as "Dan to Beersheba," "bond and free," "native and resident
    alien," and "good and evil" to suggest a totality. Nevertheless, there is simply not
    enough evidence to say with confidence that "blind and lame" of 2 Sam 5:8b is
    a synecdoche or an inclusive idiom, although the possibility ought to be kept
    in mind. As for Deut 23:2 (Eng. 1), such explanations seem less likely, given the
    evidence that the text's specific concern is the inability to procreate, as I shall
    argue.

12. Similarly Milgrom, *Leviticus 17–22*, 1828, who rejects the "visual criterion" on this
    basis, although cf. 1827: ". . . the blemishes are limited to only those that are visi-
    ble or noticeable." E. S. Gerstenberger, *Leviticus: A Commentary* (Louisville, KY:
    Westminster John Knox, 1996), 316, mentions "visible disfigurements" as charac-
    teristic of "defects." Y. Leibowitz and Y. S. Licht argue that all "defects" are visible
    ("mûm, m(')ûm," *EM* 4:726 [Hebrew]). Tracy Lemos (personal communication)

reminds me that evidence of circumcision is also not normally visible, although some texts require circumcision for ritual participation (e.g., Exod 12:48).

13. Although Milgrom seems to suggest that "skin disease" (*ṣara'at*) is included under a larger rubric of skin conditions – both polluting and nonpolluting – referred to in the biblical text as *garab* (ibid., 1828), this seems highly unlikely, given that *garab* is listed as a type of "defect" in Lev 21:20. Because the "defects" of Lev 21:17–23 are not constructed as polluting, *garab* of Lev 21:20 cannot include polluting skin conditions such as *ṣara'at*. It is clear from Num 5:2–3, an H text like Lev 21:17–23, that the presence of "skin disease" (*ṣara'at*) was not only polluting, but grounds for expulsion from the community. Thus, the term *garab*, like the term *yallepet*, can only refer to nonpolluting skin conditions in the "defect" list of Lev 21:17–23.

14. The technical vocabulary of laceration (e.g., *śereṭ*, *śaraṭet*) and tattooing or branding (e.g., *qa'aqa'*) is missing from texts listing "defects." On these activities, see, e.g., Lev 19:28; 21:5; for their relationship to "defects," see further Olyan, *Biblical Mourning: Ritual and Social Dimensions* (Oxford, UK: Oxford University Press, 2004), 118–119.

15. Why the adjective *tamîm* ("whole," "perfect") is not used readily of persons without "defects" is unclear. On this, see the discussion in n. 1.

16. The exception is stated in v. 23: *śarûa' weqalûṭ* may be sacrificed for a free will offering, but cannot be accepted to fulfill a vow. As mentioned, *śarûa'* likely means an extended limb; the meaning of *qalûṭ* remains unclear. The verse suggests that for some reason, these two conditions are less repellent to Yhwh than the others listed.

17. Compare the use of "abomination" elsewhere in Deuteronomy to describe unclean animals (14:3).

18. Exclusive because in contrast to the holy foods, which are eaten by all clean members of a priest's household (e.g., Num 18:11, 13, 19), the most holy foods are restricted to males of the priestly line alone (e.g., Num 18:10).

19. A priest's dependents, including his slave, his unmarried daughter, or his widowed or divorced daughter without progeny who has returned to his house, may eat of the holy foods according to Lev 22:10–13.

20. Although it is by no means the only formal locus, given increasing evidence for domestic cultic rites. On this subject, see, e.g., the essays in *Household and Family Religion in Antiquity: Contextual and Comparative Perspectives* (ed. John Bodel and Saul M. Olyan; Oxford, UK: Blackwell, in press).

21. The identity of the *mamzer* of v. 3 (Eng. 2) is unclear, although it seems from the context of the larger pericope that he is someone with a problematic lineage.

22. Blindness and other disabilities are not uncommon among ancient West Asian treaty curses, self-imprecations, and other curses. See, e.g., Sefire I A 39, which mentions blindness (J. A. Fitzmyer, S. J., *The Aramaic Inscriptions of Sefire* [Rome: Pontifical Biblical Institute, 1967], 14–15, for the Aramaic text and English translation); the first Hittite Soldier's Oath, paragraphs 3 and 10, which mention blindness and deafness (W. Hallo et al., eds., *The Context of Scripture. Volume I: Canonical Compositions from the Biblical World* [Leiden, The Netherlands: Brill, 1997], 165, for an English translation); the Hadad inscription from Zinjirli, where

blindness is present in a self-imprecation (*KAI* 214:29–30; see H. Donner and W. Röllig, eds., *Kanaanäische und Aramäische Inschriften* [3 vols.; 4th ed.; Wiesbaden, Germany: Harrassowitz, 1979], 1:39, for the text in Aramaic; 2:214–223 for a German translation and commentary); and the Aqhat epic from Ugarit, where blindness functions as a curse on a town (*CAT* 1.19 IV 5–6; see M. Dietrich, O. Loretz, and J. Sanmartín, eds., *The Cuneiform Alphabetic Texts from Ugarit, Ras ibn Hanbi and Other Places* [2nd enlarged ed.; Münster, Germany: Ugarit Verlag, 1995], 60, for the text in Ugaritic and S. B. Parker, ed., *Ugaritic Narrative Poetry* [Atlanta: Scholars Press, 1997], 75, for an English translation).

23. Note that Yhwh is said to be the source of disabilities according to texts such as Exod 4:11.

24. Blindness in a text such as Deut 28:28 might function emblematically, given that it is the only "defect" mentioned among the cursed conditions. On the possibility that blindness and lameness together are a synecdoche or an idiom of inclusion standing in for all "defects," see the discussion in n. 11.

25. As has often been noted, it is possible that the Jebusites are suggesting that David is so weak that even persons with physical disabilities can prevent his conquest of Jerusalem.

26. Reading *śenu'ê* with the qere rather than the impossible ketib *śane'û*. Even so, the verse remains difficult, given that *we'et happiśhim we'et ha'iwrîm śenu'ê nepeš dawid* is still not a sentence. On this, see "Anyone Blind or Lame," 219, n. 3.

27. I am unconvinced by J. C. Poirier's speculative suggestion that David's hatred for the lame and the blind "is merely a rhetorical spur" and that "David did not hate the blind and the lame of Jebus any more than he hated the rest of the inhabitants..." ("David's 'Hatred' for the Lame and the Blind [2 Sam. 5.8a]," *Palestine Exploration Quarterly* 138 [2006]:28).

28. The association of blindness with darkness is a biblical commonplace, as texts such as Deut 28:29; Isa 29:18; and 59:9–10 suggest. The association is by no means a given through time and space, however. On this, see the discussion of Kudlick, "Disability History," 790.

29. For the text in Akkadian, see R. Borger, *Die Inschriften Asarhaddons Königs von Assyrien* (Graz, Austria: Weidner, 1956), 82 (par. 53, rev. line 15). For the text in English translation, see C. Walker and M. Dick, *The Induction of the Cultic Image in Ancient Mesopotamia: The Mesopotamian Mīs Pî Ritual* (Helsinki, Finland: Helsinki University Press, 2001), 25.

30. Exod 23:8 refers to the "sighted" (*piqhîm*), while Deut 16:19 substitutes the "wise" (*hakamîm*). On the relationship of the two formulations, see M. Weinfeld, *Deuteronomy and the Deuteronomic School* (Oxford, UK: Clarendon, 1972), 245; and B. Levinson, *Deuteronomy and the Hermeneutics of Legal Innovation* (New York: Oxford University Press, 1997), 139 and n. 103.

31. On the "stranger" (lit. "one I did not know"), see n. 21 in the Introduction.

32. I made this point previously in *Rites and Rank*, 114. It was originally suggested to me in conversation by Victor Hurowitz.

33. The establishment of circumcision as the sign of Yhwh's covenant with Israel is likely a development of the sixth century BCE, as has long been argued by

many scholars, although the normativity of the practice of circumcision in Israel without the covenant connection is expressed by preexilic texts.

34. On forced shaving of beard, head, or other body hair in order to humiliate, see the examples listed in n. 7 in chapter 1.

35. Note that not all "defects" are mutilations because many "defects" are congenital or the result of accidents. In contrast, mutilations, by definition, are intentionally imposed by self or other. The same might be said of maimings. My definition of mutilation is similar in several respects to that of T. M. Lemos, "Shame and Mutilation of Enemies in the Hebrew Bible," *Journal of Biblical Literature* 125 (2006):226.

36. The same act might be mutilating in one cultural context and seen very differently in another. A useful example is the way in which circumcision was viewed by the Greeks and Romans (a repellent barbarism), in contrast to the way in which Israelites and later Jews viewed the rite (as normative and enabling). On the Greek view, see, e.g., R. G. Hall, "Epispasm and the Dating of Ancient Jewish Writings," *Journal for the Study of the Pseudepigrapha* 2 (1988):71–86. Lemos observes that even within the same society, gender differences can shape notions of what is and is not mutilating. Here she compares the regnant attitude in American society toward male circumcision on the one hand, and female genital mutilation on the other ("Shame and Mutilation of Enemies," 226 and n.3).

37. On the intent of the talion formulation in biblical and other West Asian literatures to limit punishment, see, e.g., R. Westbrook, *Studies in Biblical and Cuneiform Law* (Paris: Gabalda, 1988), 41–42, 46, 73–74. That the talion principle is not always applied literally is demonstrated by Exod 21:22–25, 26, 27 and Hammurapi par. 198–199, among other texts.

38. M. T. Roth, *Law Collections from Mesopotamia and Asia Minor* (Atlanta: Scholars, 1995), 121 for text in Akkadian and the translation that I have quoted. See also par. 197 and 200.

39. Roth, ibid., 120, for text and translation.

40. The story may in fact be longer than what survives in the MT. 4QSam[a] bears witness to a detailed description of Nahash's similar abuse of the Gadites and Reubenites and the escape of 7,000 to Jabesh-Gilead preceding the confrontation at Jabesh. P. K. McCarter, Jr., has argued for the originality of the passage (*1 Samuel* [Garden City, NY: Doubleday, 1980], 198, 199n), and is followed by Lemos ("Shame and Mutilation of Enemies," 229 and n. 11).

41. That Ammon and Israel shared a parity treaty according to the text is suggested by the accusation leveled by the Ammonite courtiers: David's seemingly appropriate acts toward a treaty partner cloak his true motive, which is conquest (10:3).

42. For Esarhaddon's succession treaty, see S. Parpola and K. Watanabe, *Neo-Assyrian Treaties and Loyalty Oaths* (Helsinki, Finland: Helsinki University Press, 1988), 57, who provide the text in Akkadian and an English translation (lines 626–631). For Sefire I A 39–40, see Fitzmyer, *Aramaic Inscriptions of Sefîre*, 14–15, who provides the text in Aramaic and an English translation.

43. E. N. von Voigtlander, *The Bisitun Inscription of Darius the Great, Babylonian Version* (London: Lund Humphries, 1978), 28, for the text in Akkadian; 57–58, for the English translation that I have quoted.

44. M. Streck, ed., *Assurbanipal und die letzten assyrischen Könige bis zum Untergange Nineveh's* (3 vols; Leipzig, Germany: J. C. Hinrich, 1916), 2:38, for the text in Akkadian. See also 42, 127, for other examples of similar mutilations (e.g., of the lips). See D. D. Luckenbill, *Ancient Records of Assyria and Babylonia* (Chicago: University of Chicago Press, 1927), 2:303–304, 306, 335, for an English translation of these passages.

45. Streck, ibid., 2:62, 14. For an English translation, see Luckenbill, ibid., 312, 294–295.

46. The form of execution remains uncertain, due to the obscure meaning of the root *yq'*, although many translators opt for impalement or some other type of hanging of the corpse in public view. See further P. K. McCarter, Jr., *II Samuel* (Garden City, NY: Doubleday, 1984), 442, who discusses the various suggestions.

47. A central point of S. Knippschild, "Spoils and Iconoclasm: The Ancient Near Eastern Tradition and Athens" (unpublished paper, 2005), 11.

48. See the discussion of C. Nylander, "Earless in Nineveh: Who Mutilated 'Sargon's' Head?" *American Journal of Archaeology* 84 [1980]:329–333, who makes this argument, which I find cogent, on 330. See also the discussion of Knippschild, ibid., 16–17, who cites Nylander's paper.

49. Streck, *Assurbanipal*, 214. For an English translation, Luckenbill, *Ancient Records*, 363. For discussion, see Knippschild, ibid., 9–10.

50. Nylander, "Earless in Nineveh," 331, and especially Knippschild, ibid., 13–16, for discussion.

51. On the Ark Narrative, of which the Dagon incident is a central part, see the discussion of McCarter, *I Samuel*, 23–26, with citations, and recently N. B. Levtow, "Images of Others: Icon Parodies and Iconic Politics in Ancient Israel" (Ph.D. dissertation, Brown University, Providence, RI, 2006), 161–177. A revised version of this work is to be published in the series Biblical and Judaic Studies from the University of California, San Diego (Eisenbrauns). The narrative is clearly an apology intended for an Israelite audience. Like other examples of literature produced by those on the losing side in a war, it justifies the loss of the divine icon (in this case, the Ark), while reasserting the agency and power of the losing side's god.

52. For the hand or arm as a symbolic locus of agency and power, see expressions such as "the hand of Yhwh was heavy upon the Ashdodites" (1 Sam 5:6) or "Edom rebelled from under the hand of Judah" (2 Kgs 8:20, 22). Sometimes, it is specifically the right hand that is mentioned (e.g., Exod 15:6, 12; Isa 41:10; Ps 20:7 [Eng. 6]; 21:9 [Eng. 8]; 77:11 [Eng. 10]; 78:54; 98:1).

53. I treat the Gibeonite episode as an internal, Israelite matter, given the way the text presents the Gibeonites as a Yhwh-worshiping minority in the land.

54. This has been emphasized in some recent scholarship. On this, see Knippschild, "Spoils and Iconoclasm," 11, and especially Lemos, "Shame and Mutilation of Enemies."

55. On the honor/shame dimensions of this text, see further, Olyan, "Honor, Shame, and Covenant Relations in Ancient Israel and its Environment," *Journal of Biblical Literature* 115 (1996):212–213. Lemos and others have suggested a gendered dimension to the shaming of David's embassy through beard mutilation. By damaging

the beard, a mark of masculinity, the Ammonites feminize David's emissaries and by extension, David himself ("Shame and Mutilation," 233).

56. Streck, *Assurbanipal*, 2:80, for the text in Akkadian; Luckenbill, *Ancient Records*, 319, for an English translation. On the low status accorded to the dog, see, e.g., the references in *CAD* 8:52. Lemos argues perceptively that the story of Adonibezek in Judg 1:4–7 also involves shaming of enemies through mutilation that results in their dehumanization ("Shame and the Mutilation of Enemies," 236–239). One might also note the parallel with Ashurbanipal's treatment of Uaite (physical mutilation + imposition of dog-like behavior).

57. Lemos has suggested that mutilations shame others in the same community by pointing to their weakness ("Shame and the Mutilation of Enemies," 230).

58. R. Campbell Thompson, *The Prisms of Esarhaddon and Ashurbanipal Found at Nineveh, 1927–8* (London: British Museum, 1931), 18, for the text in Akkadian. Luckenbill, *Ancient Records*, 212, for the translation. See similarly Streck, *Assurbanipal*, 2:127, and Luckenbill, ibid., 335, with regard to the severed head of Teumman of Elam: "The severed head of Teumman I displayed conspicuously in front of the gate inside Nineveh, that the severed head of Teumman, king of Elam, might show the people the might of Assur and Ishtar, my lords."

59. Streck, ibid., 2:62, for the text in Akkadian (*eli ša maḫri mitussu utter*). My translation. Luckenbill, ibid., 312, is less literal: "I made him more dead than he was before."

60. Streck, ibid., 2:54–56. Luckenbill, ibid., 310.

3. PHYSICAL DISABILITIES NOT CLASSIFIED AS "DEFECTS"

1. On the translation "sentient" for *piqqeaḥ*, see n. 32 in the Introduction.

2. It seems likely that Israel is the servant mentioned in this passage, as it is in several other passages in Second Isaiah (e.g., 41:8–9; 44:1–2, 21). On the interpretation of the larger pericope Isa 42:18–25, see J. Blenkinsopp, *Isaiah 40–55* (New York: Doubleday, 2000), 217–219.

3. Reading privative *min* with J. Blenkinsopp, *Isaiah 1–39* (New York: Doubleday, 2000), 406. On privative *min*, see R. J. Williams, *Hebrew Syntax: An Outline* (2nd ed.; Toronto, Ontario, Canada: University of Toronto Press, 1976), 56, par. 321.

4. Cuneiform texts also bear witness to an association of deaf and mute persons with the blind, the lame, and others with physical disabilities. An example of this is a curse from a *kudurru* (boundary) inscription directed at a violator: "May they (the gods) decree for him for all time a fate of not seeing, stopping up of the ears, and seizure of the mouth" (text and translation from *CAD* 15:68).

5. The adjectives blind (*'iwwer*), lame (*pisseaḥ*), deaf (*ḥereš*), mute (*'illem*), bald (*qereaḥ, gibbeaḥ*), hunchbacked (*gibben*), and feeble eyed (*keheh*) all share in common the same Hebrew morphological pattern. Although the blind, the feeble eyed, the lame, and the hunchbacked belong to the "defect" class, the deaf, the mute, and the bald do not. The adjective *'iṭṭer*, which also displays this form, occurs only in the fixed expression *'iṭṭer yad yemînô*, literally "bound with regard to his right hand," an idiom for left handed (Judg 3:15; 20:16). A common term of moral disapprobation, *'iqqeš*, "twisted," "perverted," shares the same

morphological pattern. I suspect that its moral usage is a secondary development from an original somatic usage. Interestingly, the term *piqqeaḥ*, "sentient," used as an antonym for both blind and deaf (e.g., Exod 4:11), also takes this form, as do *ṣiḥeh*, "parched," and *ge'eh*, "arrogant." H. Bauer and P. Leander explain the pattern as used mainly to designate physical flaws and conspicuous things (Auffälligkeiten) (*Historische Grammatik der hebräischen Sprache des Alten Testaments* [Hildesheim, Germany: Georg Olms, 1965], 477). J. Schipper anticipates me to some extent when he points out that the existence of this morphological pattern indicates that "disability was a meaningful conceptual category in the ancient world" (*Disability Studies and the Hebrew Bible: Figuring Mephibosheth in the David Story* [New York: T. & T. Clark, 2006], 67). However, the "meaningful conceptual category" is not disability, as Schipper believes, but more specifically, somatic dysfunction. In other words, the implicit native classification suggested by the morphological pattern is less broad than Schipper suggests. Schipper's detailed treatment of the morphological pattern is worth consulting, although I do not agree with a number of his specific interpretations (e.g., regarding *'iqqeš* or *qereaḥ/gibbeaḥ*; ibid., 65–69).

6. On the prophet as watchman, see Jer 6:17; Ezek 3:17; 33:7; and Hos 9:8.

7. On the infinitive absolute following the imperative expressing continuance of action in this context, see GKC, par. 113r.

8. On this text, see the bibliography in Chapter 2, n. 29. Akkadian *sukkuku* means not only "deaf," but "ignorant" as well (*CAD* 15:363, for examples of this usage). Note also the common association of the deaf with the blind, the mentally disabled (*saklu*), and others lacking understanding and knowledge in Babylonian *kudurru* (boundary) inscriptions (e.g., L. W. King, ed., *Babylonian Boundary-Stones and Memorial-Tablets in the British Museum* [London: British Museum, 1912], iii 5 41–42; iv 3 6; v 3 10–12; vi 2 34; vii 2 9; xi 2 18–19, for Akkadian text and English translation).

9. "Idol" polemics such as Isa 40:18–20 focus on other supposedly stigmatizing qualities of iconic images, such as the fact that they are made of wood and overlaid with precious metals by craftsmen. Nothing is said of the disabilities of the "idols" in this particular text.

10. For "idols" as "false" (*šeqer*), see Isa 44:20; for Yhwh as a "true," "living" god, in contrast to "idols," see Jer 10:10.

11. The MT has 3ms verb and pronoun in the second colon of v. 14. I have adjusted these for ease of translation into English.

12. On the Psalms of individual complaint, see, e.g., E. S. Gerstenberger, *Psalms, Part 1: With an Introduction to Cultic Poetry* (Grand Rapids, MI: Eerdmans, 1988), 11–14; and *Psalms, Part 2, and Lamentations* (Grand Rapids, MI: Eerdmans, 2001), xvii–xxii, for an updated bibliography.

13. The Hebrew *kol benê ḥalôp*, which I have rendered "all who are transitory," means literally something like "all who are passing on" (cf. NKB 1:321, "those who fade away [?]"). The precise referent remains unclear.

14. That the idiom *tidbaq lešônî leḥikkî* refers to muteness is made clear in Ezek 3:26.

15. For the right hand or arm as a symbol of agency and power, see Exod 15:6, 12; Isa 41:10; Ps 20:7 (Eng. 6); 21:9 (Eng. 8); 77:11 (Eng. 10); 78:54; 98:1.

16. Translation of B. J. Collins in *The Context of Scripture. Volume I: Canonical Compositions from the Biblical World* (ed. W. W. Hallo et al.; Leiden, The Netherlands: Brill, 1997), 165.

17. R. Borger, "Vier Grenzsteinurkunden Merodachbaladans I. von Babylonien," *Archiv für Orientforschung* 23 (1970):14, 20, for the Akkadian text and German translation.

18. As I argue, it is possible that the adage in 2 Sam 5:8b prohibits the blind and the lame from entering the sanctuary on account of their pollution, although this is far from clear. Pollution is certainly not associated with persons with "defects" in Lev 21:17–23 and Deut 23:2 (Eng. 1), and is never ascribed to the deaf or the mute.

19. Genital "flows" are, however, less severely treated by P in Lev 15:1–15, 25–30. Although a man or woman with such a "flow" is capable of transmitting pollution to other persons and inanimate objects that he or she has come into contact with, he or she is not expelled from the community as in Num 5:2–3.

20. Interestingly, Leviticus 13 says nothing directly about the communicability of "skin disease."

21. Other biblical texts assume the expulsion of the person with "skin disease" from the community, but may bear witness to some kind of communal living arrangement for such persons (2 Kgs 7:3; 2 Chr 26:21). Cuneiform texts also suggest removal of persons afflicted with comparable polluting skin conditions (e.g., S. Parpola and K. Watanabe, *Neo-Assyrian Treaties and Loyalty Oaths* [Helsinki, Finland: Helsinki University Press, 1988], 11 [reverse iv lines 4–6]; 45 [lines 419–421]; King, *Babylonian Boundary-Stones*, xi 3 2–5). Some cuneiform evidence suggests communal arrangements for the afflicted. On this, see K. van der Toorn, *Sin and Sanction in Israel and Mesopotamia: A Comparative Study* (Assen, The Netherlands: van Gorcum, 1985), 73, 74, and 196, n. 248.

22. The "male who grasps a spindle" (*maḫazîq bappelek*) is likely a gender nonconformist. The presence of gender nonconformity in curses is not uncommon, as the first Hittite Soldiers' Oath (par. 10) and Esarhaddon's Succession Treaty (par. 91) show. For an English translation of the first Hittite Soldiers' Oath, see Hallo, ed., *Context of Scripture I*, 166; for the Akkadian text and an English translation of Esarhaddon's Succession Treaty, see Parpola and Watanabe, ibid., 56 (lines 616A–617). On the theme of gender nonconformity, see the classic article of H. Hoffner, "Symbols for Masculinity and Femininity: Their Use in Ancient Near Eastern Sympathetic Magic Rituals," *Journal of Biblical Literature* 85 (1966):326–334. Alternatively, the expression *maḫazîq bappelek* has been understood to refer not to a gender nonconformist, but to one who "clings to a crutch." See the comments of P. K. McCarter, Jr., *II Samuel* (Garden City, NY: Doubleday, 1984), 118, who compares Phoenician *plkm* in the Karatepe inscription (*KAI* 26 A ii.6). The evidence supporting the former view (e.g., Prov 31:19 and various West Asian oaths and imprecations) is, however, stronger, although McCarter's understanding of *pelek* in 2 Sam 3:29 would provide us with a text constructing lameness as a curse, and tying the lame to persons with "skin disease" and genital "flows."

23. *Saḫaršubbu* is traditionally rendered "leprosy" in translation, as is biblical "skin disease" (*ṣaraʿat*). Like "skin disease," *saḫaršubbu* is constructed as both highly

polluting and socially isolating for those afflicted with it (e.g., Parpola and Watanabe, ibid., 11 [reverse iv lines 4–6] and 45 [lines 419–421]). For the text of the treaty in Akkadian with an English translation, see Parpola and Watanabe, ibid., 11 (reverse iv lines 4–5) and 13 (reverse vi line 2). On *saḫaršubbu*, see *CAD* 15:36–37 and the discussion of K. van der Toorn, *Sin and Sanction*, 29–30, 73–75, who compares *saḫaršubbu* and biblical "skin disease."

24. For the text of the treaty in Akkadian with English translation, see Parpola and Watanabe, ibid., 45 (lines 419–421 and 422–424).

25. Ibid., 72 (reverse line 11). *Kudurru* (boundary) inscriptions also bear witness to skin diseases among listed curses (e.g., King, *Babylonian Boundary - Stones*, viii 4 7–9; ix 1 46–48; xi 3 2–5, for the Akkadian text and an English translation).

26. See also the exhortation to treat "skin disease" with the utmost seriousness and the reference to Miriam's punishment by Yhwh in Deut 24:8–9. The implication of the text is that lax handling of an outbreak of "skin disease" will result in Yhwh using the disease itself as a way to punish those who are responsible.

27. 2 Chr 26:21 suggests that Uzziah withdrew from quotidian rule and was consigned to a special dwelling locus (*bêt haḥopšît*), presumably in an isolated place outside the community (see Lev 13:46).

28. 2 Kgs 15:4 does, however, suggest that Azariah (Uzziah), although an upright king, was not free of all transgression: "Only the high places were not removed; still the people were sacrificing and burning incense on the high places." The Chronicler must have found this insufficient to justify Yhwh's striking of Uzziah with "skin disease."

29. On *saḫaršubbu* as a divine penalty for sin in cuneiform texts, see the discussion of van der Toorn, *Sin and Sanction*, 72–75. Not surprisingly, omen texts understand the presence of such a disease at birth as an indicator of future troubles: "If a woman gives birth, and at birth (the child) is already covered with leprosy – the owner of the house will die; that house will be scattered" (E. Leichty, *The Omen Series Šumma Izbu* [Locust Valley, NY: J. J. Augustin, 1970], 66 [iv 4], translation from Leichty). The Akkadian idiom is *epqam malûm*.

30. The mention of a required reparation offering (*'ašam*) in Lev 14:12 and passim may well suggest that in P's view, all who have been afflicted with "skin disease" are transgressors who have been punished by Yhwh. For this viewpoint, see, e.g., J. Milgrom, *Leviticus 1–16* (New York: Doubleday, 1991), 822, and S. J. Melcher, "Visualizing the Perfect Cult: The Priestly Rationale for Exclusion," in *Human Disability and the Service of God: Reassessing Religious Practice* (ed. N. L. Eiesland and D. E. Saliers; Nashville, TN: Abingdon Press, 1998), 58, 65.

31. See, e.g., Milgrom, *Leviticus 1–16*, 763–4, 951, and H. Marsman, *Women in Ugarit and Israel* (Leiden, The Netherlands: Brill, 2003), 200–202, for citations and discussion. Neither Lev 12:1–8; 15:19–24; nor Num 5:2–3 explicitly require the removal of the menstruant or parturient from the community or their isolation within the domicile, in contrast to the person with "skin disease," who is to be removed from the community according to both P and H texts (e.g., Lev 13:46; Num 5:2–3), and the person with a genital "flow," whose expulsion is required by H (Num 5:2–3). Clearly, the pollution P ascribes to the parturient and menstruant in Lev 12:1–8 and 15:19–24 is less severe than that attributed to the person afflicted with

"skin disease" (Lev 13:45–46). P texts are, however, not clear about the locus of the menstruant and the parturient during their time of impurity.

32. For this understanding of Lam 1:17, see the comments of A. Berlin, *Lamentations* (Louisville, KY: Westminster John Knox, 2002), 58.

33. I make this point in *Rites and Rank: Hierarchy in Biblical Representations of Cult* (Princeton, NJ: Princeton University Press, 2000), 58.

34. Note that although severe pollution is ascribed to these persons, texts distinguish degrees of impurity and their consequences. On this, see n. 31.

4. MENTAL DISABILITY

1. For contemporary American debates regarding the definition of mental retardation as well as the criteria to be considered when defining it, see, e.g., W. L. Heward, *Exceptional Children: An Introduction to Special Education* (6th ed.; Upper Saddle River, NJ: Merrill, 2000), 202–217.

2. 2 Sam 9:13 suggests that such partial dysfunction of the legs could constitute lameness for the circles responsible for that text. The verse makes a point of noting that Meribbaal (Mephiboshet), son of Jonathan, "was lame in both of his legs," as opposed to only one. This example is noted by Avalos with similar intent (*Illness and Health Care in the Ancient Near East: The Role of the Temple in Greece, Mesopotamia, and Israel* [Atlanta: Scholars Press, 1995], 319).

3. M. V. Fox provides a useful survey of the technical vocabulary of "foolishness" and the "fool" in Proverbs, with reference to usages in other wisdom texts (*Proverbs 1–9* [New York: Doubleday, 2000], 38–43). A detailed survey of the technical vocabulary of "foolishness" in biblical wisdom generally is to be found in N. Shupak, *Where Can Wisdom Be Found? The Sage's Language in the Bible and in Ancient Egyptian Literature* (Göttingen: Vandenhoeck & Ruprecht, 1993), 199–216, including comparison with Egyptian terminology. See also the older study of T. Donald, "The Semantic Field of 'Folly' in Proverbs, Job, Psalms, and Ecclesiastes," *Vetus Testamentum* 13 (1963):285–92.

4. Fox's characterization of foolishness is apt: "The essence of folly is a lack of good judgment, with consequent distortions in moral and practical choices" (*Proverbs 1–9*, 38).

5. On the wisdom tradition in Israel and its environment, see the survey in Fox, *Proverbs 1–9*, 17–27, which includes reference to non-Israelite sources. C. L. Seow also provides a useful introduction that includes a consideration of the relationship of Ecclesiastes to other works of Israelite wisdom (*Ecclesiastes* [New York: Doubleday, 1997], 60–69).

6. Fox believes that Proverbs always holds the "simple" (*petî*) responsible for their actions, while they are "never culpable" according to other sources (*Proverbs 1–9*, 43; see also Donald, "Semantic Field," 288). He notes various texts (including Proverbs) that suggest that the "simple" are capable of learning (e.g., Pss 19:8 [Eng. 7]; 119:130; Prov 8:5; 9:6). Shupak characterizes the *petî* as an "innocent and inexperienced youth" or, alternatively, as "a foolish man whose folly stems from lack of knowledge and experience," clearly not someone, in her view, with mental retardation (*Where Can Wisdom Be Found?*, 201, 250). Seow seems more ambivalent. On the one hand, he states that the "fool" (*sakal*) "is thought to be

mentally deficient . . . a half-wit, who is not expected to succeed in society," citing Eccl 10:3, 15. On the other, he speaks of "fools" as "unsophisticated, uncultured simpletons . . . [who] are not expected to rise to the top of society" (*Ecclesiastes*, 314).

7. The terms are ambiguous because the texts in which they occur generally do not tell us in any direct way about the specific mental disabilities the terms describe. Only a close examination of the texts using the vocabulary of "madness" will allow us to begin to speak with any precision about the range of meaning to be ascribed to these terms.

8. Achish's question, "Should this one enter my household?", suggests to me that the narrative assumes that David went to Gath intending to serve the Philistine king.

9. Reading *wayšanneh 'et-ṭa'mô* for MT *wayšannô 'et-ṭa'mô*. The idiom is *šinnah ṭa'am*, literally "to change (the) judgment" or "discernment," used of mental disability, as the similar use of its Akkadian cognate in cuneiform texts makes clear. McCarter translates "he disguised his judgment," which also works well in the context, given that David is feigning mental disability (*I Samuel* [Garden City, NY: Doubleday, 1980], 354). Cf. Ps 34:1.

10. Hebrew *wayyitholel*. The Hitpael can suggest feigning or acting a role, as in 2 Sam 13:5; Prov 13:7; and possibly Esther 8:17 (WO par. 26.2f). It is not at all clear to what range of mental conditions the verb refers. I have rendered it "feigning 'madness,'" on the understanding that "madness" is an imprecise term of very limited utility, and a pejorative one at that. However, given the imprecise and pejorative ways the verb is used in the text, "madness" is not an inappropriate translation.

11. Hebrew *beyadam*, perhaps as in 2 Sam 18:2.

12. MT reads *waytaw*, "and he made marks," while LXX *kai etumpanizen*, "and he drummed," reflects a Vorlage with **wytp*. McCarter chooses to read **wytp* but derives it not from the relatively common biblical Hebrew root *tpp*, "to drum," but from another *tpp* meaning "to spit," as in Talmudic Aramaic (*I Samuel*, 355 n). The reasons for my preferring "to drum" rather than "to make marks" or "spit" will become clear in my discussion of this passage.

13. Other uses of the idiom include "to change one's mind," "mood," or "loyalty." When used to refer to mental disability, the idiom is translated by *CAD* "to become deranged, insane" (*CAD* 17:405–406, with examples of the various usages). D *šunnû* + *ṭema* can mean "to drive someone insane" or "put confusion into someone's mind" (*CAD* 17:407–408).

14. Translation from A. Heidel, *The Babylonian Genesis: The Story of Creation* (Chicago: University of Chicago Press, 1951), 40. For the text in Akkadian, see P. Talon, *The Standard Babylonian Creation Myth Enuma Eliš* (Helsinki, Finland: University of Helsinki, 2005), 54.

15. W. G. Lambert and A. R. Millard, *Atra-Hasis: The Babylonian Story of the Flood* (Winona Lake, IN: Eisenbrauns, 1999), 94, for the text in Akkadian with an English translation.

16. M. Streck, ed., *Assurbanipal und die letzten assyrischen Könige bis zum Untergang Nineveh's* (3 vols.; Leipzig, Germany: J. C. Hinrich, 1916), 2:124–125, for the text in Akkadian with German translation.

17. As in Maqlu 3:148, 5:128, and other examples listed in *CAD* 17:407–408.

18. See n. 10 for comment and citations.

19. The range of behaviors associated with this verb is not entirely clear. Each context in which it occurs must be examined carefully in any attempt to establish a possible meaning for it.

20. I am indebted to Frederik Schockaert for this information regarding strokes, drooling, and mental retardation and its functional equivalents.

21. In other words, it is not clear that one reading gave rise to the other, as is often the case in such situations.

22. I am again indebted to Frederik Schockaert for providing information on drumming as a characteristic behavior of some persons with mental disability.

23. H. Cazelles notes that the root refers to irrational behavior and is mainly pejorative in its uses ("*hll* III," *TDOT* 3:411).

24. On prophetic ecstasy, see, e.g., R. R. Wilson, *Prophecy and Society in Ancient Israel* (Philadelphia: Fortress, 1980), 6–8, 13, 33–34, 141.

25. See the apt comments of M. Cogan and H. Tadmor: "Heb. *mešugga'* describes wild, uncontrolled behavior . . . It is used disparagingly to refer to the ecstatic, dervishlike behavior in some prophetic circles" (*II Kings* [New York: Doubleday, 1988], 108). See similarly P. Mommer, with respect to 1 Sam 21:11–16 (Eng. 10–15); 2 Kgs 9:20; Deut 28:28: ". . . *šg'* refers to the condition of being 'beside oneself,' to the incapacity to control one's actions. . . . In these passages, *šg'* describes extraordinary, negatively qualified behavior, and those so described are treated contemptuously by those around them" ("*šg'*," *TDOT* 14:406).

26. This is indicated by the verb "to love," used here with political nuance, as others have noted (e.g., McCarter, *I Samuel*, 281–282).

27. McCarter mentions symptoms of paranoia and manic-depressive illness (*I Samuel*, 280–281). Avalos is reluctant to identify a specific malady, although he notes that aspects of Saul's portrait in 1 Samuel 16 (e.g., impaired ability to function in his normal role, radical changes in behavior) suggest mental illness of some kind (*Illness and Health Care*, 278–280).

28. The idiom is *werawaḥ leša'ûl*. See also Job 32:20. The Pual participle *meruwwaḥîm*, "wide, spacious," should also be noted in this regard (Jer 22:14), as well as derived nouns *rewaḥ*, "space" (physical) (Gen 32:17 [Eng. 16]) or "relief" (Est 4:14), and *rewaḥah*, "relief, respite" (Exod 8:11 [Eng. 15]; Lam 3:56).

29. The precise meaning of the expression *timhôn lebab*, translated "bewilderment," is difficult to pinpoint, although a general sense incapacitation is defensible given the range of usages attested for verbal forms from the same root (*tmh*). These suggest the loss of the ability to act decisively on account of fear or shock, as in Jer 4:9 and Ps 48:6 (Eng. 5). In Isa 13:8, the verb's meaning seems to be specifically "to stare" (in horror and incapacitation) in the context of disaster. Is "bewilderment" (*timhôn lebab*) a technical term for a type of mental disability understood to be distinct from "madness" (*šigga'ôn*)? Whatever it refers to, it is a serious enough condition to constitute a curse in and of itself, alongside "madness" and blindness.

30. The relationship of texts such as 1 Sam 13:14; 15:26, 35; and 16:1 to 16:14–23 is debated, although 16:14 states clearly that Yhwh's spirit abandoned Saul, and therefore seems to presuppose Saul has transgressed and been rejected by Yhwh.

(16:1 claims the latter directly.) Many scholars understand 1 Sam 16:14–2 Sam 5:10 as a single, apologetic work, the "History of David's Rise" (HDR), intended to justify David's accession to the throne. Some would include 1 Sam 16:1–13 and even 1 Samuel 15 in it. On this, see further the discussion of McCarter, *I Samuel*, 27–30.

31. For example, David is not referred to as "dishonored" (*niqleh*) or "despised" (*bazûy, nibzeh*) in the passage, common examples of the rhetoric of dishonor.

32. On the vocabulary and dynamics of honoring and shaming in biblical and cognate sources, see S. M. Olyan, "Honor, Shame and Covenant Relations in Ancient Israel and Its Environment," *Journal of Biblical Literature* 115 (1996):201–218.

33. "You know the man and his talk." The word I have translated "talk" is *śiaḥ*. It is not often used pejoratively, although it probably is so used in 2 Kgs 9:11, as the context and some of the versions (e.g., Peshiṭta) suggest. On the uses of this noun and related verbal forms, see further J. Hausmann, "*śyḥ*," *TDOT* 14:85–89.

34. The translation and cuneiform text in transliteration may be found in E. Leichty, *The Omen Series Šumma Izbu* (Locust Valley, NY: J. J. Augustin, 1970), 36 (i 52). The word Leichty translates "male idiot" is LÚ.LIL (*lillu*). On its usages, see *CAD* 9:189–190.

35. The translation and the cuneiform text in transliteration may be found in ibid., 70 (iv 49). The word Leichty translates "boy moron" is LÚ.LIL.LA (*lillu*).

36. On these, see L. W. King, ed., *Babylonian Boundary-Stones and Memorial-Tablets in the British Museum* (London: British Museum, 1912), iii 5 41–42; iv 3 6; v 3 10–12; vi 2 34; vii 2 9; xi 2 18–19, for Akkadian text and English translation.

37. For the Akkadian text and an English translation, see W. G. Lambert, *Babylonian Wisdom Literature* (Oxford, UK: Clarendon Press, 1960), 76–77. The word used for the person with mental disability is *lillu*, as in the omen texts. The word used for the person with physical disability is *kuṣṣudu*. The word *ḫarḫaru* is translated "bum" by von Soden (*AHw*1:325), although I have rendered it "the economically unproductive person."

38. It may be that Deut 28:29 is suggesting poverty when it claims that those who violate the covenant, who are struck with blindness, "madness," and bewilderment, will not make their ways prosper (*welo' taṣlîaḥ 'et-derakêka*). The idioms "to make the way(s) prosper" or "to prosper" are typically used in a general sense of personal advancement, or with respect to success in a particular endeavor (e.g., Gen 24:56; 39:2–3, 23; Jos 1:8; 1 Kgs 22:12, 15; Ps 1:3). Obviously, personal advancement in a general sense could include the acquisition of wealth.

5. DISABILITY IN THE PROPHETIC UTOPIAN VISION

1. What I am calling the prophetic utopian vision is not a form critical category per se, but groups several, related genres under a single rubric. Among form critics, the texts I discuss are typically associated with genres such as the prophetic announcement of salvation (e.g., Isa 29:17–21), the prophetic oracle of salvation (e.g., Isa 35:4–10), or the announcement of a royal savior (e.g., Isa 11:1–9; 33:17–24). On these genres, see, e.g., the discussion of M. A. Sweeney, *Isaiah 1–39 with an Introduction to the Prophetic Literature* (Grand Rapids, MI: Eerdmans, 1996), 514,

526, 531; C. Westermann, *Prophetische Heilswort im Alten Testament* (Göttingen, Germany: Vandenhoeck & Ruprecht, 1987), and idem., "Oracles of Salvation," in *'The Place Is Too Small For Us': The Israelite Prophets in Recent Scholarship* (ed. R. P. Gordon; Winona Lake, IN: Eisenbrauns, 1995), 98–104. Given that my interests are not form critical, and that all of the texts I discuss share a future orientation and utopian characteristics, for simplicity's sake, I refer to the passages under consideration as examples of the prophetic utopian vision.

2. The same passage occurs, with minor variations and an addition, in Mic 4:1–4. On this and on matters of date and provenance, see the discussion of J. Blenkinsopp, *Isaiah 1–39* (New York: Doubleday, 2000), 190–191. It is unlikely that the text is a product of Isaiah of Jerusalem.

3. On debate over the authorship and date of this text, see Blenkinsopp's summary in ibid., 263–264.

4. Another text of this type is Isa 42:10–17, esp. v. 16, where Yhwh promises to lead the blind "on a way they do not know," turning darkness into light before them and making rough ground flat. Presumably, the text is alluding to a return of the exiles to Judah, a central theme in the work of Second Isaiah.

5. On this, see recently, B. Becking, *Between Fear and Freedom: Essays on the Interpretation of Jeremiah 30–31* (Leiden, The Netherlands: Brill, 2004).

6. On the syntax, see R. J. Williams, *Hebrew Syntax: An Outline* (2nd ed.; Toronto, Ontario, Canada: University of Toronto Press, 1976), 39, par. 214, and WO, par. 37.6f, both comparing Gen 6:17, among other texts.

7. Reconstructing **'az hilleq 'iwwer šalal marbeh* in parallel with *pishîm bazezû baz* for MT's corrupt *'az hullaq 'ad šalal marbeh*. Both Tg. and the presence of *pishîm* in the parallel colon support reconstructing *'iwwer* as the subject, and the common graphic confusion of *dalet* and *resh* at various points in the development of Hebrew scripts suggests the possibility that *'ad* (*'d*) is a corruption of **'iwwer* (*'wr*).

8. See, e.g., Judg 5:28–30, which speaks of women awaiting the return of victorious males who have plundered the enemy.

9. Compare the Kirta epic from Ugarit, where even the blind, the nonambulatory male (*zbl*), the newly wed groom, and the only male of a household – those who normally do not go out to war – participate in Kirta's war to secure a bride (*CAT* 1.14 IV 21–28). Are the blind and nonambulatory males of Kirta transformed in some way, allowing them to serve? Or do they come along as they are, making the best of it? The point of the text seems clear: that their exemption from military service, along with that of others who do not normally serve, is suspended in this particular instance. As for the physical status of the disabled who serve, the text remains opaque. The colon mentioning the blind (*'wr mzl ymzl*) is difficult to translate because the verb's meaning is not entirely clear. The verbal root *mzl* may reflect a metathesis of *m* and *z*; J. Tropper relates it to Arabic *zml*, "to limp (behind)," translating "Der Blinde hinkte fürwahr hinterher" (*Ugaritische Grammatik* [Münster, Germany: Ugarit-Verlag, 2000], 165). If this is correct, the blind are apparently making the best of it, their condition unchanged. The colon mentioning the nonambulatory male (*zbl 'ršm yš'u*, with the noun *zbl* evidently related to Akkadian *zabalu*, "to carry" or "bear") is also somewhat of a challenge to translate. Does this person carry his bed, as some suggest (e.g., C. H. Gordon,

Ugaritic Textbook [revised reprint; Rome: Pontifical Biblical Institute, 1998], 461–462), or is he carried in it (E. L. Greenstein in *Ugaritic Narrative Poetry* [ed. S. B. Parker; Atlanta: Scholars, 1997], 15)? The G verbal form *yš'u* probably suggests that the man carries his own bed, but if he has become ambulatory, why bring the bed along at all?

10. My thanks to Frederik Schockaert for reminding me that the blind and the lame who plunder are functioning as providers for their families. On booty and its distribution among the victors in war, see, e.g., Num 31:27; Deut 20:14; Judg 5:30; and 1 Sam 30:21–25.

11. B. Sommer, *A Prophet Reads Scripture: Allusion in Isaiah 40–66* (Stanford, CA: Stanford University Press, 1998), 162–163, and n. 23, 283–284, develops this idea in some detail as he explores the dynamics of exegesis in the work of Second Isaiah.

12. The text has apparently been disturbed at this juncture.

13. The lover is described as beautiful in a number of different ways throughout the Song (e.g., 1:16; 5:10).

14. "Defects" of sacrificial animals are described as "ugly" or "disfiguring" (*ra'*) in Deut 15:21 and 17:1. As I argue in chapter 1, the same association was very likely the case for human "defects" as well.

15. On the reading of privative *min* here, see n. 3 in chapter 3.

16. Blenkinsopp believes that the deaf and blind of this passage are only metaphorically disabled, in contrast to the disabled persons of Isa 35:5–7, who are literally so, but presents no cogent evidence to support this reading. The Isaianic passages he adduces as parallels (e.g., 29:9–10; 30:9) clearly discuss persons with the ability to see and hear who choose not to do so, or who are stripped of their abilities by Yhwh, in contrast to our passage, which suggests nothing of the kind (*Isaiah 1–39*, 409).

17. Blenkinsopp, ibid., 408–409, notes the ambiguity of the passage with respect to the topographical transformation, as well as its devolutionary aspects, common to apocalyptic eschatology.

18. Mic 4:6–7 follows 4:1–3, which reproduces Isa 2:2–4 almost exactly; 4:4, which elaborates on it further; and independent material in 4:5. Thus, *bayyôm hahû'*, "on that day," which introduces 4:6–7, reads in the final form of the text as a reference back to *wehayah be'aharît hayyamîm*, "At the end of days." The time reference of Zeph 3:19 and surrounding materials is vaguer, although clearly in the immediate future (see *bayyôm hahû'* in 3:16, and *ba'et hahî'* in 3:19, 20). As for the issues of date and dependency, no consensus has emerged among specialists. Some see Zeph 3:19 as the earlier passage, whereas others view Mic 4:6–7 as older. See, e.g., the treatment of Sweeney, *Zephaniah* (Minneapolis, MN: Fortress Press, 2003), 206, who sees Zeph 3:19 as the earlier text (possibly seventh century). See also the comments of H. W. Wolff, *Micah: A Commentary* (Minneapolis, MN: Augsburg, 1990), 124, who believes both passages are ultimately dependent on Ezekiel 34.

19. "Rejected" is a guess based more on the parallelism than MT's *whnhl'h* (?), explained by BDB as a Niphal participle from a denominative root *hl'* derived from the adverb *hale'ah*, "further," "onwards" (229b), meaning "removed far off." NKB doubts the MT's reading (245b). LXX reads *ten aposmenen*, "her

that was rejected," which may suggest something like *hndḥh or *hnhl'h in the Vorlage.

20. E.g., NJPS; E. Ben Zvi, *A Historical-Critical Study of the Book of Zephaniah* (Berlin: de Gruyter, 1991), 258; and A. Berlin, *Zephaniah* (New York: Doubleday, 1994), 147. The "limping one" and the "one driven away" are both feminine, perhaps in reference to Jerusalem as "Daughter Zion" and "Daughter Jerusalem" previously in chapter 3, as Sweeney argues (*Zephaniah*, 207), or because the feminine singular is used to indicate a collective (GKC par. 122s).

21. Like many commentators, I construe *boštam* as the object of *wesamtî*, with *–m* as an enclitic. For a grammatical discussion, see, e.g., Ben Zvi, *A Historical-Critical Study*, 258–259, and Berlin, *Zephaniah*, 147.

22. Lev 22:23 makes an exception for the *śarûa'* (an animal with an extended limb) and the *qalûṭ* (?) if they are offered as a free will offering, although not to fulfill a vow. See further nn. 4 and 16 in chapter 2.

23. Others have understood v. 20 as a clarifying gloss on v. 19. For discussion, see Sweeney, *Zephaniah*, 207.

6. NON-SOMATIC PARALLELS TO BODILY WHOLENESS AND "DEFECT"

1. *Purity and Danger: An Analysis of the Concepts of Pollution and Taboo* (1966; Boston: Ark, 1984, reprinted), 51–52; "Deciphering a Meal," *Daedalus* 101 (1972):76–77. The quotation is from "Deciphering a Meal," 76–77.

2. Note that although priests with a "defect" (*mûm*) are disqualified from altar service by H, they are not removed from the sanctuary, nor are they barred from consuming holy and most holy foods (Lev 21:22). Similarly, although "defective" sacrificial animals are proscribed for most sacrifices by H, certain ones are permitted as free will offerings according to Lev 22:23. For further critique of Douglas's erroneous assumptions, see, e.g., J. Milgrom, *Leviticus 1–16* (New York: Doubleday, 1991), 720–721.

3. Other texts differ from these. On this, see ahead. Exod 20:25 is 20:22 in traditional Hebrew Bibles, although not in BHS.

4. The Book of the Covenant (Exod 20:22–23:33 in its final form) is often viewed as the oldest biblical legal collection (e.g., Y. Osumi, *Die Kompositionsgeschichte des Bundesbuches Exodus 20,22b–23,33* [Freiburg, Switzerland: Universitätsverlag; Göttingen, Germany: Vandenhoeck & Ruprecht, 1991]); at minimum, one can say that it predates the Deuteronomic laws, which use it as a source, and recast material from it (B. M. Levinson, *Deuteronomy and the Hermeneutics of Legal Innovation* [New York: Oxford University Press, 1997]).

5. Other biblical sources describe different sorts of altars for burnt offerings. For example, according to P, the altar is to be made of acacia wood covered with bronze and to have four horns (Exod 27:1–2). An altar found at Iron II Arad was constructed of a combination of field stones and earth. On this, see, e.g., the discussion of Z. Zevit, *The Religions of Ancient Israel: A Synthesis of Parallactic Approaches* (New York: Continuum, 2001), 159–161, 169–170.

6. The term *gazît* refers to finished ashlar blocks, well known from excavations (see ahead). I have translated *ḥereb* "tool" rather than "sword," given the context.

NKB renders "chisel" (349b). See my upcoming discussion on profanation of that which is holy.

7. The context of Deut 27:5–6 is an address to the people telling them what to do when they cross the Jordan into the land of Canaan. The option of building an earthen altar, noted in Exod 20:24, goes unmentioned in Deut 27:5–6, which requires the erection of a stone altar at Mount Ebal.

8. See the commonplace opposition of derivatives of the roots *qdš* and *ḥll* (e.g., the nouns *qodeš*, "holiness," and *ḥol*, "profaneness" or "commonness" in such texts as Lev 10:10; Ezek 22:26; 42:20; 44:23; 48:15). Holiness is the divine quality par excellence. According to P and H, it is shared with priests (e.g., Exod 30:30; Lev 21:6–8; Num 16:1–17:5 [Eng. 16:1–40]); the sanctuary itself, often called a "holy place" (e.g., Lev 21:23); and items of the cult such as the Ark, table, vessels, lamp stand, incense altar, altar of burnt offerings, and incense (e.g., Exod 30:22–29, 34–38). On holiness, see my treatment in *Rites and Rank: Hierarchy in Biblical Representations of Cult* (Princeton, NJ: Princeton University Press, 2000), 15–37.

9. P's list of sanctified cultic items is explicit in this regard because it includes the altar of burnt offerings (Exod 30:28).

10. On the polyvalence of the root *šlm*, see W. Eisenbeis, *Die Wurzel šlm im Alten Testament* (Berlin: De Gruyter, 1969) and S. M. Olyan, "Hašalôm: Some Literary Considerations of 2 Kings 9," *Catholic Biblical Quarterly* 46 (1984):652–668.

11. In Lev 21:17, 18, 21, 23, only the formulation *mûm bô* or *bô mûm*, "a defect (is) in him," is used of the "defective" priest; the implied opposite formulation, which would parallel *tamîm/temîmah*, "whole" or "non-defective," is *'ên mûm bô* or *lo' hayah mûm bô*, "no defect (is) in him," as in 2 Sam 14:25, Song of Songs 4:7, and Dan 1:4, with respect to the bodies of nonpriests.

12. The terms are thus specialized in their usages and overlap.

13. The word *massaʿ* is generally understood to mean "quarry," although it is a hapax legomenon. This understanding is based on causative verbal forms of the root *nsʿ*, which mean "to quarry stone" (1 Kgs 5:31 [Eng. 17], which refers to ashlar; Eccl 10:9). The syntax of the verse is not altogether clear, however. On this, see further M. Noth, *Könige* (Neukirchen-Vluyn, Germany: Neukirchener, 1968), 98–99.

14. We know that the quarried blocks of 1 Kgs 6:7 were unfinished because the text makes a point of saying that no tools were heard at the site, where the finishing would have been done, and because the term ashlar (*gazît*) is avoided in the text. On the difference between finished ashlar and newly quarried limestone blocks, which are rough and unshaped after quarrying, see H. Schult, "Zum Bauverfahren in 1. Könige 6, 7," *Zeitschrift des deutschen Palästina-Vereins* 88 (1972):53–54, and especially Y. Shiloh, *The Proto-Aeolic Capital and Israelite Ashlar Masonry* (Jerusalem: Hebrew University, 1979), 61–62, and fig. 84, who reconstructs the stages from rough quarrying to finished ashlar.

15. See Y. Shiloh and A. Horowitz, "Ashlar Quarries of the Iron Age in the Hill Country of Israel," *Bulletin of the American Schools of Oriental Research* 217 (1975):37–48.

16. Nothing is said explicitly in Leviticus 22 or Numbers 18 about the holiness or lack of same of "defective" sacrifices.

17. That which is sanctified cannot come into contact with that which is unclean, and sanctified sacrifices such as the firstlings are normally to be consumed in

the sanctuary according to Deut 15:20. Therefore, the claim of Deut 15:22 that "defective" firstlings may be eaten outside the sanctuary by unclean persons indicates that "defective" firstlings are common or profane rather than holy.

18. If the "defects" were congenital, as seems likely, it is probable that the firstlings were never sanctified, so we cannot legitimately speak of them losing their holiness; rather, it seems best to state simply that they are profane rather than holy, or that they lack holiness.

19. For priestly sanctification in H, see, e.g., Lev 21:6–8; in P, see Exod 30:30. On the difference between the holiness of priests and the holiness of the people according to H, see my discussion in *Rites and Rank*, 121–122.

20. On profanation generally and the limited instances of licit profanation, see my discussion in ibid., 25–27.

21. Other texts also claim that ashlar was used for building purposes at the Jerusalem temple. See, e.g., 1 Kgs 6:36; 1 Chr 22:2; cf. Ezek 40:42. Obviously, the biblical anthology, and even the sources of the Deuteronomistic History itself, present conflicting claims regarding the materials used to build the temple.

22. On this, see, e.g., Shiloh, *The Proto-Aeolic Capital*, 50–59.

23. On the incense altars, see the study of S. Gitin, "Incense Altars from Ekron, Israel, and Judah: Context and Typology," *Eretz-Israel* 20 (1989):52*–67*. The Beersheba altar was published by Y. Aharoni, "The Horned Altar of Beer-sheba," *Biblical Archaeologist* 37 (1974):2–6. See recently, Zevit, *Religions of Ancient Israel*, 171–174.

24. On the use of ashlar for constructing various elements of sanctuaries at Iron II sites such as Tel Dan and Megiddo, see, e.g., B. A. Nakhai, *Archaeology and the Religions of Canaan and Israel* (Boston: American Schools of Oriental Research, 2001), 177, 184–185 and Zevit, ibid., 180–191.

7. EXEGETICAL PERPETUATIONS, ELABORATIONS, AND TRANSFORMATIONS: THE CASE OF QUMRAN

1. I focus on the Dead Sea Scrolls because they constitute our richest single corpus of exegetical materials from the Second Temple period, yet the size of the corpus permits a fairly thorough chapter-long survey of the representation of disability at Qumran. Thus, a comprehensive treatment of the representation of disability in the larger corpus of Jewish works from the period of the Second Temple remains a desideratum. Because the sectarian texts from Qumran frequently quote, paraphrase, or allude to scripture, often creatively, I speak of the writers of those texts as biblical interpreters. As a recent, influential reference work on the Dead Sea Scrolls aptly states, "[n]early all of the writings of the Qumran community, whether formally linked with scripture or not, are pervaded with scriptural interpretation.... Regardless of whether there was a biblical 'canon' at Qumran and what its contents might have been, it is generally conceded that, however it was defined by the Qumranites, and whatever books it contained, the books of what is now known as the Hebrew scriptures frequently functioned as both the source and the framework for what the Qumran writers wanted to say and the way in which they said it" (M. J. Bernstein, "Interpretation of Scriptures," *Encyclopedia of the Dead Sea Scrolls* [2 vols.; ed. L. H. Schiffman and

J. C. VanderKam; New York: Oxford University Press, 2000], 1:376). It must be emphasized that although scholars frequently speak of a single, Qumran corpus, the literature comprising this corpus is extremely varied, and the ideas expressed in that literature are not always consistent. This observation will become clearer as I discuss the varied representations of disability in the relevant texts.

2. On this tendency, see, e.g., J. L. Kugel, *Traditions of the Bible: A Guide to the Bible As It Was at the Start of the Common Era* (Cambridge, MA: Harvard University Press, 1998); idem., *In Potiphar's House: The Interpretive Life of Biblical Texts* (San Francisco: HarperCollins, 1990); and S. M. Olyan, *A Thousand Thousands Served Him: Exegesis and the Naming of Angels in Ancient Judaism* (Tübingen, Germany: Mohr/Siebeck, 1993).

3. J. H. W. Dorman's study "The Blemished Body: Deformity and Disability in the Qumran Scrolls" (Ph.D. dissertation, University of Groningen, Groningen, The Netherlands, 2007) came into my possession as I was completing the final form of this manuscript for publication. In contrast to my investigation, Dorman focuses exclusively on physical, non–illness-related disabilities such as blindness and lameness and their role in Qumran texts. Her careful study of MMT is particularly worthy of consultation, although I do not agree with all of her conclusions. Note also the recent article of K. Berthelot, "La place des infirmes et des 'lépreaux' dans les textes de Qumrân et les évangiles," *Revue biblique* 113 (2006):211–241, cited by Dorman (ibid., 11). To Berthelot's credit, she includes persons with "skin disease" in her discussion.

4. All translations in this chapter are my own. The Hebrew (and occasionally, Aramaic) texts of the Qumran documents translated or cited in this chapter may be found conveniently in F. García Martínez and E. J. C. Tigchelaar, *The Dead Sea Scrolls Study Edition* (2 vols.; Leiden, The Netherlands: Brill, 1997), with English translations provided.

5. On the Pseudo-Daniel materials from Qumran, including 4Q245, see J. J. Collins, "Daniel, Book of: Pseudo-Daniel," *EncDSS* 1:176–178.

6. These are probably to be understood as nonphysical. On this, see my upcoming discussion.

7. The Hebrew "into it" (*lah*) is ambiguous, but the larger context indicates clearly that "it" refers to the sanctuary city (see *bah* "in it," referring to the city of the sanctuary ['*îr hammiqdaš*] in the previous statute [11Q19 45:12]).

8. I translate '*iwwer* as a plural for the sake of consistency because the following verbs and pronouns are plural.

9. Given their classification with other polluters in this passage, it seems highly likely that the blind here are viewed as polluting in and of themselves. The alternative understanding, that they are excluded on account of their inability to know that they have had contact with a polluting thing, is not suggested by the arrangement of the text. Such an understanding, however, is evidenced in the treatment of blind priests in 4QMMT B 49–54, which I discuss ahead. E. Qimron understands the Temple Scroll's proscription to be grounded in the assumption that the blind cannot know that they might be impure (E. Qimron and J. Strugnell, *Qumran Cave 4.V: Miqṣat Ma'aśe Ha-Torah* [Oxford, UK: Clarendon Press, 1994], 160–161).

10. I am not the first to notice the use made of Num 5:3 in the construction of 11Q19 45:12–14. See, e.g., Y. Yadin, *The Temple Scroll* [Jerusalem: Israel Exploration Society/Shrine of the Book, 1983], 1:290, 2:193.

11. I prefer to understand *'arel weṭame'* as a hendiadys construction ("the uncircumcised who are unclean"), given that the subject of the text to which Isa 52:1 alludes (*beliya'al*, "a worthless man") is singular, not plural. On the allusion to Nah 2:1 (Eng. 1:15) in Isa 52:1, see the discussion of B. D. Sommer, *A Prophet Reads Scripture: Allusion in Isaiah 40–66* (Stanford, CA: Stanford University Press, 1998), 82–84.

12. Yadin anticipates my argument here regarding the possibility of a synecdochic understanding of the "blind" in 11Q19 45:12–14 (*The Temple Scroll*, 1:291).

13. The mention of *ṭaharat hammiqdaš*, apparently a reference to the holy foods consumed by priests in the sanctuary, suggests that the blind and deaf persons of interest to the text are priests. I discuss the restriction on deaf priests in the second part of this chapter. On *ṭaharat hammiqdaš* as the Qumran Hebrew equivalent of biblical *qodašîm*, the holy foods, see the discussion in Qimron and Strugnell, *Qumran Cave 4.V: Miqṣat Ma'aśe Ha-Torah*, 138 (5.3.2.1) and 168, n. 166. See also H. Harrington's lucid treatment of priestly and lay food terminology in the Scrolls ("Purity," *EncDSS* 2:725). For the text of 4QMMT, I follow Qimron's and Strugnell's composite reconstruction in ibid., 50–52, with translation and commentary. On the vocalization *ṭaharah* as opposed to biblical *ṭohorah*, see Qimron, *The Hebrew of the Dead Sea Scrolls* (Atlanta: Scholars Press, 1986), 17 and 100. The ruling in 4QMMT B 49–54 may also refer to blind and deaf members of priestly households who are not priests themselves, as priestly dependents routinely eat holy (although not most holy) foods according to Lev 22:10–13. Harrington believes that the text refers to "Jews of any status" who "because of their lack of vision and hearing, might accidentally defile holy offerings . . ." ("Holiness in the Laws of 4QMMT," in *Legal Texts and Legal Issues: Proceedings of the Second Meeting of the International Organization for Qumran Studies, Cambridge 1995* [ed. M. Bernstein et al.; Leiden, The Netherlands: Brill, 1997], 123). However, the text seems to speak of the routine, permitted access of blind and deaf persons to holy foods, a circumstance that suggests to me priests or priestly dependents rather than laypersons unconnected to priestly households (*wehemmah ba'îm leṭaharat hammiqdaš*). Dorman, "The Blemished Body," 213–214, believes the reference is most likely to priests, although she does not make an argument based on access to the holy foods, as I do. (She believes *ṭaharat hammiqdaš* has a wider reference, to pure objects belonging to the sanctuary, which may include holy foods [ibid., 205].) See also the discussion of Berthelot, who considers the possibility that priestly foods are at issue ("Infirmes et lépreaux," 221).

14. The word *ḥigger*, used here along with *pisseaḥ*, is also usually translated "lame." The context suggests however that there may well be some difference between the person described as *pisseaḥ* and the person described as *ḥigger*, although what this difference might be is unclear.

15. On the nonbiblical category of the "permanent defect" (*mûm 'ôlam*), see my upcoming discussion.

16. Others have anticipated me in this claim (e.g., Yadin, *Temple Scroll*, 1:290).

17. Reading *'el* for consonantal *'lh*, a common – although not universal – emendation. For discussion, see S. M. Olyan, "The Exegetical Dimensions of Restrictions on the Blind and the Lame in Texts from Qumran," *Dead Sea Discoveries* 8 (2001):44, n. 19, and Dorman, "The Blemished Body," 73–74 and nn. 81–83.

18. Compare Deut 23:2 (Eng. 1) ". . . shall not enter the assembly of Yhwh" to 1QS^a 2:3–11 ". . . shall not enter the assembly of God," evidently a direct echo of the rhetoric of Deut 23:2 (Eng. 1). Compare also ". . . shall not enter to station themselves in the midst of the congregation. . . ."

19. It may be that the text is suggesting that muteness and deafness are also to be understood as "defects," a major innovation. On this, see my upcoming discussion.

20. All participants in the eschatological war must be "'whole' with respect to spirit and flesh" (*temîmê rûaḥ ûbaśar*), according to 1QM 7:4.

21. It may be that in 1QS^a, deafness and muteness have been recast as "defects," as I discuss in the next section.

22. Why the young child of 4Q266 must be excluded on account of the presence of the holy angels remains unclear to me. As for the stumbling old man of 1QS^a, he is likely understood as not unlike the lame, in that he cannot walk effectively. A. Shemesh believes that the old man is excluded because of both his physical disability and his weakness ("'The Holy Angels are in their Council': The Exclusion of Deformed Persons from Holy Places in Qumranic and Rabbinic Literature," *Dead Sea Discoveries* 4 [1997]: 196).

23. Milgrom, however, is convinced that the Qumran sectarians "included deafness as a defect," citing 4QMMT B 52–54 (*Leviticus 17–22* [New York: Doubleday, 2000], 1826).

24. Including the stumbling old man of line 7.

25. The word "stricken" (*menugga'*) is used in 1QM 7:4 only with respect to the unclean: *'îš menugga' beṭum'at beśarô*. 11Q19 48:14–15 (*menugga'îm beṣara'at*) and 45:17–18 (*ṣarûa' ûmenugga'*) use the word in a similar manner.

CONCLUSION

1. Some patterns of association are more common than others. For example, although the deaf and the blind, or deafness and blindness, are commonly classified together in biblical, cuneiform, and Qumran literatures, the association of blindness or other "defects" with polluting skin conditions is less common.

2. The minibiography includes 2 Sam 4:4; 9:1–13; 16:1–4; 19:25–31 (Eng. 24–30). C. Fontaine anticipates me in making this point and citing the example of Meribbaal (Mephiboshet) ("Disabilities and Illness in the Bible: A Feminist Perspective," in *A Feminist Companion to the Hebrew Bible in the New Testament* [ed. A. Brenner; Sheffield, UK: Sheffield Academic Press, 1996], 292). On the Meribbaal (Mephiboshet) narrative, see especially the detailed study of J. Schipper, *Disability Studies and the Hebrew Bible: Figuring Mephibosheth in the David Story* (New York: T. & T. Clark, 2006).

3. See similarly Gen 27:1 regarding Isaac, and 1 Sam 2:22; 3:2 regarding Eli the priest of Shiloh, both of whom are said to be blind on account of old age.

4. "You shall not sacrifice to Yhwh your god a bull or sheep in which there is a 'defect' (*mûm*) – any ugly thing – for it is an abomination of Yhwh" (Deut 17:1).

5. To this one might compare rabbinic texts that suggest that deaf and mute persons are "little better than a corpse" as J. Z. Abrams puts it (*Judaism and Disability: Portrayals in Ancient Texts from the Tanach through the Bavli* [Washington, DC: Gallaudet University Press, 1998], 43–44).

6. Nonnative explanations for the stigmatizing of persons with disabilities through time and space abound. These are usually framed broadly as explanations for stigmatizing in general, a process that some have claimed is universal. R. Garland Thomson discusses phenomenological, historicist, and psychological approaches, among others, remaining agnostic with regard to explaining motivation (*Extraordinary Bodies: Figuring Physical Disability in American Culture and Literature* [New York: Columbia University Press, 1997], 31–32). B. Major and C. P. Eccleston, "Stigma and Social Exclusion," in *Social Psychology of Inclusion and Exclusion* (ed. D. Abrams et al.; New York: Psychology Press, 2005), 67–70, survey various psychological and social psychological explanations, including contemporary evolutionary approaches, with critique of each approach. Like others, I, too, remain agnostic with regard to explaining what combination of factors might motivate the stigmatization of disabilities cross-culturally and through time.

7. For example, Garland Thomson, ibid., 9, 27–29, and C. J. Kudlick, "The Outlook of *The Problem* and the Problem with the *Outlook*," in *The New Disability History: American Perspectives* (ed. P. K. Longmore and L. Umansky; New York: New York University Press, 2001), 201–202, citing Garland Thomson.

8. The identity of the *mamzer* of Deut 23:3 (Eng. 2) is, as I have mentioned, unclear. He is traditionally understood to be the issue of an illegitimate sexual union.

Bibliography

Abrams, J. Z. *Judaism and Disability: Portrayals in Ancient Texts from the Tanach through the Bavli*. Washington, DC: Gallaudet University Press, 1998.

Ackerman, S. *Warrior, Dancer, Seductress, Queen: Women in Judges and Biblical Israel*. New York: Doubleday, 1998.

Aharoni, Y. "The Horned Altar of Beer-sheba." *Biblical Archaeologist* 37 (1974):2–6.

Altman, B. M. "Disability Definitions, Models, Classification Schemes, and Applications." Pages 97–122 in *Handbook of Disability Studies*. Edited by G. L. Albrecht et al. Thousand Oaks, CA: Sage, 2001.

Avalos, H. *Illness and Health Care in the Ancient Near East: The Role of the Temple in Greece, Mesopotamia, and Israel*. Atlanta: Scholars Press, 1995.

———, S. Melcher, and J. Schipper, eds. "This Abled Body: Rethinking Disabilities in Biblical Studies." *Semeia* in press.

Bauer, H., and P. Leander. *Historische Grammatik der hebräischen Sprache des Alten Testaments*. Hildesheim, Germany: Georg Olms, 1965.

Baynton, D. C. "Disability and the Justification of Inequality in American History." Pages 33–57 in *The New Disability History: American Perspectives*. Edited by P. K. Longmore and L. Umansky. New York: New York University Press, 2001.

Becking, B. *Between Fear and Freedom: Essays on the Interpretation of Jeremiah 30–31*. Leiden, The Netherlands: Brill, 2004.

Ben Zvi, E. *A Historical-Critical Study of the Book of Zephaniah*. Berlin: de Gruyter, 1991.

Berlin, A. *Zephaniah*. New York: Doubleday, 1994.

———. *Lamentations*. Louisville, KY: Westminster John Knox, 2002.

Bernstein, M. J. "Interpretation of Scriptures." Pages 375–383 in vol. 1 of *Encyclopedia of the Dead Sea Scrolls*. Edited by L. H. Schiffman and J. C. VanderKam. 2 vols. New York: Oxford University Press, 2000.

Berquist, J. L. *Controlling Corporeality: The Body and the Household in Ancient Israel*. New Brunswick, NJ: Rutgers University Press, 2002.

Berthelot, K. "La place des infirmes et des 'lépreaux' dans les texts de Qumrân et les évangiles." *Revue biblique* 113 (2006):211–241.

Blenkinsopp, J. *Isaiah 1–39*. New York: Doubleday, 2000.

———. *Isaiah 40–55*. New York: Doubleday, 2000.

————. *Isaiah 56–66*. New York: Doubleday, 2003.

Bodel, J. and S. M. Olyan, eds. *Household and Family Religion in Antiquity: Contextual and Comparative Perspectives*. Oxford, UK: Blackwell, in press.

Borger, R. *Die Inschriften Asarhaddons Königs von Assyrien*. Graz, Austria: Weidner, 1956.

————. "Vier Grenzsteinurkunden Merodachbaladans I. von Babylonien." *Archiv für Orientforschung* 23 (1970):1–26.

Brenner, A. *The Intercourse of Knowledge: On Gendering Desire & 'Sexuality' in the Hebrew Bible*. Leiden, The Netherlands: Brill, 1997.

Brown, F., S. Driver, and C. Briggs. *The Brown-Driver-Briggs Hebrew and English Lexicon*. Peabody, MA: Hendrickson, 2000, Reprinted.

Cassuto, U., et al., eds. *'enṣîqlopedyah miqra'ît*. Jerusalem: Mossad Bialik, 1965–1988.

Cazelles, H. "*ḥll* III." Pages 411–413 in vol. 3 of *Theological Dictionary of the Old Testament*. Edited by G. J. Botterweck and H. Ringgren. Translated by J. T. Willis et al. 14 vols. Grand Rapids, MI: Eerdmans, 1978.

Ceresko, A. R. "The Identity of 'the Blind and the Lame' ['iwwer upisseaḥ] in 2 Samuel 5:8b." *Catholic Biblical Quarterly* 63 (2001):23–30.

Cogan, M., and H. Tadmor. *II Kings*. New York: Doubleday, 1988.

Collins, J. J. "Daniel, Book of: Pseudo-Daniel." Pages 176–178 in vol. 1 of *Encyclopedia of the Dead Sea Scrolls*. Edited by L. H. Schiffman and J. C. VanderKam. 2 vols. New York: Oxford University Press, 2000.

Dietrich, M., O. Loretz, and J. Sanmartín, eds. *The Cuneiform Alphabetic Texts from Ugarit, Ras ibn Hani and Other Places*. 2nd enlarged ed. Münster, Germany: Ugarit Verlag, 1995.

Dohmen, C., and D. Rick. "*r*"." Pages 560–588 in vol. 13 of *Theological Dictionary of the Old Testament*. Edited by G. J. Botterweck et al. Translated by D. E. Green. 14 vols. Grand Rapids, MI: Eerdmans, 2004.

Donald, T. "The Semantic Field of 'Folly' in Proverbs, Job, Psalms, and Ecclesiastes." *Vetus Testamentum* 13 (1963):285–292.

Donner, H., and W. Röllig, eds. *Kanaanäische und Aramäische Inschriften*. 4th ed. 3 vols. Wiesbaden, Germany: Harrassowitz, 1979.

Dorman, J. H. W. "The Blemished Body: Deformity and Disability in the Qumran Scrolls." Ph.D. dissertation, University of Groningen, Groningen, The Netherlands, 2007.

Douglas, M. *Purity and Danger: An Analysis of the Concepts of Pollution and Taboo*. Original, 1966. Boston: Ark, 1984, Reprinted.

————. "Deciphering a Meal." *Daedalus* 101 (1972):61–81.

Eisenbeis, W. *Die Wurzel šlm im Alten Testament*. Berlin: de Gruyter, 1969.

Fitzmyer, J. A., S. J. *The Aramaic Inscriptions of Sefire*. Rome: Pontifical Biblical Institute, 1967.

Fontaine, C. "Disabilities and Illness in the Bible: A Feminist Perspective." Pages 286–300 in *A Feminist Companion to the Hebrew Bible in the New Testament*. Edited by A. Brenner. Sheffield, UK: Sheffield Academic Press, 1996.

Fox, M. V. *A Time to Tear Down and a Time to Build Up: A Rereading of Ecclesiastes*. Grand Rapids, MI: Eerdmans, 1999.

————. *Proverbs 1–9*. New York: Doubleday, 2000.

Frymer-Kensky, T. *In the Wake of the Goddesses: Women, Culture and the Biblical Transformation of Pagan Myth*. New York: Free Press, 1992.

García Martínez, F., and E. J. C. Tigchelaar. *The Dead Sea Scrolls Study Edition*. 2 vols. Leiden, The Netherlands: Brill, 1997.

Garland, R. *The Eye of the Beholder: Deformity and Disability in the Greco-Roman World*. Ithaca, NY: Cornell University Press, 1995.

Garland Thomson, R. *Extraordinary Bodies: Figuring Physical Disability in American Culture and Literature*. New York: Columbia University Press, 1997.

George, A. R. *The Babylonian Gilgamesh Epic. Introduction, Critical Edition and Cuneiform Texts*. 2 vols. Oxford, UK: Oxford University Press, 2003.

Gerstenberger, E. S. *Psalms, Part 1: With an Introduction to Cultic Poetry*. Grand Rapids, MI: Eerdmans, 1988.

———. *Leviticus: A Commentary*. Louisville, KY: Westminster John Knox, 1996.

———. *Psalms, Part 2, and Lamentations*. Grand Rapids, MI: Eeerdmans, 2001.

Gilders, W. *Blood Ritual in the Hebrew Bible: Meaning and Power*. Baltimore: The Johns Hopkins University Press, 2004.

Gitin, S. "Incense Altars from Ekron, Israel, and Judah: Context and Typology." *Eretz-Israel* 20 (1989):52*–67*.

Goffman, E. *Stigma: Notes on the Management of Spoiled Identity*. Englewood Cliffs, NJ: Prentice Hall, 1963.

Gordon, C. H. *Ugaritic Textbook*. Rev. reprint. Rome: Pontifical Biblical Institute, 1998.

Hall, R. G. "Epispasm and the Dating of Ancient Jewish Writings." *Journal for the Study of the Pseudepigrapha* 2 (1988):71–86.

Hallo, W., et al., eds. *The Context of Scripture. Volume I: Canonical Compositions from the Biblical World*. Leiden, The Netherlands: Brill, 1997.

Harrington, H. "Holiness in the Laws of 4QMMT." Pages 109–128 in *Legal Texts and Legal Issues: Proceedings of the Second Meeting of the International Organization for Qumran Studies, Cambridge 1995*. Edited by M. Bernstein et al. Leiden, The Netherlands: Brill, 1997.

———. "Purity." Pages 724–728 in vol. 2 of *Encyclopedia of the Dead Sea Scrolls*. Edited by L. H. Schiffman and J. C. VanderKam. 2 vols. New York: Oxford University Press, 2000.

Hausmann, J. "ṣyḥ." Pages 85–89 in vol. 14 of *Theological Dictionary of the Old Testament*. Edited by G. J. Botterweck et al. Translated by D. W. Stott. 14 vols. Grand Rapids, MI: Eerdmans, 2004.

Heidel, A. *The Babylonian Genesis: The Story of Creation*. Chicago: University of Chicago Press, 1951.

Hendel, R. S. "The Exodus in Biblical Memory." *Journal of Biblical Literature* 120 (2001):601–622.

Heward, W. L. *Exceptional Children: An Introduction to Special Education*. 6th ed. Upper Saddle River, NJ: Merrill, 2000.

Hoffner, H. "Symbols for Masculinity and Femininity: Their Use in Ancient Near Eastern Sympathetic Magic Rituals." *Journal of Biblical Literature* 85 (1966):326–334.

Holden, L. *Forms of Deformity*. Sheffield, UK: JSOT Press, 1991.

Hunt, L., ed. *The New Cultural History*. Berkeley: University of California Press, 1989.
───── and V. E. Bonnell, eds. *Beyond the Cultural Turn: New Directions in the Study of Society and Culture*. Berkeley: University of California Press, 1999.
Kautzsch, E., and A. E. Cowley. *Gesenius' Hebrew Grammar*. 2nd ed. Oxford, UK: Clarendon Press, 1910.
Kellermann, D. "*šemo'l*." Pages 137–141 in vol. 14 of *Theological Dictionary of the Old Testament*. Edited by G. J. Botterweck et al. Translated by D. W. Stott. 14 vols. Grand Rapids, MI: Eerdmans, 2004.
King, L. W. *Babylonian Boundary-Stones and Memorial-Tablets in the British Museum*. London: British Museum, 1912.
Knippschild, S. "Spoils and Iconoclasm: The Ancient Near Eastern Tradition and Athens." Unpublished paper, 2005.
Knohl, I. *The Sanctuary of Silence: The Priestly Torah and the Holiness School*. Minneapolis, MN: Fortress, 1995.
Koehler, L., and W. Baumgartner. *The Hebrew and Aramaic Lexicon of the Old Testament*. Trans. M. E. J. Richardson et al. 5 vols. Leiden, The Netherlands: Brill, 1994.
Kudlick, C. J. "The Outlook of *The Problem* and the Problem with the *Outlook*." Pages 187–213 in *The New Disability History: American Perspectives*. Edited by P. K. Longmore and L. Umansky. New York: New York University Press, 2001.
─────. "Disability History: Why We Need Another 'Other.'" *The American Historical Review* 108 (2003):763–793.
Kugel, J. L. *Traditions of the Bible: A Guide to the Bible As It Was at the Start of the Common Era*. Cambridge, MA: Harvard University Press, 1998.
─────. *In Potiphar's House: The Interpretive Life of Biblical Texts*. San Francisco: HarperCollins, 1990.
Lambert, W. G. *Babylonian Wisdom Literature*. Oxford, UK: Clarendon Press, 1960.
───── and A. R. Millard. *Atra-Hasis: The Babylonian Story of the Flood*. Winona Lake, IN: Eisenbrauns, 1999.
Leibowitz, Y., and Y. S. Licht. "mûm, m(')ûm." Pages 724–727 in vol. 4 of *'enṣîqlopedyah miqra'ît*. Jerusalem: Mossad Bialik, 1962. (Hebrew)
Leichty, E. *The Omen Series Šumma Izbu*. Locust Valley, NY: J. J. Augustin, 1970.
Lemos, T. M. "Shame and Mutilation of Enemies in the Hebrew Bible." *Journal of Biblical Literature* 125 (2006):225–241.
Levinson, B. *Deuteronomy and the Hermeneutics of Legal Innovation*. New York: Oxford University Press, 1997.
Levtow, N. B. "Images of Others: Icon Parodies and Iconic Politics in Ancient Israel." Ph.D. dissertation, Brown University, Providence, RI, 2006.
Lincoln, B. *Discourse and the Construction of Society: Comparative Studies of Myth, Ritual, and Classification*. New York: Oxford University Press, 1989.
Linton, S. *Claiming Disability: Knowledge and Identity*. New York: New York University Press, 1998.
Longmore, P. K., and L. Umansky, eds. *The New Disability History: American Perspectives*. New York: New York University Press, 2001.
Luckenbill, D. D. *Ancient Records of Assyria and Babylonia*. Chicago: University of Chicago Press, 1927.

Major, B., and C. P. Eccleston. "Stigma and Social Exclusion." Pages 63–87 in *Social Psychology of Inclusion and Exclusion*. Edited by D. Abrams et al. New York: Psychology Press, 2005.

Marsman, H. *Women in Ugarit and Israel*. Leiden, The Netherlands: Brill, 2003.

Marx, T. C. *Disability in Jewish Law*. London: Routledge, 2002.

McCarter, P. K., Jr. *I Samuel*. Garden City, NY: Doubleday, 1980.

———. *II Samuel*. Garden City, NY: Doubleday, 1984.

Melcher, S. J. "Visualizing the Perfect Cult: The Priestly Rationale for Exclusion." Pages 55–71 in *Human Disability and the Service of God: Reassessing Religious Practice*. Edited by N. L. Eiesland and D. E. Saliers. Nashville, TN: Abingdon Press, 1998.

Meyers, C. *Discovering Eve: Ancient Israelite Women in Context*. New York: Oxford University Press, 1988.

Milgrom, J. *Leviticus 1–16*. New York: Doubleday, 1991.

———. *Leviticus 17–22*. New York: Doubleday, 2000.

Mommer, P. "*šgʿ*." Pages 405–408 in vol. 14 of *Theological Dictionary of the Old Testament*. Edited by G. J. Botterweck et al. Translated by D. W. Stott. 14 vols. Grand Rapids, MI: Eerdmans, 2004.

Nakhai, B. A. *Archaeology and the Religions of Canaan and Israel*. Boston: American Schools of Oriental Research, 2001.

Noth, M. *Könige*. Neukirchen-Vluyn, Germany: Neukirchener, 1968.

Nylander, B. "Earless in Nineveh: Who Mutilated 'Sargon's' Head?" *American Journal of Archaeology* 84 (1980):329–333.

Olyan, S. M. "Hašalôm: Some Literary Considerations of 2 Kings 9." *Catholic Biblical Quarterly* 46 (1984):652–668.

———. *A Thousand Thousands Served Him: Exegesis and the Naming of Angels in Ancient Judaism*. Tübingen, Germany: Mohr Siebeck, 1993.

———. "Honor, Shame, and Covenant Relations in Ancient Israel and Its Environment." *Journal of Biblical Literature* 115 (1996):201–218.

———. "'Anyone Blind or Lame Shall Not Enter the House': On the Interpretation of Second Samuel 5:8b." *Catholic Biblical Quarterly* 60 (1998):218–227.

———. *Rites and Rank: Hierarchy in Biblical Representations of Cult*. Princeton, NJ: Princeton University Press, 2000.

———. "The Exegetical Dimensions of Restrictions on the Blind and the Lame in Texts from Qumran." *Dead Sea Discoveries* 8 (2001):38–50.

———. *Biblical Mourning: Ritual and Social Dimensions*. Oxford, UK: Oxford University Press, 2004.

Oppenheim, A. L., et al., eds. *The Assyrian Dictionary of the Oriental Institute of the University of Chicago*. Chicago: Oriental Institute, 1956–2007.

Osumi, Y. *Die Kompositionsgeschichte des Bundesbuches Exodus 20,22b–23,33*. Freiburg, Switzerland: Universitätsverlag; Göttingen, Germany: Vandenhoeck & Ruprecht, 1991.

Parker, S. B., ed. *Ugaritic Narrative Poetry*. Atlanta: Scholars Press, 1997.

Parpola, S., and K. Watanabe. *Neo-Assyrian Treaties and Loyalty Oaths*. Helsinki, Finland: Helsinki University Press, 1988.

Poirier, J. C. "David's 'Hatred' for the Lame and the Blind (2 Sam. 5.8a)." *Palestine Exploration Quarterly* 138 (2006):27–33.

Preuss, H. D. "*bô*'." Pages 20–49 in vol. 2 of *Theological Dictionary of the Old Testament*. Edited by G. J. Botterweck and H. Ringgren. Translated by J. T. Willis. 14 vols. Grand Rapids, MI: Eerdmans, 1975.

Propp, W. H. C. *Exodus 1–18*. New York: Doubleday, 1999.

Qimron, E. *The Hebrew of the Dead Sea Scrolls*. Atlanta: Scholars Press, 1986.

───── and J. Strugnell. *Qumran Cave 4.V: Miqṣat Ma'aśe Ha-Torah*. Oxford, UK: Clarendon Press, 1994.

Raphael, R. *Biblical Corpora: Representations of Disability in Hebrew Biblical Literature*. New York: T. & T. Clark, in press.

"Review Essays: Beyond the Cultural Turn." *American Historical Review* 107 (2002):1475–1520.

Rose, M. L. *The Staff of Oedipus: Transforming Disability in Ancient Greece*. Ann Arbor: University of Michigan Press, 2003.

Roth, M. T. *Law Collections from Mesopotamia and Asia Minor*. Atlanta: Scholars Press, 1995.

Schipper, J. "Reconsidering the Imagery of Disability in 2 Samuel 5:8b." *Catholic Biblical Quarterly* 67 (2005):422–434.

─────. *Disability Studies and the Hebrew Bible: Figuring Mephibosheth in the David Story*. New York: T. & T. Clark, 2006.

Schult, H. "Zum Bauverfahren in 1. Könige 6,7." *Zeitschrift des deutschen Palästina-Vereins* 88 (1972):53–54.

Scott, J. Wallach. "Gender: A Useful Category of Historical Analysis." Pages 28–50 in *Gender and the Politics of History*. New York: Columbia University Press, 1988.

Seow, C. L. *Ecclesiastes*. New York: Doubleday, 1997.

Shemesh, A. "'The Holy Angels Are in Their Council': The Exclusion of Deformed Persons from Holy Places in Qumranic and Rabbinic Literature." *Dead Sea Discoveries* 4 (1997):179–206.

Shiloh, Y. *The Proto-Aeolic Capital and Israelite Ashlar Masonry*. Jerusalem: Hebrew University, 1979.

───── and A. Horowitz. "Ashlar Quarries of the Iron Age in the Hill Country of Israel." *Bulletin of the American Schools of Oriental Research* 217 (1975):37–48.

Shupak, N. *Where Can Wisdom Be Found? The Sage's Language in the Bible and in Ancient Egyptian Literature*. Göttingen, Germany: Vandenhoeck & Ruprecht, 1993.

Skehan, P. W., and A. A. di Lella. *The Wisdom of Ben Sira*. New York: Doubleday, 1987.

Smith, J. Z. "Fences and Neighbors: Some Contours of Early Judaism." Pages 1–18 in *Imagining Religion: From Babylon to Jonestown*. Chicago: University of Chicago Press, 1982.

─────. "Classification." Pages 35–43 in *Guide to the Study of Religion*. Edited by W. Braun and R. T. McCutcheon. London: Cassell, 2000.

Sommer, B. *A Prophet Reads Scripture: Allusion in Isaiah 40–66*. Stanford, CA: Stanford University Press, 1998.

Streck, M., ed. *Assurbanipal und die letzten assyrischen Könige bis zum Untergange Nineveh's*. 3 vols. Leipzig, Germany: J. C. Hinrich, 1916.

Sweeney, M. A. *Isaiah 1–39 with an Introduction to the Prophetic Literature*. Grand Rapids, MI: Eerdmans, 1996.

─────. *Zephaniah*. Minneapolis, MN: Fortress Press, 2003.

Talon, P. *The Standard Babylonian Creation Myth Enuma Eliš*. Helsinki, Finland: University of Helsinki, 2005.

Thompson, R. C. *The Prisms of Esarhaddon and Ashurbanipal Found at Nineveh, 1927–8*. London: British Museum, 1931.

Tropper, J. *Ugaritische Grammatik*. Münster, Germany: Ugarit-Verlag, 2000.

van der Toorn, K. "Judges XVI 21 in the Light of the Akkadian Sources." *Vetus Testamentum* 36 (1986):248–253.

———. *Sin and Sanction in Israel and Mesopotamia: A Comparative Study*. Assen, The Netherlands: van Gorcum, 1985.

van der Woude, A. S. "*šem* name." Pages 1356–1357 in vol. 3 of the *Theological Lexicon of the Old Testament*. Edited by E. Jenni and C. Westermann. Translated by M. E. Biddle. 3 vols. Peabody, MA: Hendrickson, 1997.

Vargon, S. "The Blind and the Lame." *Vetus Testamentum* 46 (1996):498–514.

von Soden, W. *Akkadisches Handwörterbuch*. 3 vols. Wiesbaden, Germany: Harrassowitz, 1965–1981.

von Voigtlander, E. N. *The Bisitun Inscription of Darius the Great, Babylonian Version*. London: Lund Humphries, 1978.

Walker, B., and M. Dick. *The Induction of the Cultic Image in Ancient Mesopotamia: The Mesopotamian Mīs Pî Ritual*. Helsinki, Finland: Helsinki University Press, 2001.

Waltke, B. K., and M. O'Connor. *An Introduction to Biblical Hebrew Syntax*. Winona Lake, IN: Eisenbrauns, 1990.

Weinfeld, M. *Deuteronomy and the Deuteronomic School*. Oxford, UK: Clarendon Press, 1972.

Weitzman, S. "Plotting Antiochus's Persecution." *Journal of Biblical Literature* 123 (2004):219–234.

Wendell, S. *The Rejected Body: Feminist Philosophical Reflections on Disability*. New York: Routledge, 1996.

Westbrook, R. *Studies in Biblical and Cuneiform Law*. Paris: Gabalda, 1988.

Westermann, C. *Prophetische Heilswort im Alten Testament*. Göttingen, Germany: Vandenhoeck & Ruprecht, 1987.

———. "Oracles of Salvation" Pages 98–104 in '*The Place Is Too Small for Us': The Israelite Prophets in Recent Scholarship*. Edited by R. P. Gordon. Winona Lake, IN: Eisenbrauns, 1995.

White, H. *The Content of the Form: Narrative Discourse and Historical Representation*. Baltimore: The Johns Hopkins University Press, 1987.

Williams, R. J. *Hebrew Syntax: An Outline*. 2nd ed. Toronto, Ontario, Canada: University of Toronto Press, 1976.

Wilson, R. R. *Prophecy and Society in Ancient Israel*. Philadelphia: Fortress, 1980.

Wolff, H. W. *Micah: A Commentary*. Minneapolis, MN: Augsburg, 1990.

Yadin, Y. *The Temple Scroll*. Jerusalem: Israel Exploration Society/Shrine of the Book, 1983.

Zevit, Z. *The Religions of Ancient Israel: A Synthesis of Parallactic Approaches*. New York: Continuum, 2001.

Subject Index

Abigail, 17, 24
Absalom, 16, 18, 138n.6
Achish, 66–67, 73–74
afterlife and punitive mutilation, 45
Ahijah, 9–10, 126
altars, 94–97, 158n.5
Ammonites, 32–33, 40, 43, 147n.55,
    148n.55
angels, holy, 107–108, 113–116
animals
    corpses left to, 41
    "defective" sacrificial, ugliness of, 19–21,
        90
    sacrifices of "defective," forbidden,
        19–20, 30, 90, 93–94, 97, 126–127,
        138n.11, 139n.11
    transformations of, 80–81
Aqhat epic, 145n.22
archeological material remains, 133n.12,
    134n.12
Ark Narrative, 41–42, 147n.51
Ark of Yhwh, 42
ashlar blocks, 94–95, 96, 97, 98–99
Ashurbanipal and mutilation, 40–41, 43,
    45
Ashurnirari V, 55
assembly see community's assembly
Assyria, 41, 44, 55
Atra-Hasis, 67
Azariah (Uzziah), 56, 125, 151n.27,
    151n.28

"Babylonian Theodicy," 75
bad judgment see ignorance

baldness, 20
beards, 17, 43, 138n.7, 147n.55, 148n.55. See
    also depilation; shaving
beauty
    female, 5, 17–19, 24, 140n.27
    human preference for, 23
    male, 5, 15–17
    and perfection, 21–22
    as sign of Yhwh's favor, 23
    and ugliness, 22, 24–25
    vocabulary of, 22
    in West Asian literature, 139n.20
    and wholeness, 18–19, 138n.1
Beersheba, 99
Benjaminites, 21
bewilderment, 72, 154n.29
binary discourses, 5–6, 22, 30–31, 121
Bir-Ga'yah, 40
Bisitun Inscription, 40
blindness and the blind
    of Ahijah, 9–10
    associated with corruption and bad
        judgment, 7
    associated with ignorance, 7, 35, 51, 54,
        102–103, 120–122
    associated with mental disability, 72
    associated with the deaf and the mute,
        49–52
    associated with the poor, 35–36,
        120–122
    associated with weakness and
        ineffectuality, 82–83
    associated with wickedness and
        falsehood, 103–104

171

Biblical and Non-Biblical Citation Index